Presidential Debates

Presidential Debates

THE CHALLENGE OF CREATING
AN INFORMED ELECTORATE

Kathleen Hall Jamieson

David S. Birdsell

NEW YORK   OXFORD

OXFORD UNIVERSITY PRESS

1988

To Margaret Surratt and
Dale and Myrtle Birdsell

Oxford University Press

Oxford   New York   Toronto
Delhi   Bombay   Calcutta   Madras   Karachi
Petaling Jaya   Singapore   Hong Kong   Tokyo
Nairobi   Dar es Salaam   Cape Town
Melbourne   Auckland

and associated companies in
Berlin   Ibadan

Published by Oxford University Press, Inc.,
200 Madison Avenue, New York, New York 10016

Oxford is a registered trademark of Oxford University Press

Library of Congress Cataloging-in-Publication Data
Jamieson, Kathleen Hall.
Presidential debates.
Bibliography: p.   Includes index.
1. Presidents—United States—Election. 2. Campaign
debates—United States. 3. Television in politics—
United States. I. Birdsell, David S. II. Title.
JK524.J37   1988   324.7   88-12548
ISBN 0-19-505539-X

2 4 6 8 9 7 5 3 1
Printed in the United States of America
on acid-free paper

Acknowledgments

We wish to gratefully acknowledge: Valerie Aubrey, editor and adviser; Niko Pfund, patient detail-person; Steve Bedney, copy editor extraordinaire; the G. B. Dealey family and the Belo Corporation whose generous support made research assistance possible: Deanna Matthews, who unscrambled the messes created by DOS and us on the computer; John Pauley and Kevin Dean who tracked elusive articles; Seamus Neary who located photos; Baruch's Martha Kessler for support and assistance; UT Communication Dean Robert Jeffrey for limiting his meetings with chairs to two hours a week; UT Vice President Gerhard Fonken for aiding when not abetting; Baruch College for release time; Rosemary Wellner for editing and handholding; Tony Schwartz for advice and FAX; Beth Macom for proofing; and especially Benjamin Page, Dennis Davis, and Ernest Bormann whose careful critiques saved us from more foolishness than we dare admit; Karlyn Kohrs Campbell for counsel about things feminist; Rod Hart, Max McCombs, Mark Knapp, and Rick Cherwitz who tolerate the eccentricities of one of us with good humor; and our families for all the inexpressible things that families do and ours do particularly well. Finally, we wish to thank Margaret Surratt and Myrtle and Dale Birdsell—to whom this book is dedicated—the first for making it possible to both chair and write, the second two for understanding when a son needs a good meal.

Austin, Texas   K. H. J.
New York, New York   D. S. B.
March 1988

Contents

Presidential Debates

Introduction

The Vietnam war was not an issue in the 1964 presidential campaign. Four years later, public opposition to his handling of that war prompted Lyndon Johnson's decision to withdraw from the presidential race. In 1976 few in the audience could identify Ayatollah Khomeini; yet in 1980, his holding of U.S. hostages cast a shadow over the campaign.

Elections invite voters to become fortune-tellers. We must guess how a candidate would act in circumstances we may not even be able to imagine. An Arab oil cartel is formed or disintegrates. A Soviet leader is ousted or dies; Brezhnev gives way to Gorbachev. A Berlin Wall is built. Soviet missiles are moved to Cuba.

How can we know whom to entrust with the nation's highest elected office? Answers are elusive. If a long, distinguished legislative career is a useful guide, then how could we have forecast the successes of Lincoln or Eisenhower? Military prowess has yielded such dissimilar presidents as Taylor, William Henry Harrison, and Andrew Jackson. What about Wilson would have predicted his failures and successes?

When presidents were chosen by the elite few, intimate knowledge could guide electors. Trust in George Washington was confirmed in this way. But as the electorate grew, such knowledge became inaccessible to most. As parties emerged to select nominees, certification by one sort of peer replaced another. The rise of the broadcast media cut the umbilical cord that tied candidates to party platforms. The job of determining the qualifications of those who aspired to the presidency fell to the press and public. For evidence, they had words and images—aggregations of lines on paper or dots on a television screen.

What these images and words promised was not necessarily what they delivered. The presumed "peace candidate" in 1964 delivered an expanded land war in Asia. The candidate who in 1968 touted a secret plan to stop that war had not found a way to honorably end it by 1972.

When voters report, as they have since the early 1970s, that their voting decisions are more influenced by the character of the candidate than by stands on issues or party affiliation, they are revealing, in part, the extent to which party and promises are insufficient to allay the fears engendered by unforecast policies and unanticipated presidential behaviors: two presidents of opposite parties who lied to the American people; a succession who promised and failed to deliver full employment and a balanced budget without tax increases.

This book focuses on presidential debates to determine "What can we know and how can we know it?"

In a televised world filled with pre-timed, candidate-packaged messages, a world surfeiting in speech writers, media masters, and press aides, the electorate otherwise is hard pressed to know that what it sees is what it will get as president.

So skillful have candidates and their consultants become at choreographing themselves for news, that news can no longer assume the complete burden of disclosing the person who would be president. Biased toward dramatic, digestive, visual messages and preoccupied not with the substance of speeches but with their effect and strategic intent, broadcast news is more likely to focus on the race than on the decisive similarities and differences between the candidates. So do ads. As a result, a phalanx of consultants and advisers can hide a candidate behind carefully scripted and staged speeches and professionally produced ads.

Those who reduce the substance of campaigns to spot ads and situate these snippets within programming, tacitly acknowledge that the audience for ads is an inadvertent one. Audiences are unaccustomed to pondering the meaning and evidence harbored in ads for deodorants, discount records, denture creams, and toilet bowl cleaners. Framing political ads with "L.A. Law" and laxatives equates the presidency with escapist melodrama and disposable products and also invites viewers to see the claims of the candidates as unworthy of attention in their own right.

The audience that views debates has not been tricked into attention by its desire to learn the Venus Butterfly. By virtue of being ad-free, sustained encounters, debates assert the seriousness of the judgment they and the candidates court.

Not only do debates invite a focused attention uncharacteristic of ads but they also create a climate in which even those otherwise disposed to shun political messaging are expected to be able to converse about political data. "For days after the 1960 debates," recalled columnist David Broder before the 1980 debates, "there was intensive private conversation about the debates."[1] After the first debate of 1976, for example, eight of ten people reported that they had discussed the exchange.[2] The social pressure to take a sustained view of both candidates creates a climate more conducive to political learning than any other which the typical voter will seek or chance upon.

In a campaign season chock full of spot ads and news snippets viewers turn to debates to provide sustained analysis of issues and close comparisons of candidates. "Debate" has become a buzzword for "serious politics." Yet, after pulling out of the Democratic primary race in February 1988, former Arizona governor Bruce Babbitt bemoaned what he called the candidates' failure to address the most important issues. "We haven't really joined a debate. You know, you listen to the candidates and you think, they're all just talking."[3] Within the month, other candidates had joined in the chorus. "Some way must be found to get past the slogans," said Gary Hart in the Houston debate held in late February 1988. "We're trapped in these 90-second sound bites trying to say things that make a difference," added Jesse Jackson. But, countered debate moderator Linda Ellerbee, the format of this debate was put together by members of the campaign staffs of the candidates. "Your people agreed that this was the fairest way to do it." Whenever longer treatments of issues are proposed, added veteran television analyst Walter Cronkite, the opponents are the network executives and the campaign consultants.[4]

These charges occurred in a primary campaign featuring more candidate debates than any other in the history of presidential politics. If the candidates did not "really" join in debate, it was certainly not for lack of nationally televised events described as debates. By February 17, the date of Babbitt's withdrawal, the Democrats had met one another in such encounters at least twenty-two times, and one more was scheduled for the following evening. The programs were moderated by a representative of either the media or a national interest group; at least four of the candidates were present. By the conventions, the omnipresence of the debates had elicited parodies and jokes by candidates.

Many analysts suggest that the central problem is that these "joint press conferences" are not really debates at all.[5] Much can be said for this point of view. In the most common of the current formats, moderators and/or press panelists come between those who might otherwise argue directly among themselves. Sustained consideration of important issues is at best difficult when the topics shift rapidly, the emphases are determined by noncontestants, and the time is short. On the other hand, what we now know as candidate debates do provide politicians with a national forum in which to take their cases to the people. Presidential hopefuls gain some opportunity to spar if only by poking at one another in stolen asides. Debates in some senses and individual performances in others, these moderated confrontations defy simple classification.

Quite another question is whether these events—however labeled—are in the best interests of a nation faced with choosing a leader. Do they test knowledge and vision? Do they sort good ideas from bad? Do they reveal important character traits and habits of mind? In short, do they provide voters with what they need to know to choose a president?

Because they are national events, hyped by the campaigns and heralded by the media, and because, until the advent of cable, competing programming was minimal, debates were the fulcrum of the presidential campaigns in which they occurred. By 1976, over 98% of the homes in America owned televisions, so debates were accessible. Aired during a time when most are accustomed to viewing television, the prime-time general election debates are difficult to ignore. When debates are announced, movement in the polls slows; in anticipation, the electorate suspends its willingness to be swayed by ads and news. Here is the opportunity to see the candidates side by side, unfiltered and unedited.

The nation's experience with televised presidential debates dates from the 1960 election when John Kennedy faced Richard Nixon. The four sessions held in that year were not only the first televised presidential debates, but the first face-to-face debates of any sort between the nominees of the major parties.

If the idea of presidential candidate debates was new, the concept of political debating, even debating in presidential campaigns, was not. The great deliberative assemblies of the eighteenth and nineteenth centuries were in part debate societies constituted to enable the elected representatives of the people to meet one another to plead their cases for the best interests of the nation. Though contemptuous of electioneering, some individuals contesting for seats in the U.S. House of Representatives felt the need to debate on the campaign trail as early as 1788. Since the House was elected by direct popular vote, such appeals made sense. Early in the country's history two of its founders and future presidents—James Madison and James Monroe—engaged in debate for a congressional seat from Virginia. Some of these debates became legendary. In 1838, John T. Stuart and Stephen A. Douglas held joint debates in all the county seats of their Illinois congressional district. Each was a recognized champion of his party. Stuart was elected to Congress by a mere eight votes.

Occasionally debate was prompted not by a forthcoming election but a pending national issue. In 1854, Lincoln, who had held a single term in the House, took on incumbent Senator Stephen Douglas over the Kansas–Nebraska bill. Douglas spoke for the bill at the 1854 Illinois State Agricultural Fair; Judge Trumbell of Alton, a famous anti-Nebraskan Democrat, failed to arrive on time to deliver his scheduled reply; Lincoln, the most prominent of Illinois' anti-Nebraskan Whigs, countered Douglas' speech that evening. Earlier that year, Lincoln had rebutted Calhoun—another pro-Nebraska Democrat.

Because U.S. senators were not elected by popular vote but by the legislature, the Lincoln–Douglas debates of 1858 were controversial. "The present political canvass in Illinois is a singular one, and, I think, without a parallel in the history of electioneering campaigns in this country," wrote a correspondent for the New York *Evening Post* on October 21, 1858. "I say it is without parallel, for I do not believe that another instance can be shown where two individuals have entered into a personal contest before the public for a seat in the United States Senate—an office not directly in the gift of the people, but their representatives." "The members of the coming Legislature of Illinois will be just as free to exercise their own will in the choice of a Senator, as if neither Mr. Douglas nor Mr. Lincoln had perigrinated the State from lake to river, wrangling over what they are pleased to consider great national issues," sniffed the Cincinnati *Commercial* on September 23 of the same year. "The whole country is disgusted with the scene now exhibited in the State of Illinois," opined the Washington, D.C., *Union* (September 2, 1858). "The paramount object" of legislative selection "was to place the selection of a senator beyond the reach of the maddening issues of the hour to which the members of the lower house were exposed. But the spirit of the constitution is now being violated in Illinois." Two who had debated in House campaigns broke the taboo on such contests between senatorial opponents. History repeated itself in 1960. The first two major party nominees to debate each other had gained their House or Senate seats by besting incumbents in debate.

Although presidential candidates were thought to be above campaigning for themselves, surrogates for the candidates debated vigorously throughout the 1800s. In 1856, for example, Abraham Lincoln took to the stump in support of presidential contender John C. Frémont. But decorum dictated that presidential candidates themselves not debate. So William Jennings Bryan did not engage McKinley when his campaign brought him to McKinley's home town of Canton, Ohio. Nor did William Howard Taft and TR clash in person when they passed through the same town in the bitter campaign of 1912.

The debates that did occur were closely followed by voters who bought thousands of copies of the more famous speeches and read newspapers packed with detailed accounts of local contests. Political debating took place in a culture that valued debate as a means of educating leaders and elevating the character of the citizenry.

None of this means the system was flawless. Some partisans left after hearing the speech of their favorite. "Today we listened to a 3½ hour's speech from the Hon Abram Lincoln, in reply to that of Judge Douglas of yesterday," wrote a reporter for the *Chicago Democratic Press* on October 6, 1854. "He made a full and convincing reply and showed up squatter sovereignty in all its unblushing pretensions. We came away as Judge Douglas commenced to reply to Mr. Lincoln." Partisan newspapers accused each other of distorting the words of their candidate. "[I]t seems, from the difference between the two versions of Lincoln's speech, that the Republicans have a candidate for the Senate of whose bad rhetoric and horrible jargon they are ashamed, upon which, before they would publish it, they called a council of 'literary' men, to discuss, re-construct and re-write," observed the *Chicago Tribune* on August 25, 1858. "[T]hey dare not allow Lincoln to go into print in his own dress; and abuse us, the *Times,* for reporting him literally." Then as now the charge "all style and no substance" was heard.

Douglas' speeches "are plainly addressed to an excited crowd at some railway station, and seem uttered in unconsciousness that the whole American People are virtually deeply interested though not intensely excited auditors," noted the *New York Tribune* on November 9. "They are volcanic and scathing but lack the repose of conscious strength, the calmness of conscious right. They lack forecast and are utterly devoid of faith." Nor was news coverage necessarily substantive. "On the way to the railway track the procession of the Judge was met by Abe, who in a kind of nervous-excited manner tumbled out of his carriage, his legs appearing sadly in the way or out of place," reported the *Missouri Republican* (August 1, 1858). "Lincoln is looking quite worn out, his face looks even more haggard than when he said it was lean, lank and gaunt."

Then as now sports and battle metaphors abounded. "Illinois is regarded as the battle-ground of the year" wrote the *New York Semi-Weekly Post* (August 18, 1858). "The real battle has begun, by broadsides too, from the heaviest artillery," observed the *Louisville Democrat* (September 5, 1858)."We hope that Mr. Lincoln will continue to follow up Senator Douglas with a sharp stick, even if it does make his organ howl with rage," exclaimed the *Illinois State Journal* (July 23, 1858).

In his speech at Havana, Illinois, on August 13 (*Chicago Tribune,* August 25, 1858), Lincoln joked about the inappropriateness of the fight metaphor:

> I am informed [said he] that my distinguished friend yesterday became a little excited—nervous, perhaps—[laughter]—and said something about *fighting*, as though referring to a pugilistic encounter between him and myself. . . . I am informed, further, that somebody in *his* audience, rather more excited or nervous than himself, took off his coat, and offered to take the job off Judge Douglas's hands, and fight Lincoln himself. . . . Well, I merely desire to say that I shall fight neither Judge Douglas nor his second [great laughter]. I shall not do this for two reasons, which I will now explain. In the first place, a fight would *prove* nothing which is in issue in this contest. It might establish that Judge Douglas is a more muscular man than myself, or it might demonstrate that I am a more muscular man than Judge Douglas. But this question is not referred to in the Cincinnati platform, nor in either of the Springfield platforms [great laughter]. . . . My second reason for not having a personal encounter with the Judge is, that I don't believe he wants it himself. [laughter] He and I are about the best friends in the world, and

when we get together he would no more think of fighting me than of fighting his wife.

The extended history of political debate in America provides a record against which to assess the qualities of contemporary televised debates. In this book, we offer a review of past practices in an effort to discover how present debates serve the body politic and how they might be changed to be more helpful. Political debates have been important for more than two hundred years and respond to the history of that experience. By examining the role of debate in different historical and cultural circumstances, we can gain a clearer idea of the implications of format, the role of advocates, and the inherent qualities of debate as a form.

From the welter of competing formats, several characteristics emerge to define debate. Rhetorical scholar J. Jeffrey Auer identified five in his review of the 1960 presidential debates. Traditionally, debates have involved "(1) a confrontation, (2) in equal and adequate time, (3) of matched contestants, (4) on a stated proposition, (5) to gain an audience decision."[6] To Auer's list we would add a sixth: debates are rule governed.

These six characteristics enable debate to embody basic democratic assumptions and commit political leaders to them while calling forth a response from the audience that is consistent with them. Our country's belief in free speech is given substance in the words of the candidates, the panelists, the sponsors of the event, the news commentators, and the citizens whose opinions are reflected in polls. The notion that government derives its just powers from the consent of the governed is implied by the presence of a national audience. Where the constitutional debates were held in secret and their proceedings veiled in mystery, the country gradually came to accept that in a democracy debate should take place in the open, before the people. The records of those early constitutional debates were released. Senate and House proceedings were transcribed and published.

The belief that our system entails democratic choice is evident in the presence of two or more candidates whose task is to demonstrate that one would better represent the country than the others. Throughout the debates, the candidates will agree that the problems facing the country are solvable, that its institutions are functional, and that the people rule. The simultaneous presence of two candidates invites a focus on the office of president as well as those who aspire to hold it and a concentration on presidential relations with Congress as an institution regardless of the particular persons who represent the citizenry in the House and Senate.

Although the ideal of debate has rarely been realized in practice, it was useful for those who had just founded a new country. Debate flourished in the early days of this country because the country had to reestablish order after overthrowing one set of institutions for another. The new institutions needed to demonstrate that they were more legitimate than those they had replaced. Where the colonists had remonstrated and pleaded without response from George III, here would be a system responsive to the voices of the aggrieved.

The rhetoric of "we, the people" and "governments derive their just powers from the consent of the governed" was powerful stuff. The founders—a landed, educated elite—set in motion a system that would bind the conduct of subsequent generations of elites and would eventually empower the broader population to take part in government. Power would not transfer by bloodline but election. Power would be checked by other power. At the heart of "checks and balances" was a confidence in the ability of the best ideas to triumph if strongly presented by forceful advocates in a fair forum. Accordingly, the veto message of a president would be read into the record of Congress. Congress would then *reconsider* the legislation it had offered for signature.

The founders held George III accountable for his actions. The notion of presidential accountability to the people also emerged gradually. As we will argue, the form in which it emerged—the presidential press conference/debate—may not be well suited to accomplish this important objective. Since we will compare alternative forms of political communication to the classical concept of debate, let us briefly describe each of its characteristics.

A Confrontation

Debate gains its vitality from direct challenge. Advocates who disagree meet one another face to face to argue their differences. Misrepresentation invites immediate response. Unprepared debaters risk embarrassment and audience rejection. The great debates of history such as Madison–Lansing, Webster–Hayne, and Lincoln–Douglas pitted one against the other in the same place at the same time.

Debaters enter such confrontation in the belief that the stronger side will prevail, truth will triumph over falsehood, *logos* over *pathos*. The tangible fact of the opponent's presence acts as a check on discourse.

Alone on the stump, the politician runs few risks in padding his or her own record or hiding behind ambiguous appeals. By giving contesting candidates the opportunity to reinterpret, rebut, or take exception before a common audience, traditional debate raised the risks in distorting, dissembling, or hiding behind platitudes. So, for example, when the dominance of a single party silenced political debate in the South after the Civil War, a long-time Southern politician pined for the good old days. "Forty years ago," recalled Reuben Davis, "constant practice had made our public speakers so skillful in debate that every question was made clear even to men otherwise uneducated. For the last twenty years this practical union between politicians and people has not existed. Only one party is allowed to speak, and the leaders of that party no longer debate, they simply declaim and denounce." As a result, "The people follow with confidence the misleading and uncontrolled assertions of their leaders, and act upon false impressions, to their own prejudice and the injury of the common good."[7]

The Rule-governed Nature of Debate

By engaging in an orderly, rule-governed debate about ideological differences, individuals establish that they can resolve their disagreements peacefully. They can respectfully agree to disagree. Debate is a rule-bound activity with its peculiar protocols, time limits, and organization. All debates are structured, some more highly than others. The rules governing a debate are negotiated in advance, made plain to the audience, and accepted by the debaters. These rules usually specify the speaking order, length, and function of speeches as well as the overall structure of the exchange. The role of other participants such as the moderator may also be defined. By agreeing in advance to specified rules of procedure, debaters minimize dispute over such things, dispute that could detract seriously from the discussion at hand.

But debate is also bound by implied rules. Reason is privileged over emotion. Argument is considered superior to assertion. Tests of evidence exist. They guide judges to reject demagoguery and polemic for the reasoned case.

If truth can overcome falsehood in a fair encounter, and such fairness is ensured by the rules of debate, then there is no need for an elite to arbitrate political disagreements. The stronger arguments should prove persuasive. The merits of two-sided exchanges were recognized by G. B. Shaw who claimed that "The way to get at the merits of a case is not to listen to the fool who imagines himself impartial, but to get it argued with reckless bias for and against."

The point of debate is not to win but to let the truth emerge and prevail. By defining them as games and assessing their outcome as a win for one side or the other, we make of debates something they were not originally intended to be. By focusing on gaffes, appearance, and strategy but not the logic of the argument or the cogency of the evidence, we reduce debates to contests. By dismissing good argument as a mere rehash of old stump speeches, we deny that the end of debate is advancing a sense of which case is stronger and educating the audience in the process of making that determination.

Equal and Adequate Time

All parties enter a debate with equal standing. The more powerful faction is given the same time and governed by the same rules as the less powerful. Equal time is a fundamental principle in debate. Audiences cannot make useful comparisons of advocates who are granted different lengths of time. Moderators of televised general election debates cleave to this rule rigorously, timing candidates to the second and objecting strenuously when they run over.

The fact of equal time implies that various factions will listen to the positions advocated by their opponents and will then respond. There is an implied respect for the legitimacy of the other side and for the right of its advocates to carry forward its case. By requiring "listening" and encouraging engagement, debates become a means of educating all sides in the strengths and weaknesses of opposing positions.

The rule-governed nature of debate and its guarantee of equal time protect the minority. Unpopular views will not be suppressed but will instead be aired.

Matched Contestants

Successful debate hinges on a rough equality between advocates. Unmatched contestants provide a poor test of the ideas at issue. Academic debate preserves equality by pairing debaters of similar experience and skill against one another. Such a separation of accomplished and less accomplished participants requires shared criteria of what constitutes good debating and a clear method of tracking wins and losses.

The notion that contestants should be matched reveals the extent to which debate is designed to adjudicate issues, not to determine which advocate is the better leader. The focus of the Lincoln–Douglas debates was an issue and only incidentally concerned the people who took the opposite sides on it. Voters who agreed with the side championed by Lincoln would presumably vote for him.

A Stated Proposition

By engaging the same proposition, debaters focus their exchange. Tangents are minimized. Agenda switching is discouraged.

Academic debaters argue a specific proposition, such as "The United States should significantly increase its foreign military commitments," or "The federal government should adopt a comprehensive policy of land use control in the United States."[8] An affirmative team defends the proposition, a negative argues against it. As more than a topic area, the proposition provides an explicit focus for the debate, deepening the quality of the discussion and letting the audience know what the debaters are trying to prove. Their success will be measured by their ability to support or reject the resolution, not by smaller arguments or personal idiosyncracies unrelated to that task.

An Audience Decision

Lawyers arguing cases before the Supreme Court are debaters of a sort, adapting themselves to the infinite complexity of the legal code, the decisions of prior courts, and the etiquette appropriate for the nation's premier judicial body. The judges couch their decisions not in the language of personal preference, but of precedent, rule, and technical argumentation. Formal debating organizations such as intercollegiate societies also emphasize judicial neutrality. Judges are expected to suspend their ideological dispositions and vote for the more cogently argued side.

The audience for presidential debating is far less directed and accountable than the legal and intercollegiate judging pools. No written rules govern a decision on who "won" or "lost" a presidential debate. Audiences are free to vote preference rather than performance, and usually do. The audience probably employs some set of standards, but these are informal and inexplicit; candidates cannot easily make appeal to the "rules" in the course of argument.

One problem with the rules governing audience decision is that presidential debates require no formal decisions. Polling provides an idea of who looked best to the voters. But voters' partisan dispositions influence their judgment. On the simple dimensions of win and loss, debates are meaningless unless they translate into votes. Votes, in their turn, are poor indications of success or failure in debate. The decision to support or reject a candidate rests only partly, if at all, on debate performance.

Summary

In this book we argue that by minimizing confrontation, requiring brief responses, and spreading discussion across a smorgasbord of topics, televised presidential debates sacrifice much of their power to educate voters about the substance of issues. Even so, these "joint press conferences" remain powerful vehicles both for informing and for exposing an often-maligned but nonetheless important characteristic of candidates disparaged as image. Among our goals is determining what voters do and could learn about the content of public policy and the character of those who would shape it.

In the first three chapters, we will review the character and contributions of debates before the broadcast age. Chapter 1 seats political debate in the broad cultural context of the young nation. Many of the expectations applied to debate, then and now, were generated in colleges and public debating societies not directly connected with political enterprises. Along with the similarities between today's debates and those of the eighteenth and nineteenth centuries are some important differences. These are as much historical and cultural as they are specific to debate. We have already noted the variation in time, format, and the direct confrontation of the earlier debates. Important also is the question of who debates. In the nineteenth century, surrogates shouldered that responsibility in the presidential elections. Today, the candidates themselves take to the podium. Chapters 2 and 3 explore the contributions and limitations of the older format. These debates established points of difference between candidates but occasionally polarized issues needlessly. The debates involved the most prominent citizens in impassioned argument, but that very involvement bloodied some participants to the point that they could no longer assume the mantle of a president who must lead all. In short, some of the virtues of debate, when taken to extremes, can become vices.

Chapters 4, 5, and 6 examine the factors introduced in the broadcast era, reassessing the benefits of the debate form in its mass mediated incarnation. By contrasting the new with the old, we will attempt to sift the characteristics of debate from the uses to which the activity is put in an effort to determine how we might best use the form. Chapter 7 suggests ways to improve debating in particular and campaigning in general. We do not view debate as a panacea for the nation's political problems; indeed, we believe that debate, per se, is unequal to the tasks now asked of it. We do hold, however, that improved debates can strengthen the political process. The emphasis in the final chapter is not on creating the perfect conditions to support some ideal vision of presidential debates, but on practical responses to the realities of the contemporary campaign.

CHAPTER 1

◆

Characteristics
of Prebroadcast Debates
in America

The American political system grew up with debate. Colonial assemblies debated revolution, the Constitutional Convention debated the Constitution, and Congress debated the law. These contests produced memorable speeches and launched political careers. But debate was more than a political tool in early America; it was also a means of educating the young, honing professional skills, demonstrating personal worth, and enlightening the citizenry. These different purposes, overlapping in some respects and conflicting in others, combined to form the debate traditions of the early national period and some of the expectations that remain today.

Because training in debate was thought to produce sound habits of mind, skillful debating was taken as a sign of breeding and talent. From the colleges, legal moots, and lyceums, citizens carried the lessons of forensic education into political practice. Debate would not only teach the young, but guide the decisions of the nation as well.

Education

Though education in debate began as a university activity, available to very few colonists, it soon spread into a means of professional training. Educational societies held debates and encouraged the participation of every class of citizen. Debate was seen as a means of social advancement and a bulwark for independent thinking.

Academic and Civic Training

From the Latin disputations of the great British universities, Americans inherited debate as a means of training young scholars. In these disputations, students defended opposite sides of a question in syllogisms phrased in Latin. The result was undeniably elegant, but extremely formal and ill-suited to the rough-and-tumble life in the American colonies. Nevertheless, by the 1650s, most colonial colleges required the disputations, which were seen as the best way to pursue all three legs of the Roman trivium—rhetoric, logic, and grammar—in a single exercise. Competence in the disputations signaled a student's readiness to move on to more esoteric studies and ensure that these too could be presented in an arcane form unique to academe.

Beginning about 1750, colonial educators introduced more flexible forms of argumentation, in English.[1] At first, these complemented the disputations. The comparatively colloquial language and the emphasis on issues of the day generated enthusiasm for debating in the colonial colleges. Students pursued debates in the curriculum and in extracurricular clubs. The practice lasted well beyond the Revolution, and can still be found on many college campuses.

Curricular debates usually were supervised by a faculty member. When Thomas Jefferson was a student, George Wythe oversaw the debates at William and Mary. In addition to Jefferson, Wythe trained Henry Clay and John Marshall.[2] Yale's President Timothy Dwight published a book devoted entirely to comments on issues debated by the senior class in the 1813–14 academic year.[3] Though Dwight did not treat all the debates in precisely the same way, his standard practice was to offer some practical suggestions for the students on each side and then launch into a discussion of the main question with little reference to what the debaters may have said. All in all, the senior class held forty disputes between November 2 and April 20, a little more than six debates per month. Topics ranged from government ("Is Party spirit beneficial?" January 5, 1814), to education ("Ought emulation to be encouraged in schools?" February 5, 1814), to the supernatural ("Do spectres appear?" March 23, 1814). The president's decisions were written in a broadly instructive tone, emphasizing relevant literature and the importance of moral choice.

But the debates served as more than a forum for moral improvement. In the case of the lighter topics particularly, the debating societies were also a form of entertainment. In 1795, Harvard's Hasty Pudding Club debated the breach of promise in the case of *Dido* v. *Aeneas*.[4] Extracurricular societies were often run by the students without faculty assistance. John Quincy Adams participated in two such groups during his sojourn at Harvard. He must have enjoyed himself; complaining that he was too sick to attend the lectures of the day on November 12, 1786, he somehow managed to make a presentation that same evening.[5]

The comparatively limited goals of the disputations were radically expanded in the more open forensic form. Debate became known as the best way to develop the character and skills required of the citizens of a republic. As with the formal disputations, the conviction that debate and democracy are conjoined had its beginnings in England, appearing most often in pleas for the study of eloquence. Thomas Sheridan's *Course of Lectures on Elocution and the English Language* emphasized the many opportunities to put oratorical skills to good use. Sheridan was aghast that the English schools paid so little attention to the development of skills in the students' native tongue, saying that "the English are the only civilized people, either of ancient or modern times, who neglected to cultivate their language, or to methodize it in such a way, as that the knowledge of it might be regularly acquired."[6]

> These neglects are the more astonishing, because, upon examination, it will appear, that there neither is, nor ever was a nation upon earth, to the flourishing state of whose constitutional government, such studies were so absolutely necessary. Since it must be obvious to the slightest enquirer, that the support of our establishment, both ecclesiastical and civil, in their due vigour, must in a great measure depend upon the powers of elocution in public debates, or other oratorical performances, displayed in the pulpit, the senate–house, or at the bar.[7]

Americans were willing to buy the argument outright in all respects save geography. For them, the United States—not England—was the nation where such skills were most necessary. In his inaugural lecture for the Boylston Chair of Rhetoric at Harvard, John Quincy Adams reminded his audience of the power and responsibility enjoyed by the eloquent in a "pure" republic. "Under governments purely republican, where every citizen has a deep interest in the affairs of the nation, and, in some form of public assembly or other, has the means of delivering his opinions, and of communicating his sentiments by speech; where government itself has no aims but those of persuasion; where prejudice has not acquired an uncontrolled ascendency, and faction is yet confined within the barriers of peace, the voice of eloquence will not be heard in vain."[8] Adams' father also linked oratorical skill with personal success. "Eloquence will become the instrument for recommending men to their fellow citizens, and the principal means of advancement through the various ranks and offices of society."[9]

Private organizations encouraged the development of the skills that offered mastery and not a little mystery. New York's Forum was one such organization operating in the early nineteenth century. I. P. C. Sampson, the outgoing president, eulogized the speaker as a god.

> In the senate, eloquence assumes a graver aspect . . . when he rises in the midnight debate, every eye is fixed, every ear listens. Wearied attention fastens on his words. By degrees, attention becomes astonishment, astonishment conviction. His hearers wonder at their former doubts; till, as he rises to the meridian of his eloquence, they lose themselves in transport and enthusiasm. . . . His eloquence is not the display of sentiment . . . his true character is force, and he delights to exert it; like the tempest, swelling and rising with the roar of the chafed element.[10]

These sentiments held firm throughout the nineteenth century. Touting the values of a debating society for young men in 1890, Charles Cuthbert Hall continued the virtual deification of the debater. "There is something truly magnificent in the caution, quickness, prowess and pluck of a good debater. His eye flashes with mental fire; his face is radiant with the play of ideas; his muscles are tense with their grasp of the theme; he wrestles not with flesh and blood, but with principalities and powers of the human intellect. Is there a nobler sport for men, the highest of all God's creatures?"[11]

Beyond developing great orators debate was thought to benefit the common folk. Hall prized debate as an "antidote to dogmatism of newspapers, the crowded mode of living [and] the subtle power of personal prejudice."[12] At the grass-roots level, debate was valued as the guarantor of the "sacred right of private judgment." Thus, on the one hand, debate was a means of improving the quality of decision making, and, on the other, a means by which, theoretically, all opinions could gain some standing in the community.

The notion that debate provided access to the political life of the nation bore important implications for an expanding democracy. If popular wisdom lodged power with the debater and all citizens could debate, then meaningful social power was available to all members of the society; the individual's only choice was whether to develop and use the skill. Debate did not have to function perfectly as a powerful social leveler. There were enough reputations founded on debate to characterize it as an important instigator of social change. Making use of this avenue for empowerment required would-be advocates to adapt to some of the more conservative conventions of the day. Debaters submitted to an authority governing most aspects of the activity, from order of procedure and speaking time to rendering a decision. Rather than threatening the system, debate helps to conserve it.

Outside the schools, people from all walks of life flocked to the speaking and debating societies that grew up in tandem with the citizen education societies known as lyceums. By 1831, more than one thousand lyceums dotted the landscape.[13] The Boston Lyceum, one of the oldest and most active organizations in the nation, offered regular classes in debate.[14] Through the 1840s, the Concord and Manchester lyceums were organized almost entirely around debates.[15] Walt Whitman served as secretary for the Smithtown Debating Society in 1837 and 1838. Two years before his death, Thomas Jefferson wrote an approving letter to the organizer of a Massachusetts debating society founded in his name.

> I have duly received your favor of the 6th instant, informing me of the institution of a debating society in Hingham, composed of adherents to the republican principles of the Revolution; and I am justly sensible of the honor done my name by associating it with the title of the society. The object of the society is laudable, and in a republican nation, whose citizens are to be led by reason and persuasion, and not by force, the art of reasoning becomes of first importance.[16]

The distinction between the lyceum and the debating society was a useful one in the early nineteenth century. Historian Carl Bode reports that most lyceum constitutions forbade the introduction of overtly political topics; the debating society was a natural recipient of the political overflow.[17] In practice, by the end of the nineteenth century, lyceums hosted a number of controversial speakers whose presence if not their presentations excited partisan reaction. Despite the strictures on political debate written into lyceum bylaws, political topics found their way into programs during the antebellum period as well. Politicians such as Lewis Cass and abolitionists such as Frederick Douglass were regular speakers on the lyceum circuit. Lyceum meetings often centered on questions of political economy that bore direct implications for partisan politics. For instance, in 1850, the Glasgow Lyceum met to consider whether "the signs of the times indicate a dissolution of the present Political Parties."[18]

Whatever the explicit political content, the lyceums were popular and influential. Members dedicated themselves to "mutual education," teaching and being taught through joint participation in a series of discussions and lectures. The meetings were geared for self-improvement, but served as entertainment also, the nineteenth century's version of public broadcasting. In some rural areas, the lyceum or debating society was the only legal public entertainment.

The societies dovetailed neatly with the capabilities and prejudices of the young nation. With self-improvement as a stated goal, they fit comfortably within the reformist enthusiasms of antebellum society. The opportunity for universal involvement was consistent with a government "of the people, by the people, and for the people."

Youngsters were raised on the examples of the great debates. In addition to the desktop "readers" and "spellers," most students were given a "speaker," brimming with selections from America's great speeches. By the latter half of the nineteenth century, popular texts included the *Young America Speaker,* the *Young Folks Speaker,* and McGuffey's *New Juvenile Speaker.* In these volumes and in the readers, students were introduced to American oratory with the William Wirt version of Patrick Henry's speech on the Stamp Act and Webster's reply to Hayne.[19] The speeches were memorized and delivered in class as part of regular lessons. From an early age, children were taught the majesty of debate and edified with tales of the success of those who debated well. Advanced students might go on to James McElligott's *The American Debater,* an early text on debate technique. McElligott stressed the unique importance of debate to an American citizen. In language similar to Adams' or Hall's, he extolled debate as a duty of citizenship that held the promise of greatness for everyone. "The occasions for the use of deliberative eloquence are now more numerous and important than they ever have been in any previous age of the world. Wherever the will of the people is the law of the land, wherever republican principles prevail to any considerable extent, there deliberative assemblies must often be convened."[20]

Legal Training

Many of America's politicians began their professional lives as attorneys and were schooled in face-to-face advocacy in this role. The country's legal tradition has always been adversarial, based on the assumption that justice is most likely to occur when plaintiff and respondent present the strongest possible cases before a neutral judge and jury. A vote for the winning argument provides the best means of ensuring justice. "We believe that truth is apt to emerge from this crucible," said attorney Joseph N. Welch, counsel for the Army during the Army–McCarthy hearings. "It usually does."[21]

Legal-debating societies involved prominent citizens in colonial America. John Jay was a member of two such organizations. In 1768, he participated in the plainly titled Debating Society of New York City. The members considered the debates "particularly valuable training for attorneys," but ranged over topics of interest beyond the bar. Accounts remain of the group's efforts to answer the question, "Was Virginius morally justified in putting his daughter, Virginia, to death to preserve her from violation by Appius?"[22]

The Moot, an organization holding debates in New York from 1770–1775, was more tightly tied to legal questions, such as jurisdiction, the authority of lesser courts, and the proper wording for contracts.[23] Participants saw the Moot as a means of continuing their legal education and providing answers to questions important to the legal community. These were not school exercises, but adult activities taken seriously by the leading attorneys in New York. That they would take time away from their practices during such a volatile period is ample testimony to the value the profession attributed to debate skills.

Thomas Jefferson stressed the importance of debate to young attorneys. Writing in the same year he was admitted to the Virginia bar, Jefferson advised aspirants to find a "neighbor engaged in the same study, take each of you different sides of the same cause, and prepare pleadings according to the customs of the bar, where the plaintiff opens, the defendant answers, and the plaintiff replies."[24] He also recommended a study of the principles of rhetorical practice, citing particularly Hugh Blair's *Lectures on Rhetoric and Belles Lettres* (London, 1783) and Thomas Sheridan's *Course of Lectures on Elocution and the English Language* (London, 1759) as useful texts.

Success at the bar and the rostrum often coincided. Patrick Henry and John Adams were two of the more highly compensated lawyers in the colonies. Daniel Webster argued several famous cases before the Supreme Court and continued to draw a substantial income from his law practice well into his career in the Senate. On the other hand, Jefferson's legal career was comparatively inglorious. Admitted to the bar in 1767, he closed his practice in 1774. Biographer Merrill Peterson notes, kindly, that Jefferson "never achieved the celebrity of his folksy friend, Patrick Henry."[25] Some attribute his difficulties to problems in debate. "He had all the other qualifications; but his voice became gutteral [*sic*] and inarticulate in moments of great excitement, and the consciousness of his infirmity prevented him from risking his reputation in debate."[26]

Despite these problems, Jefferson remained convinced of the importance of debate. He advocated training in style as well as technical argumentation. Jefferson encouraged a style that would allow advocates to appeal directly to the common man. "State a moral case to a ploughman and a professor. The former will decide it as well, and often better than the latter, because he has not been led astray by artificial rules."[27] The third president considered verbal style one of the most important elements shaping the character of a legal career. In a letter to James Madison written in the last year of his life, Jefferson linked the study of law to the generation of political principle.

> In the selection of our Law Professor, we must be rigorously attentive to political principles. You will recollect that before the Revolution, Coke Littleton was the universal elementary book of law students, and a sounder Whig never wrote, nor of profounder learning in the orthodox doctrines of the British Constitution, or in what were called English liberties. You remember also that our lawyers were then all Whigs. But when his black-letter text and uncouth but cunning learning got out of fashion, and the honeyed Mansfieldism of Blackstone became the student's hornbook, from that moment, that profession (the nursery of our Congress) began to slide into toryism, and nearly all the young brood of lawyers now are of that hue.[28]

More than a refined sense of oratory, Jefferson's interest in style reflected his agrarian ideals and his concern that deliberation be directed toward the people. To involve the simple citizens, from whom he thought the best impulses in the nation would derive, style in law and politics had to remain plain.

The image of the lawyer as debater continued in a more or less straight line from Patrick Henry in the eighteenth century to Daniel Webster in the nineteenth, Clarence Darrow in the twentieth, and Louis Nizer today. We have added the notion of the lawyer as carefully briefed technocrat, and were moving in that direction as early as the 1920s, but even this dimension of the profession assumes the kind of responsive argumentation that was once prosecuted orally and orally alone.[29] The importance of debate in law and the prominence of lawyers in the political system reinforce the procedural and personal impact of debate as an evaluative tool.

Politics

Educators' assertions that debates would be central to the political life of the American democracy were borne out in the eighteenth and nineteenth centuries. However, determining what the period of "great debates" might tell us about our modern practices is problematic. The first difficulty has to do with the forum. Most of the great debates were not campaign debates in any direct sense; they took place in deliberative bodies such as the Constitutional Convention, the colonial and state assemblies, and the Congress. The purposes and pressures of debating questions of policy in a body of peers differ rather dramatically from those confronting presidential candidates debating qualifications for office before an audience of voters. A second problem has to do with participants. Candidates at any level rarely debated one another directly in the prebroadcast era; presidential nominees never did. Finally, the culture was very different. In a world unaffected by the technology of electronic media and yet to undergo the ideological upheavals of the twentieth century, debates spoke to the sensibilities and conditions of a time that cannot easily be compared with ours.

The legacy of the great debates is nevertheless interesting for several reasons. Legislative debates were political arguments conducted under specific rules to gain an audience decision. They were prominent and closely attended; by the standards of the day, they were media events. The need to argue simultaneously before knowledgeable colleagues and the public remains an ongoing problem for debate. Presidential campaign debates involved battles by surrogates. The strengths and limitations of the surrogate tradition pose an illuminating counterpoint to contemporary candidate debates. A critical assessment of the way that debate worked then—in an age more accustomed, through training and practice, to the rigors of traditional debate—can offer a better understanding of what might be possible.

The complexity and sheer number of legislative debates make a complete treatment impossible in this volume. We have opted instead to examine the characteristics most relevant to modern presidential debating. We will begin this section by describing the expectations and practices of legislative debate with an eye to the roles of character and argumentative style. A discussion of election debates follows.

Debates in Deliberative Assemblies

Debate satisfied a powerful social need for the new nation. The balanced, oppositional character of the government that emerged from the Constitutional Convention of 1787 expressed itself naturally in the give and take of policy debate. "The people were not an order organically tied together by their unity of interest but rather an agglomeration of hostile individuals coming together for their mutual benefit to construct a society," argues historian Gordon Wood.[30] Such a system requires a way to express and resolve competition in a socially responsible fashion. Madison framed the problem in *The Federalist* #10 when he said that "The regulation of these various and interfering interests forms the principal task of modern legislation and involves the spirit of party and faction in the necessary and ordinary operations of government."[31] Debate provided a form readymade for the political arena. The Congress institutionalized the expression and resolution of sectional interests in the new nation. Provided that national leaders trusted one another as men of decency and honor, debate could serve as a direct expression of political differences within the context of a shared social and political commitment.

Central to the notion of resolving disputes in an orderly fashion was the use of faction against faction in an open forum. The founding fathers thought faction most mischievous when it was hidden, and debate is quintessentially public. However, "public" was thought by some to refer to the open exchange of opinions among equals, not the dissemination of those exchanges to common citizens. The difference is related to competing visions of democracy. Operating on the assumption that knowledge is a kind of power, those who defended disclosure effectively defended a broader political system.

The public character of argument became an issue in the debates over adoption of the Constitution.

The debates at the Constitutional Convention over the New Jersey and Virginia proposals for representation illustrate the delegates' use of debate to gain perspective and reach resolution. In these confrontations the delegates opted for lengthy examination of the plans in general session rather than solutions negotiated in committee "in order that a comparative estimate might be had of the two."[32] The records of these debates are still sought for guidance on the framers' "original intent" for the new Constitution. James Madison, who took his role as recorder seriously, apparently intended the debates to serve as the measure of the wisdom of the delegates. Writing in the Preface to his *Notes of Debates in the Federal Convention of 1787*, he claimed that "of the ability and intelligence of those who composed the convention, the debates and proceedings may be a test; as the character of the work which was the offspring of their deliberations must be tested by the experience of the future."[33]

That was not, however, the way they were treated at the time. The Constitutional Convention of 1787 that produced the U.S. Constitution was conducted behind closed doors, the records of its debates deposited in the custody of the president and kept from the people who were called on to ratify the document. In deciding to shield the debates from public view, the convention adopted the sentiments of Benjamin Franklin, who noted,

> The opinions I have had of its errors, I sacrifice to the public good. I have never whispered a syllable of them abroad. Within these walls they were born, and here they shall die. If every one of us in returning to our Constituents were to report the objections he has had to it, and endeavor to gain partizans in support of them, we might prevent its being generally received, and thereby lose all the salutary effects and great advantages resulting naturally in our favor among foreign Nations as well as among ourselves, from our real or apparent unanimity.[34]

The recordkeepers heeded Franklin's advice for more than fifty years; Madison's notes went unpublished until 1840. Some scholars feel that Madison did not publish them himself because he did not want his arguments for broad federal authority to be marshalled against his own later defenses of state sovereignty. Irving Brant believes that some of the alterations in the manuscript resulted from the fourth president's embarrassment over what he had actually said in the Constitutional Convention debates.[35]

Those opposing ratification underscored the extent to which open deliberation was a shared premise of the infant government. Writing against adoption (October 11, 1787) by New York, George Clinton rebutted an advocate pseudonymously labeled Caesar saying, "He shuts the door of free deliberation and discussion, and declares that you must receive this government in manner and form as it is *proffered*."[36] Six days after Pennsylvania became the second state to ratify the Constitution, the anti-Federalists published their dissent. "The convention sat upward of four months. The doors were kept shut, and the members brought under the most solemn engagements of secrecy. Some of those who opposed their going so far beyond their powers, retired, hopeless, from the convention; others had the firmness to refuse signing the plan altogether; and many who did sign it, did it not as a system they wholly approved but as the best that could be then obtained; and notwithstanding the time spent on this subject, it is agreed on all hands to be a work of haste and accommodation."[37]

After ratification, the spectre of the secret convention was raised by those advocating amending the Constitution, Melancton Smith of New York among them. Under the pseudonym "A Plebian," he claimed, "While it was agitated, the debates of the Convention were kept an impenetrable secret, and no opportunity was given for well-informed men to offer their sentiments upon the subject."[38] The subsequent deliberation revealed the faith in open public debate. "Since that, it has been the object of universal attention—it has been thought of by every reflecting man—been discussed in a public and private manner, in conversation and in print; its defects have been pointed out, and every objection to it stated; able advocates have written in its favor, and able opponents have written against it. And what is the result? It cannot be denied but that the general opinion is that it contains material errors and requires important amendments."

Abstract evaluation of the ideas expressed in the Constitution was an important, but insufficient test of its value. Debate, if not secret, offered an opportunity to assess the document in terms of personal commitments. In the eighteenth and nineteenth centuries, reputation was an important component of argument. By dichotomizing "image" and "issue," contemporary theorists have lost sight of the role that character can and has played in the assessment of claims. "Reflect," urged John Jay in support of the Constitution, "that the present plan comes recommended to you by men and fellow citizens who have given you the highest proofs that men can give of their justice, their love for liberty and their country; of their prudence; of their application; and their talents. They tell you it is the best that they could form; and that in their opinion it is necessary to redeem you from those calamities which already begin to be heavy upon us all. You find that not only those men but others of similar characters, and of whom you have also had very ample experience, advise you to adopt it. . . . They perceive not those latent mischiefs in it, with which some double-sighted politicians endeavor to alarm you."[39] Character was marshalled on the other side as well. Speaking against ratification, Patrick Henry noted, "A number of characters of the greatest eminence in this country object to this government for its consolidating tendency. This is not imaginary. It is a formidable reality."[40]

The debates that followed the constitutional disputes of the 1780s perpetuated the close linkage of character and claim. Advocates lent their own authority to their positions; debate was a means of comparing not only policy, but public persona as well. The great debaters, such as John Calhoun, Daniel Webster, Stephen Douglas, and others, spent a good deal of time preparing their arguments and placed great importance on the outcomes. The debates committed members to positions and established the parameters within which solutions negotiated in smaller groups would need to fit.

Some of the more important debate speeches became identified as definitive national positions. One of the nineteenth century's greatest debates began as a digression. A proposal to limit the sale of public lands and abolish the office of Surveyor General occasioned the wide-ranging deliberation on the Constitution, the Union, and the nature and scope of the powers of the federal government known as the Webster–Hayne Debate. Webster's Second Reply to Hayne, delivered January 26–27, 1830, "the most widely read and most influential utterance of its time," came to stand for the unionist position against the nullificationist challenge.[41] James Madison claimed that the speech crushed nullification and "must everywhere hasten the abandonment of secession."[42] The fame Webster achieved through this and other debates did not win him the presidency, nor did the debates ensure the success of his legislative agenda, but they were significant rallying points that established political alignments and elicited popular support. The Second Reply to Hayne, for example, drove a wedge between western and southern Democrats over specific questions of public works and over more general concerns over patriotism and nationhood.

Although the growing split may not have given Webster the victories he sought, it was an important event in the political history of the nation. Webster's reply to Hayne was significant not only for the issues it addressed, but for the words he chose. Numerous advocates of nationhood had asserted the importance of the union. By couching the arguments in memorable rhetoric, Webster located the rationale for union in a popularly accessible form. Consider his argument for the supremacy of the people in the reported version of the Second Reply to Hayne.

Sir, whence is this supposed right derived of the State authorities to interfere with the action of this government? It has its foundation, in my opinion, in a total mistake of the origin of this government. I hold it to be a popular government coming from the people, created by the people, responsible to the people, capable of [being] amended and modified in such manner as the people may prescribe; just as popular, just as much emanating from the people as the State governments and there is no more authority in the State governments to interfere and arrest the action of any law of Congress because they think it unconstitutional, than Congress has to arrest the action of any law of any State because it is contrary to the Constitution of that State. Sir, I go the whole length. This Government has not dependence on the State governments. We the People of the United States made this Government. It is as pure an emanation of popular opinion as any State Government whatever. . . . This government came from the people, is responsible to them, and is an independent fruit of the popular [will?] How is it then that the State Governments have a right to interfere in the action of the government?[43]

Tarred with aristocratic sentiments early in his career, Webster here offers a vision of popular democracy that both responds to Hayne's efforts to link northern Whigs with the Hartford Convention and coopts the populism of the secessionists. He bases his analysis on the Constitution, but bases the Constitution in turn on the will of the people. Democrats who suborn the will of the national government do not protect, but rather usurp, the rights of individual Americans. Coinciding as they did with the rapid expansion of popular democracy under Andrew Jackson, the arguments resonated not only with Webster's natural constituency in New England, but with swelling democratic feelings throughout the nation.

Turning quickly from the people to patriotism, he closed the speech with a personal pledge to nationhood.

> I hope I may not see the standard raised of separate State rights, star against star, and stripe against stripe; but that the flag of the Union may keep its stars and its stripes corded and bound together in indissoluble ties. I hope I shall not see written, as its motto, *First* Liberty, and *then* Union. I hope I shall see no such delusive and deluted motto on the flag of that Country. I hope to see spread all over it, blazoned in letters of light and proudly floating over Land and Sea that other sentiment, dear to my heart, "Union *and* Liberty, now and forever, one and inseparable."[44]

By offering an opportunity to respond to personal charges in kind, debate permitted the identification of people with doctrines and framed personal testimony as a strong impetus to action. Webster could performatively negate the charges of elitism for himself and his party in the act of espousing his patriotic alternatives. The image of the maligned patriot aroused on behalf of his country grasped attention at the level of personality as well as issue. Cultural historian Daniel Boorstin notes the importance of such riveting moments in the development of national character. "The brevity of the American tradition and the scarcity of sacred political texts gave the Great Debates (Webster–Hayne, Lincoln–Douglas, etc.) a peculiar role in helping the nation publicly discover itself."[45]

The role of debating changed substantially by the late nineteenth century; the dramatic expansion of the committee system backed more and more legislative work off the floors of the House and Senate into smaller rooms lacking galleries, size, and formality.[46] With much of the legislative burden undertaken in committee, there was less opportunity to attempt to persuade the larger bodies of the Congress in floor debate. The volume of work moved into committee between 1820 and 1905 is reflected in the rising number of committees. In 1821, there were thirty-eight standing committees in the Congress. In 1836, that number had risen to forty-nine. There were one hundred six standing committees in 1895, and one hundred fifteen by 1903.[47] Debate remained important even as the committee system grew, but its character changed. Legislative harangues outside the explicitly elective context were less well publicized. The smaller and more specialized audiences encouraged a kind of Capitol Hill argot that was not as accessible as the more self-consciously public language of debates in the antebellum period.

Woodrow Wilson believed that the committee system demeaned

ROBERT HAYNE

the deliberative process. Writing in *Congressional Government* near the turn of the century he condemned the tendency of the houses of Congress to rubber-stamp committee recommendations without careful debate.[48] Nor did the deliberations within the standing committees satisfy him. "They have about them none of the searching, critical, illuminating character of the higher order of parliamentary debate, in which men are pitted against each other as equals, and urged to sharp contest and masterful strife by the inspiration of political principle and personal ambition, through the rivalry of parties and the competition of policies." In the committees Wilson found "a joust between antagonist interests." Without the general melee of the full legislature, these could not be brought around to serve the will of the people. Wilson's regret for the loss of a style in which "men are pitted against each other" reflects the shift from a highly individualistic, personalized conception of debate to a more technical means of doing business. Whether the product of workload or zeitgeist, the burgeoning committee system

DANIEL WEBSTER

Daniel Webster turned a debate on western lands into the definitive case for union. His Second Reply to Hayne became the most widely read political document of its time.

was largely responsible for shifting high profile personality struggles from the rostrum to the backroom.

Election Debates

Beyond the strictly deliberative applications of argumentation, debate has been an important element of elections in America from 1788 through the twentieth century. That is not to say, however, that the earliest election debates looked very much like our own. Presidential candidates did not campaign for the office in person until late in the nineteenth century. Even Winfield Scott's single speech defending himself against opponents' accusations in 1840 occasioned a fuss over propriety. Not until William Jennings Bryan assumed a high profile in his 1896 race against McKinley did a presidential candidate campaign in a way we would recognize today.

The Lincoln–Douglas debates in 1858 were the most famous of the candidate election debates, but they were certainly not the first. James Madison and James Monroe debated in pursuit of a House seat from Virginia in 1788. Madison undertook his debating responsibilities reluctantly, writing to Thomas Jefferson that "The trip [to campaign in Virginia] is in itself very disagreeable, both on account of its electioneering appearance and the sacrifice of the winter."[49] Madison and Monroe stumped together across Orange, Spotsylvania, Louisa, Culpeper, and Albemarle counties, debating face to face at each stop. Madison later conceded that the effort proved worthwhile. "I am persuaded, however, that my appearance in the district was . . . necessary. In truth, it has been evinced by the experiment that my absence would have left a room for the calumnies of anti-federal partizans, which would have defeated much better pretensions than mine."[50] Twelve years later, presidential candidate Thomas Jefferson was able to leave the stumping to others. The *Virginia Argus* reported "A meeting of candidates for electors of the President and Vice President of the United States . . . for the purpose of haranguing the people of the county."[51]

Debate remained an important element of campaigning throughout the nineteenth century. William Jennings Bryan's first campaign for the House revolved around "a series of joint debates with his Republican opponent."[52] Some observers attribute his nomination at the 1896 Democratic national convention to his debating skills.

Ben Tillman of South Carolina had been engaged in a vigorous debate with Senators Hill and Vilas and former Governor Russell over the currency plank of the party platform. Arranging to be heard last, Bryan delivered his well-practiced "Cross of Gold" speech. A tremendous demonstration followed the speech. One observer claimed that the moment "was an emotional high that was remembered, like hearing Patti or Jenny Lind," the popular singers of the nineteenth century.[53]

In focusing attention during this period in American politics on the "boom"—the rowdy, shouting support for favored candidates—observers such as Ostrogorski have neglected the role of debates in the elections of the late nineteenth century.[54] Bryan's clever use of the debate format to display his skills favorably in direct and compelling contrast with more established party members allowed him to be taken seriously in a way that he might not have been able to arrange through other means. The debate form allowed him to show the "Cross of Gold" speech to advantage in contest with an opponent, a display of the sort of skill, knowledge, and leadership expected of a president.

More common than direct candidate debates in the nineteenth century was the practice of surrogate debating, a phenomenon important in presidential elections. Numerous election debates were conducted by surrogates acting on behalf of the major party candidates. These stand-ins were often prominent, talented members of the Congress or major political figures in their respective states. Former presidential aspirants Clay and Webster also stumped for the Whig candidates. In the election of 1836, two obscure Illinois politicians joined the fray when Abraham Lincoln, representing the Whigs, debated Democrat John I. Calhoun in Illinois. Lincoln debated Calhoun again in 1840 and 1844. Contemporary newspaper accounts followed the give and take of the debate closely. On March 18, 1844, the *Sangamo Journal* reported that "Though Mr. Calhoun triumphantly established the first proposition, yet Mr. Lincoln had the hardihood to assert that [the cost of the tariff] might *probably* fall upon the manufacturer, after Mr. Calhoun had shown that it positively fell upon the consumer. . . . Mr. Lincoln very candidly acknowledged his inability to prove that the tariff had anything to do with the *late* low prices throughout this country and Europe."[55] The surrogate debates illustrated the influence of party politics of the time. Barred by custom from campaigning on his own behalf, a presidential candidate could not be elected without the efforts of the party stalwarts stumping the land. This had the dual effect of binding established candidates to the party platform and giving younger politicians national exposure.

Surrogate debaters often raised character questions, charging that their opponents were all style and no substance. Stand-ins who were not yet prominent members of the national party engaged freely in personal attack. When Democrats blamed the Whigs for hanging on to Taylor's "military coattails," Lincoln responded on the floor of the House of Representatives. "Your campaign papers have constantly been 'Old Hickories' with rude likenesses of the old general upon them; hickory poles and hickory brooms, your never-ending emblems; Mr. Polk himself was 'Young Hickory' 'Little Hickory' or something so; and even now, your campaign paper here, is proclaiming that Cass and Butler are of the true 'Hickory Strips.' No, sir, you dare not give it up."[56]

Party leaders thought the proxy arguments extremely important, and paid close attention to their opponents' claims. This was true even of House and Senate races, in which candidates campaigned personally. Concerned about the vigorous assaults on his candidacy and his ticket in the Illinois elections of 1858, Stephen Douglas insisted on the importance of help on the hustings. In a letter to Charleston's Postmaster, Jacob I. Brown, Douglas wrote, "It is important that Gen. Linder should take the stump immediately, and the 'genteel thing' will be done with him. Tell him to [meet?] me at my first appointment, wherever it may be, after his return from Indiana, prepared to take the stump from that time until the election. . . . The Democrats are thoroughly aroused, and well united, and a glorious triumph awaits us as certain as the day of election comes. Yet our friends should not be idle but should put forth effort that will overcome those that are made against us."[57] This letter highlights the role of stand-ins even in nonpresidential races. Despite ample opportunities to debate Abraham Lincoln face to face in 1858, Douglas thought that surrogate activity was essential to his own candidacy and the overall success of the Democratic party in Illinois. The use of surrogates in such a contest shows that the pressure for surrogacy went beyond efforts to protect the delicate sensibilities of those who campaigned for the presidency in the early national period.

The publication of responses and selections from debate speeches served as an important adjunct to political campaigning. Though not debates in the strict sense, campaign publications were often rendered as if they were, serving to extend the influence of the form. Like the face-to-face arguments, these print debates were invested with a sense of order and propriety. When in the summer of 1788 Andrew Brown revived his paper, the *Federal Gazette,* the inaugural issue of October 1 contained an anonymous letter from "A Friend to the Union." The Friend, later identified as Benjamin Rush, articulated a basic premise regarding fair conduct in print debates: Both sides should have access to the same audience. "If a printer offends you, attack him in your paper, because he can defend himself with the same weapons with which you wound him. Type against type is fair play; but to attack a man who has no types nor printing press, or who does not know anything about the manual of using them, is cowardly in the highest degree. If you had been in twenty Bunker Hill battles instead of one, and had fought forty duels into (sic) the bargain, and were afterwards to revenge an affront upon a man who was not a printer in your newspaper, I would not believe that you possessed a particle of true courage."

Summary

In the classroom and the Congress, the lyceum and the legislature, debate proved the mettle of policies and persons. In politics, debating reveals problem-solving abilities, habits of mind, and electoral appeal. The prominent debaters of the early national period were powerful members of their parties whose arguments digested the legislative battles of their time. Their cases were delivered on the floors of the House and Senate as well as in newspapers and town meeting halls. The wide reach of the debate form and its importance in capturing the voters catapulted talented young surrogates to national attention. Besides revealing the power of a set of ideas, the information gained from the debates allowed voters to judge the worth of those who would one day seek elective office. Public access to debate extended the sense of citizen engagement in the affairs of the democracy.

Debate served well in some respects, poorly in others. Though well adapted to deliberating questions of policy, the quality of debate often suffered when turned to purposes beyond assessing the merits of a proposition. Debate improved the character of discussion on some important issues during the early days of the American republic, but it did not salvage wisdom from rancor or produce a clear answer to every difficult question. In Chapters 2 and 3, we will examine the benefits and pitfalls of debate as it was practiced in the prebroadcast era.

◆

CHAPTER 2

The Contributions
of American Debate,
1770-1920

Prominent Americans have ascribed various benefits to debate. Thomas Jefferson named "free argument and debate" the "natural weapons" of truth, "errors ceasing to be dangerous when it is permitted freely to contradict them."[1] Woodrow Wilson believed that debate discouraged demagoguery. In Britain, he observed, debate had produced decades of leaders, but few demagogues. In parliamentary debate, orators were judged by their "readiness of resource," "clearness of vision," "grasp of intellect," "courage of conviction," and "earnestness of purpose." Accordingly, at each of the universities where he taught, Wilson advocated debating societies patterned on the Oxford Union.[2] Though debate often fell short of these grand promises, prebroadcast debates in America contributed to the development and preservation of the political system and educated the electorate about the issues and personalities of the day.

Our analysis of the contributions of debate begins with a discussion of formal and informal structure. Participants in a debate subject themselves to certain rules of procedure and assessment. In Jefferson's rules of order, for example, members of Congress could speak on an issue only twice in the same day. Abraham Lincoln and Stephen Douglas were restricted to one and one-half hours each in their debates of 1858. The rigors of format are a constant reminder to debaters and audiences that debates—no matter how rancorous— are fundamentally lawful activities, bound by agreements that go beyond the issues of the moment.

This lawfulness makes each debate a demonstration of controlled disagreement, at once exciting because it generates passion, and reassuring because it buttresses social and political conventions. By showcasing differences in a context that highlighted the orderly resolution of disputes, debates helped to conserve the political system and educate the electorate. People paid attention to the clash between famous people and the ideas they espoused, providing an opportunity to disseminate information both on issues of the day and the partisan stands of the advocates. In behaving in the manner expected of an audience, or in violating those norms, spectators participated in shaping the terms of the social and political contests of the young nation.

Debates Helped Conserve the Political System

Debates allowed politicians to vent their disagreements without overthrowing the political system. Political disputes could lead to debate without endangering the fundamental assumptions underlying the government. As more than a means of conflict resolution, debate became a release valve for the pressures of constituency and faction. This is not to say that politicians accepted defeats quickly or gracefully; parliamentary procedure leaves too many resources to the loser to make capitulation attractive. On the other hand, the cycle of debate offered clash without disaster and simultaneously affirmed the value and legitimacy of the political structure that made debate possible.

To arrive at consensus in debate required that villification and *ad hominem* arguments be rejected. This characteristic of the form was apparent even before the national government's authority was clarified. In the debates at the Constitutional Convention, liberality "as well as prudence induced [the delegates] to treat each other's opinions with tenderness," recalled John Jay, "to argue without asperity, and to endeavor to convince the judgment without hurting the feelings of each other. Although many weeks were passed in these discussions, some points remained on which a unison of opinions could not be effected. Here again that same happy disposition to unite and conciliate induced them to meet each other; and enable them, by mutual concessions, finally to complete and agree to the plan they have recommended."[3]

The deliberative process at the convention was threatened when accepted standards of civility and decorum broke down. In the debate over representation, argument grew heated as delegates favor-

ing a weaker national government pressed the advocates of a strong
federal system for assurances that groups of states would not combine to abuse the rights of smaller states. John Lansing, Jr., of New
York, spoke on behalf of perfectly equal representation among the
states, regardless of size. James Madison, architect of the Virginia
proposal, lost patience and replied heatedly. "Can any of the lesser
States be endangered by an adequate representation?" he asked.
"Where is the probability of a combination? What the inducements?
Where is the similarity of customs, manners or religion? If there
possibly can be a diversity of interest it is the case of the three large
States. Their situation is remote, their trade different. The staple
of Massachusetts is fish, and the carrying trade; of Pennsylvania,
wheat and flour; of Virginia, tobacco. Can States thus situated in
trade ever form a combination?"[4]

Delegates were accustomed to attacks on positions, such as the
claim illustrated in Alexander Hamilton's subsequent support of
Madison's argument. He specified problems with the reasoning
rather than deficiencies of the reasoner. "He deduces from [these
principles] the necessity that states entering into a confederacy must
retain the equality of votes. This position cannot be correct."[5] The
advocate is insulated from direct attack by Hamilton's emphasis on
the claim. Madison violated the implicit rule by specifying slov-
enly habits of mind and attributing them to the thinkers rather
than focusing on the argument, claiming, "Those gentlemen who
oppose the Virginia plan do not sufficiently analyze the subject.
Their remarks, in general, are vague and inconclusive."[6] Sensitive
to the prospect of insult and disruption, Benjamin Franklin rose
to propose reflection on the uniqueness of the problem and the need
to seek divine grace. He suggested prayer.[7] A later commentator
observed that "this timely and gracious advice of the aged diplomat
produced its desired effect, and the debate resumed the highly im-
personal tone of its early stages."[8] Lansing eventually left the convention, but by staying long enough to put his case many times,
he bolstered its authority.

The lessons learned in such clashes were shared in memoirs and
autobiographies. Ben Franklin recalled:

> When another asserted something that I thought an error I deny'd my-
> self the pleasure of contradicting him abruptly, and of showing im-
> mediately some absurdity in his proposition; and in answering I began
> by observing that in certain cases of circumstances his opinion would
> be right, but in the present case there appear'd or seem'd to me some

difference, etc. I soon found the advantage of this change in my manner; the conversations I engag'd in went on more pleasantly. The modest way in which I propos'd my opinions procur'd them a readier reception and less contradiction; I had less mortification when I was found to be in the wrong and I more easily prevail'd with others to give up their mistakes and join with me when I happened to be in the right.[9]

Not all politicians copied Franklin's example. Insults were common in the Congress and on the campaign trail. Even insult, however, was governed by informal rules. Responding to a scathing attack from Senator Charles Sumner, Stephen Douglas delineated the boundaries of decorum. "I can pay great deference to the frailties and the impulses of an honorable man, when indignant at what he considers to be a wrong. If the Senator, betraying that he was susceptible of just indignation, had been goaded, provoked, and aggravated, on the spur of the moment, into the utterance of harsh things, and then apologized for them in his cooler hours, I could respect him." Sumner's great trespass, according to Douglas, was to have planned his calumnies.

[I]t has been the subject of conversation for weeks, that the Senator from Massachusetts had his speech written, printed, committed to memory, practiced every night before the glass with a negro boy to hold the candle and watch the gestures, and annoying the boarders in the adjoining rooms. . . . The libels, the gross insults which we have heard to-day have been conned over, written with cool, deliberate malignity, repeated from night to night in order to catch the appropriate grace, and then he came here to spit forth that malignity upon men who differ from him—for that is their offence.[10]

Rules governed style as well as content and bore direct implications for the quality of debate. In the eighteenth and early nineteenth centuries, debaters were loath to read any portion of the speeches, let alone personal attacks. "To speak from a text before mid-[nineteenth] century was to court laughter," reports historian Thomas C. Leonard.[11] Influential speakers delivered their remarks extemporaneously or from memory. George Washington's manuscript delivery of his first inaugural address disappointed his admirers. "This great man was agitated and embarrassed more than ever he was by the leveled cannon or pointed musket," recalled William Maclay.[12] "He trembled, and several times could scarce make out to read, though it must be supposed he had often read it before. . . . I felt hurt that he was not first in everything."

Washington's discomfort illustrates the comparative unimportance of communicative skills for early presidents. Both of the Adamses, Madison, and Lincoln were skilled advocates, but they were the exceptions in the antebellum presidency. Presidents did not campaign for themselves and they communicated more often from the page than the platform, more often still through surrogates.

Extemporaneous delivery was prized in part because it allowed spontaneous response to argument. Debate was valued in turn for its ability to generate immediate give and take, an exchange very difficult to engineer when using manuscripts. The development of stenographic techniques in the nineteenth century changed the equation. Because speeches could be transcribed with considerable accuracy, the press would be more likely to disseminate verbatim passages rather than reconstructed accounts of debate. This encouraged careful manuscripting on the part of debaters in and out of the Congress. Many contemporary observers abhorred the practice. A Washington correspondent for a Boston paper, Benjamin Perley Poore, "hated that prepared speech that had become the mechanism for discussing the fate of the Union. . . . Political debate was a sham, and so compromise was impossible when congressmen refused to address one another."[13]

The observance of formal and informal rules in debate is more than a matter of simple decorum. By agreeing to submit their grievances to the elaborate procedural requirements of structured argumentation, advocates bind themselves to mutual interests and commitments that go beyond the matters of the moment. While participants remain within the pale of accepted practices, debate is not only an exposition of disagreements en route to a resolution, but a demonstration of the authority of the political system sponsoring the debate. Members of Congress may feel passionately about their constituencies and convictions, but will nonetheless yield the floor to a point of order; they will, by and large, take their seats when required to do so. Issues change, but the rules are perennial; acting under them reinforces the collective commitment to the process of resolving disputes under the given system.

As a result, even the most divisive arguments in a sense can conserve the political system. The arguments over states' rights in the U.S. Congress during the mid-nineteenth century expressed the bitter divisions that ultimately split the nation in the Civil War. Until that war, however, the sectional debates had a thirty-year career of binding in argument what would be sundered in war.

Occasioned by a number of specific actions and a variety of theories, such as nullification, secession, and compact theory, the controversy was at base an argument over the authority of the federal government. It continued well past the Constitutional Convention and became a central feature of American politics up to the Civil War. Proponents of the strong states' rights positions claimed, with varying degrees of vehemence, that a state had the right and the obligation to nullify noxious federal legislation. Analogous to a line-item veto, nullification suggested the possibility of agreeing with the bulk of what the Congress would decide, but preserved the right to eliminate particulars. Secession, the progeny of nullification, went further to claim that the states had the right to dissolve the government piecemeal. The consent that constituted the government could be withdrawn. More than an arcane legal dispute, states' rights lay at the center of the tensions leading to the Civil War.

The argumentative career of states' rights involved a number of reversals and, until the brink of war, constant recourse to the Congress to air positions. Alignments shifted frequently and unpredictably; arguments originally offered by one side were often appropriated to support the other. For example, though the South was the haven of nullificationist and secessionist sentiment throughout the antebellum period, the first major group of prominent citizens accused of plotting secession was the northern leadership of the Hartford Convention of 1814–15. Nullification itself, formulated by southerners as a response to the tariff controversies of 1828 and beyond and relied on as a hedge against the feared abolitionist legislation, was employed most effectively by northern legislatures "nullifying" the Fugitive Slave Law. Given the passions on both sides, the lengthy debate on states' rights is something of a surprise. This was, after all, a debate over the prerogatives of the central government; that those who disputed such rights would continually return to the forums of the central government to press the issue speaks to the power of the institution and its devices. By offering the prospect for some sort of resolution and allowing participants to vent passion while channeling dissent into rather than against the system, the debate form made possible the extended controversy.

The Hartford Convention was convened in 1814 to assess the proper course of action for northern states suffering gross abuses under the "oppressions of Government."[14] The delegates, by and large a conservative group bemoaning the decline in relations with England and the country's coziness with France, expressed particular concern over the effects of Republican embargoes on the North and the prosecution of the war. Linking these problems to questions about the form of the Constitution, they insisted on the necessity for state action. The Report of the Convention held that, "when emergencies occur which are either beyond the reach of the judicial tribunals, or too pressing to admit of the delay incident to their forms, States which have no common umpire must be their own judges, and execute their own decisions."[15]

The Hartford Convention's rhetoric sounded a great deal like an argument for secession, and it was precisely that flavor that alarmed contemporaries and prompted Robert Hayne's blistering observations on the New England representatives some fifteen years later. His choice of words reflects the difficulties of the nullificationist position, difficulties Daniel Webster was to capitalize on immediately. Note the thinly veiled personal accusations that had become fairly standard practice by the time Hayne delivered his speech in 1830. Had he been the butt of this attack, the sensitive Lansing would have been aghast.

When the Government seemed to be almost tottering on its base, when Great Britain, relieved from all her other enemies, had proclaimed her purpose of "reducing us to unconditional submission"—we beheld the peace party in New England . . . pursuing a course calculated to do more injury to their country and to render England more effective service than all her armies. Those who could not find it in their hearts to rejoice at our victories sang "Te Deum" at the King's Chapel in Boston at the restoration of the Bourbons. Those who would not consent to illuminate their dwellings for the capture of the Guerriere could give visible tokens of their joy at the fall of Detroit. The "beacon fires" of their hills were lighted up, not for the encouragement of their friends, but as signals to the enemy; and in the gloomy hours of midnight the very lights burned blue. Such were the dark and portentous signs of the times which ushered into being the renowned Hartford Convention. That convention met, and from their proceedings it appears that their chief object was to keep back the men and money of New England from the service of the Union and to effect radical changes in the Government—changes that can never be effected without a dissolution of the Union.[16]

In reminding conservative northern politicians of their secessionist pasts, Hayne sought to blunt the attack on nullification. By so doing, he gave Webster the chance to repudiate the Hartford Convention and to cast himself as a champion of the people. At the same time, Hayne's assertion that the states' rights position was cowardly and treasonous invited reply in kind over his own defense of southern intransigence in the face of the tariff.

The ancestry of the individual arguments, however, is less important than the function served by congressional debate overall. If Congress could contain disagreements over the very nature of the federal compact, then its authority was broad indeed. Had there not been an opportunity to parlay positions in the legislature, considerably more local agitation might have occurred in the states, with secession arguments bandied over pitchforks rather than state briefs. Without a sanctioned forum in which arguments from polar positions could be aired, war could well have come earlier. Debate is, in essence, the intellectual vehicle promising the prospect of change for those dissatisfied with the system but unwilling to break with it.

In addition to undergirding the values of the political system, debates legitimized those who participated. Though sometimes gaining prominence through arguments that fall outside the stricter definitions of debate, advocates could, by goading a hostile audience, attract the attention of a nation that might not have paid attention otherwise. Many who had no legislative power rose to prominence on the strength of their rhetorical skills and their talents for controversy.

Nineteenth-century abolitionists were particularly adept at gaining prominence through public arguments conducted in person and in print. Debate moved marginal positions into the political mainstream and articulated deep divisions within the movement. The most significant dispute within abolition was the break between the immediate abolitionists, who wanted to abolish all aspects of the slave system at once, and the gradualists, who supported a slower process. Both groups captured public recognition, with the immediatists hectoring and employing hyperbole, the gradualists more consistent with the argumentative traditions of the time. The confrontational style of the immediatists invited short-term prominence far in excess of their numbers. The gradualists achieved more lasting influence, due in part to their stated willingness to work within the social, political, and juridical structure authorizing debate.

William Lloyd Garrison, firebrand of immediate abolitionism and publisher of *The Liberator,* gained his reputation in part because his vehement style elicited a strong counterattack from southerners. In the paper and in his speeches, Garrison lashed out against social, religious, and political institutions that condoned slavery.

The U.S. government—for Garrison, no better than an agent legitimizing slavery—came under fierce attack. It was not enough that the government might be turned to the goals of abolition; the example of this nation allowing bondage in any section, but particularly in its capital, corrupted its mission to the world. "It is expedient that slavery at the Capitol should be abolished," he said, "because its toleration brings into contempt our nation's boasted love of equal rights, justly exposes us to the charge of hypocrisy, paralyzes the power of our free principles, and cripples our moral efforts for the overthrow of oppression throughout the world. . . . [B]y cherishing in the heart of the republic such a system of cold-blooded oppression, as the sun has rarely seen, we have rolled back the tide of reform in other nations, and cut the sinews of struggling humanity."[17]

Garrison did not protest as a friend of tradition. His sarcasm cut at concepts central to America's history and pride and established the tone of immediate abolitionism. In one Fourth of July address, he mocked the nation, its liberties, and its gods.

> Fellow Citizens: What a glorious day is this! What a glorious people are we! This is the time-honored, *wine*-honored, toast drinking, powder wasting, tyrant-killing fourth of July—consecrated, for the last sixty years, to bombast, to falsehood, to impudence, to hypocrisy. It is the great carnival of republican despotism, and of christian impiety, famous the world over! Since we held it last year, we have kept securely in their chains, the stock of two millions, three hundred thousand slaves we then had on hand, in spite of every effort of fanaticism to emancipate them; and, through the goodness of God, to whom we are infinitely indebted for the divine institution of negro slavery, have been graciously enabled to steal some seventy thousand babes, the increase of that stock, and expect to steal a still greater number before another "glorious" anniversary shall come round![18]

The Liberator never enjoyed a large paid circulation; many of its copies were mailed to the editors of other newspapers. Historians Gilbert Barnes and Dwight Dumond report that most northern editors ignored it, "but Southern editors, with slaveholding constituencies already 'in a state of phrensy' over the approach of emancipation in the West Indies, quoted it with enthusiasm."[19] The southerners took on Garrison as if he were the voice of the North, though this was far from the case. The willingness of these editors to engage him in debate made his position the rallying point for southern fears that the North meant violence to the southern way of life. *The Liberator*'s fierce denunciations of the government lent credence to the slaveholders' claims that abolitionists were merely Jacobins masquerading as social reformers. Garrison's radical rejection of the bases of union polarized the debate between slaveholders and abolitionists along lines that would culminate in the Brownlow–Pryne confrontation.

Garrison's insistent immediatism did not reflect the gradualist mainstream of the abolition movement. Yet, like Garrison, many gradualists gained fame through debate. A single set of debates and the reaction to them guaranteed the reputation of the gradualist abolitionist group known as the Lane Rebels. Similarly, their speeches and debates brought Sarah and Angelina Grimké to public attention. Theodore Weld also was a noted speaker and debater. Their more moderate views fit neatly into the traditions of American rhetoric.[20]

The substantive differences between the gradualists and the immediatists were reflected in their attitudes toward debating. Garrison's views were too extreme for negotiation; they could not fit comfortably within the kind of extended give and take necessary for legislative debates in a democracy. His polarizing debating style garnered attention, but forfeited the opportunity to employ the debate form as an instrument of influence. For the gradualists, debate was not only a means of attaining policy goals, but an enactment of the goal in and of itself. In his defense of the Lane debates, Theodore Weld credited discussion alone with the capacity to bring about sweeping change. Weld wrote, "A subject so deeply freighted with human interests as that of slavery, cannot be investigated and discussed intelligently and thoroughly without amplifying and expanding the intellect and increasing the power of its action upon all subjects. Let all our institutions engage in discussing subjects of great moment, such as slavery, temperance and moral reform; let them address themselves to the effort, let it be persevered in through an entire course, and they will introduce a new era in mind—the era of disposable power and practical accomplishment."[21] For the gradualists, debate was not only a means of gaining attention, but a means of retaining influence as well. Nevertheless, Garrison became the more famous advocate because his arguments were taken up by southern opponents.

Debates Educated the Electorate

Not only did debates stir up editors and clerics, they aroused common citizens as well, involving them in the issues of the day. Debates were major events, eagerly anticipated and well attended. The participants—visiting politicians and other notables—were celebrities. An observer in the early twentieth century called political debate "at once public business and also entertainment; an attractive political orator had some of the glamour that heroes of the stage and the movies came to have later."[22] Thousands came to hear Lincoln and Douglas debate in Illinois in 1858. Claques shouted support for their favorite; the text of the Lincoln–Douglas debates is littered with the candidates' responses to cheers and cat-calls. Such debates provided an opportunity for the electorate to become involved with the process of governance. Voters could see their candidates perform and join them in demonstrations of political faith.

We already have discussed the use of debate to improve the citizenry. Equally important was debate's usefulness in exposing advocates and audiences to differing points of view. "Many a man has discovered in himself," said debate promoter Charles Cuthbert Hall, "and has educated for subsequent success, powers of deliberation and powers of verbal expression, which have made him at length to some extent a leader of men, a persuasive and compelling counsellor in the legislature of his country, or in the general assembly of his church."[23] Debate impressed Hall not only as a study in form, but an opportunity to gain an understanding of content as well. By providing an opportunity to dispute party positions, debate forced participants to "gather . . . sift and weigh and decide upon the evidence."[24] This is not to say that all debates resulted in the "fair, fine comity that holds us loyal each to his own convictions, yet each generous and kind to those whose convictions oppose his own" that Hall envisioned for his debate societies.[25] Many debates prompted displays of partisanship and intimidation; however, all but the most violent afforded citizens the chance to hear the arguments of opposing factions.

Because debates were events, they were covered by newspapers. Some were reproduced in detail and others merely described. The papers, more overtly partisan in the eighteenth and nineteenth centuries than in the twentieth, presented surprisingly even-handed

At no time in the nineteenth century did a presidential candidate debate his opponent. For most of that century, candidates avoided campaigning on their own behalf. Nonetheless, Lincoln's senatorial debates with Douglas proved decisive when the two faced each other in the presidential race two years after Lincoln's defeat for the Senate. (*Library of Congress*)

accounts of debates and, often, fairly thorough statements of opposing positions. The *Virginia Argus,* which supported James Madison for the presidential nomination in 1808, printed lengthy letters from James Monroe's Corresponding Committee. From September to October, Madison enthusiasts were treated to an extended debate on the candidates' respective characters, prospects, and positions.

In the 1844 presidential election, surrogate debaters Calhoun and Lincoln stumped across Illinois. The Whig *Sangamo Journal* called the arguments of Democrat Calhoun "unanswerable," praising Lincoln for a "hardy" but apparently unconvincing response.[26] We might assume that Lincoln had lost some of the force that carried him through an earlier series of debates with Calhoun in 1836 when the *Sangamo Journal* reported that, "At one fell stroke, [Lincoln] broke the ice upon which we have seen Mr. Calhoun standing, and left him to contend with the chilling waters and merciless waves."[27] Some of the partisan flavor remained, but the arguments were dutifully placed before the electorate. The least that can be said of such published debates is that they allowed opponents to come to know well the position of the other side.

Politicians did not rely exclusively on the newspaper editors to carry their party's case to the voters. Many debates and speeches were published in pamphlet form. For some of the more important issues, the politicians oversaw publication themselves. Before his second reply to Hayne, Webster asked Joseph Gales, the editor and publisher of the *National Intelligencer,* to take the notes himself. He did not permit publication until he had spent a month revising the stenographic record.[28] "Within the next few months," writes Webster's biographer, Daniel Current, "the public printers distributed forty thousand copies, and from other presses at least twenty different editions soon appeared. Never before had a speech in Congress been so widely read."[29] Perhaps none were so widely read, but many were as extensively amended. Gales and his partner, William Winston Seaton, made a practice of submitting their stenographic notes to politicians for editing and revision.[30]

By arranging arguments in opposition to one another, the debate pamphlets educated partisans on the points of difference between their party and their opponents'. During the election of 1840, Lincoln published a pamphlet containing his speeches from a debate with John Calhoun in December 1839. "I now only ask the audience," Lincoln pleaded, "when Mr. Calhoun shall answer me, to hold him to the questions. Permit him not to escape them. Require him either to show, that the Sub-Treasury would not injuriously affect the currency, or that we should in some way, receive an equivalent for that injurious effect. Require him either to show that the Sub-Treasury would not be more expensive as a fiscal agent, than a Bank, or that we should, in some way be compensated for that additional expense. And particularly require him to show, that the public money would be as secure in the Sub-Treasury as in a National Bank, or that the additional insecurity would be overbalanced by some good result of the proposed change."[31] The underlinings, all of which appear in the original, call attention to the important issues. Voters are invited to pay close attention to particular answers. Although Lincoln implies that Calhoun cannot respond, he does not dismiss the Democrat's case out of hand; instead, he encourages a reasoned evaluation. This emphasis on the issues educated the public about the Whig positions and reinforced the image of government as a forum for the competition of ideas and values rather than personalities. Citizens were educated simultaneously in the traditions of the political systems and the issues of the day.

For political and deliberative applications alike, debate produced information both about the participants and the issues. The Lincoln–Douglas debates of 1858, conducted in the heat of the Illinois summer, exhausted the range of legal arguments about the extension of slavery to the territories.[32] The candidates showed not only their grasp of the issues, but their personalities as well. From these debates we can glean information that reveals habits of mind in a distinctly political context. Throughout the debates, Lincoln's sly, self-deprecating humor contrasted sharply with Douglas' bombast. When a heckler at the first debate, in Ottawa, yelled to Lincoln to "Put on your specs," he replied, "Yes sir, I am obliged to do so. I am no longer a young man."[33] Douglas did not respond equally well to heckling. In the course of the fourth debate, at Charleston, the Little Giant was interrupted while indicting Lincoln for merely repeating the charges of others. A heckler asked, "How about the charges?" Douglas replied caustically, "Do not trouble yourselves, I am going to make my speech in my own way, and I trust, as the Democrats listened patiently and respectfully to Mr. Lincoln that his friends will not interrupt me when I am answering him."[34] After a charged, personal attack from Douglas in the sixth debate, in Quincy, Lincoln joked about time. "Since Judge Douglas has said to you in his conclusion that he had not time in an hour and a half to answer all that I had said in an hour, it follows of course that I will not be able to answer in a half an hour all that he said in an hour and a half."[35] Douglas' opening in the same debate was the more pedantic: "Permit me to say that unless silence is observed it will be impossible for me to be heard by this immense crowd, and my friends can confer no higher favor upon me than by omitting all expressions of applause or approbation. I desire to be heard rather than to be applauded. I wish to address myself to your reason, your judgment, your sense of justice, and not to your passions."[36]

Both debaters presented elaborate arguments. During the fifth debate, in Galesburg, Lincoln asked that the audience consider a syllogism regarding the Dred Scott decision. Lincoln was trying to pin Douglas down on the doctrine of popular sovereignty. Douglas held that a state has the right to choose how it will deal with blacks: free, slave, or somewhere in between. Lincoln wanted to show that the policy was inconsistent with the Democrats' own interpretations of constitutional law and would ensure a permanent acceptance of slavery. The following passage illustrates the attention Lincoln demanded of his audience as he argued his position in detail. The style is alien to today's public political debates.

In the second clause of the sixth article, I believe it is, of the Constitution of the United States, we find the following language: "This Constitution and the laws of the United States which shall be made in pursuance thereof; and all treaties made, or which shall be made under the authority of the United States, shall be bound thereby, any thing in the Constitution or laws of any State to the contrary notwithstanding."

The essence of the Dred Scott case is compressed into the sentence which I will now read: "Now, as we have already said in an earlier part of this opinion, upon a different point, the right of property in a slave is distinctly and expressly affirmed in the Constitution." I repeat it. *"The right of property in a slave is distinctly and expressly affirmed in the Constitution!"* . . . What follows as a short and even syllogistic argument from it?

Nothing in the Constitution or laws of any State can destroy a right distinctly and expressly affirmed in the Constitution of the United States.

The right of property in a slave is distinctly and expressly affirmed in the Constitution of the United States.

Therefore, nothing in the Constitution or laws of any State can destroy the right of property in a slave.

I believe that no fault can be pointed out in that argument; assuming the truth of the premises, the conclusion, so far as I have any capacity to understand it, follows inevitably. There is a fault in it as I think, but the fault is not in the reasoning; but the falsehood in fact is a fault of the premises. I believe that the right of property in a slave *is not* distinctly and expressly affirmed in the Constitution, and Judge Douglas thinks it *is*. I believe that the Supreme Court and the advocates of that decision may search in vain for the place in the Constitution where the right of a slave is distinctly and expressly affirmed. I say, therefore, that I think one of the premises is not true in fact. But it is true with Judge

Douglas. It is true with the Supreme Court who pronounced it. They are estopped from denying it, and being estopped from denying it, the conclusion follows that the Constitution of the United States being the supreme law, no constitution or law can interfere with it. It being affirmed in the decision that the right of property in a slave is distinctly and expressly affirmed in the Constitution, the conclusion inevitably follows that no State law or constitution can destroy that right. I then say to Judge Douglas and to all others, that I think it will take a better answer than a sneer to show that those who have said that the right of property in a slave is distinctly and expressly affirmed in the Constitution, are not prepared to show that no constitution or law can destroy that right.[37]

This passage reveals Lincoln's assumptions that his audience could follow a syllogistic argument, but not recall the language of the Constitution or the Dred Scott decision. He did not "play the house," but rather presented the whole of his case en route to proving that Douglas' position was in essence an endorsement of slavery. This small section of a much longer speech suggests the wealth of information and the close reasoning characteristic of arguments given before voters.

Douglas also demanded a great deal of the voters' attention; but instead of emphasizing the course of the argument per se, he filled his speeches with references to yet other speeches, his own, Lincoln's, and those of third parties. In the sixth debate, he attacked Lincoln's goals as unworkable for a nation composed of many states. He also wanted to demonstrate Lincoln's "inconsistency" in answering questions about the rights and status of blacks.

Read the speech of Speaker Orr, of South Carolina, in the House of Representatives, in 1856, on the Kansas question, and you will find that he takes the ground that while the owner of a slave has a right to go into a Territory, and carry his slaves with him, that he cannot hold them one day or hour unless there is a slave code to protect him. He tells you that slavery would not exist a day in South Carolina, or any other State, unless there was a friendly people and friendly legislation. Read the speeches of that giant in intellect, Alexander H. Stephens, of Georgia, and you will find them to the same effect. Read the speeches of Sam Smith, of Tennessee, and of all Southern men, and you will find that they all understood this doctrine then as we understand it now. Mr. Lincoln cannot be made to understand it, however. Down at Jonesboro, he went on to argue that if it be the law that a man has a right to take his slaves into territory of the United States under the Constitution, that then a member of Congress was perjured if he did not vote for a slave code. I ask him whether the decision of the Supreme Court is not binding on him as well as on me? If so, and he holds that he would be perjured if he did not vote for a slave code under it, I ask him whether, if elected to Congress, he will so vote? I have a right to his answer, and I will tell you why. He put that question to me in Egypt, and did it with an air of triumph. . . . I answered him that a fundamental article in the Democratic creed, as put forth in the Nebraska bill and the Cincinnati platform, was non-intervention by Congress with slavery in the States and Territories, and hence, that I would not vote in Congress for any code of laws, either for or against slavery in any Territory. I will leave the people perfectly free to decide that question for themselves.[38]

The passage is dense with references to people, places, and agreements. It typifies Douglas' tendency to center arguments on individuals and their commitments rather than the character of the ideas themselves. The audience got a good deal of information about the supporters of the Democratic position and the kind of thinking underlying Douglas' positions, learning about the issues and the politician.

Though Douglas won the Senate seat, the debates launched Lincoln in national politics and created a host of problems for Douglas. Already unpopular with southern Democrats because of his stand on Kansas' Lecompton Constitution, Douglas lost further ground after the debates. He was stripped of his chairmanship of the committee on territories in December 1858. Historian Robert Johannsen believes that his role in the debates denied him the presidency.[39] Lincoln, on the other hand, increased his surrogate activities in response to party demand. He recognized his debates with Douglas as the key to his newfound national fame. Much as Webster had vetted the dissemination of his second reply to Hayne, Lincoln oversaw publication of his debates with Douglas. After collecting the newspaper accounts in a scrapbook, Lincoln offered the debates for publication in 1859. The debates, along with earlier speeches of both Lincoln and Douglas, were released in book form in 1860 and circulated as campaign literature.[40]

These exchanges helped to clarify issues for the electorate as well as the participants. The debates magnified Douglas' failure to unite his party under "popular sovereignty" and exposed the difficulties inherent in the position. Popular sovereignty—which held that each state had the right to pass its own judgments on slavery—pleased neither the slaveholders nor the abolitionists. Lincoln understood this when he said, in accepting the nomination to run against Douglas, " 'A house divided against itself cannot stand.' I believe this government cannot endure permanently half slave and half free."[41] One of his goals in the debates was to get Douglas to admit that, under popular sovereignty, the best that the nation could hope for would be a continuation of the division so hateful to North and South alike. He came close to getting that admission in the sixth debate, at Quincy. In his rejoinder to Douglas he pounced on Douglas' use of language to prove his point. "I wish to return to Judge Douglas my profound thanks for his public annunciation here today, to be put on record, that his system of policy in regard to the institution of slavery *contemplates that it shall last forever*. We are getting a little nearer the true issues of this controversy, and I am profoundly grateful for this one sentence. Judge Douglas asks you, 'Why cannot the institution of slavery, or rather, why cannot the nation, part slave and part free, continue as our fathers made it *forever*?' "[42] Although Lincoln went on to dispute Douglas' understanding of our "fathers'" intent, the more telling point had already been made.

Even Debates that Violate the "Rules" Can Focus Political Questions

The Lincoln–Douglas debates worked well as debates. They were orderly and closely attended. Both advocates were serious and articulate. They addressed themselves to a discrete set of political concerns. The debates advanced the issues, illuminating areas of both agreement and disagreement. The contest continues to occupy a special place in the national mythology. A debate does not have to satisfy a platonic standard of truth and reasonableness, however, to merit attention or clarify issues. Major flaws in debate, such as digression, obfuscation, rancor, and *ad hominem* attack, can be revealing in and of themselves.

The sublime rhetoric of the Webster–Hayne debate was followed by an era of far less gentlemanly partisanship in the legislature. Southerners were quick to take offense at any perceived infringement of their "constitutional right" to hold slaves as property. The issue of abolition or emancipation was so central to the South's sense of identity and survival that the southern members of Congress often threatened to quit the assembly rather than participate in discussions, let alone legislation, so thoroughly inimical to their privileges and interests.

John Calhoun summarized the southern position on slavery in the minority report from a committee established to investigate the wisdom of suppressing anti-slavery agitation in the Congress. "He who regards slavery in those States simply under the relation of master and slave, important as that relation is, viewed merely as a question of property to the slaveholding section of the Union, has a very imperfect conception of the institution and the impossibility of abolishing it without disasters unexampled in the history of the world. . . . The two races have long lived in peace and prosperity, and if not disturbed, would long continue so to live. . . . To destroy the existing relations would be to destroy this prosperity and to place the two races in a state of conflict which must end in the expulsion or extirpation of one or the other."[43] Such apocalyptic rhetoric expressed feelings ill suited to the spirit of compromise that commends debate as a vehicle for decision making. Such rhetoric also indicated the intractability of the differences separating North and South.[44]

The debate over the right to petition the Congress exemplifies the extreme positions assumed by the advocates. In 1836, the House of Representatives adopted gag rules, banning its members from introducing any resolutions or petitions on the subject of slavery. Northern legislators had been in the habit of reading into the record petitions for emancipation, African repatriation, gradual abolition, and other such proposals for ridding the nation of its peculiar institution. Most petitions focused on the District of Columbia because the Congress could do something about that jurisdiction directly, without having to trouble over a state government. The debate on the gag rule was, in essence, a debate on debate, demonstrating the centrality of the concept of open argument to the definition of nationhood.

Incensed at the prospect of limitations on the right of debate, John Quincy Adams attacked the proposal as nothing less than the suppression of free speech. "Will you introduce a resolution that the members of this House shall not speak a word in derogation of the sublime merits of slavery? You must have a resolution of this kind, to follow the one laid upon your table this morning—a resolution that no member of this House shall dare to utter an incendiary sentiment?" Adams quickly projected beyond members of the House to the free speech of all Americans, not only in debate but in the press as well.

And what is that incendiary sentiment? Why, it is, in substance, the contents of these pamphlets. Well, sir, you begin with suppressing the right of petition; you must next suppress the right of speech in this House; for you must offer a resolution that every member who dares to express a sentiment of this kind shall be expelled, or that the speeches shall not go forth to the public—shall not be circulated. What will be the consequence then? You suppress the right of petition; you suppress the freedom of speech; the freedom of the press and the freedom of religion; for, in the minds of many worthy, honest, and honorable men—fanatics if you so please to call them—this is a religious question, in which they act under what they believe to be a sense of duty to their God; and, however erroneous may be their conclusions, it is not for me, nor for this House, to judge them. Therefore, sir, in deference to the respect which is due to the right of petition, and the respect which is due to the right of freedom of speech, freedom of the press, and freedom of religion, I hope that this petition will be left where it has been placed by the House, in the possession of the Committee on the District of Columbia, and that we shall hear no more about it.[45]

Although Adams framed the petition in terms somewhat less agitated than Calhoun's, they were equally apocalyptic and equally self-defining. The freedoms that had come, even as early as 1836, to embody the nation were imperiled by the southern resolution. As Adams phrased it, this was not yet explicitly an argument between North and South, but an argument over the relationship of the whole to an aggrieved part.

Responding to Adams, Waddy Thompson of South Carolina chose to inflame, rather than ameliorate, sectional tensions. "I do, with a full knowledge of all my responsibilities, declare that, in my opinion, nothing will satisfy the excited, the almost frenzied, South but an indignant rejection of these petitions; such a rejection as will, at the same time that it respects the right of petitioning, express the predetermination, the foregone conclusion, of the House on the subject—a rejection, sir, that will satisfy the South and serve as an indignant rebuke to the fanatics of the North. . . . Fanatics, did I say, sir? Never before was so vile a band dignified with that name. They are murderers, foul murderers, accessories before the fact, and they know it, of murder, robbery, rape, infanticide."[46] Adams afforded speakers such as Thompson an opportunity to justify the suppression of the petitions in national terms. Like Thompson, most chose not to do so. Their concerns were regional and justified as such. The broadest gag rule passed the

JOHN QUINCY ADAMS

As a member of the House of Representatives, former President
John Quincy Adams led the battle to keep congressional debate
open for anti-slavery petitions.

House 117 to 68. All petitions would be immediately tabled without comment or commitment to the record.

In the next session of Congress, Adams tested the gag rule by presenting a petition. Southern members were outraged and demanded that he be censured. Their anger was increased by Adams' disingenuous claims that he was innocent of any effort to contravene the rules of the House. He never did state clearly what the petition contained. Southern members first jumped to the conclusion that it was a petition by slaves in Fredericksburg, Virginia, to ban slavery. It was then thought that the petition came from "free negroes." Adams finally revealed that the petition *endorsed* slavery. The confusion is expressed in one of the many resolutions for censure. "Resolved, That the honorable John Quincy Adams, a member of this House, by stating in his place that he had in his possession a paper purporting to be a petition from slaves, and inquiring if it came within the meaning of a resolution heretofore adopted (as preliminary to its presentation), has given color to the idea that slaves have the right of petition, and of his readiness to be their organ; and that for the same he deserves the censure of this House."[47]

Julius Alford of Georgia disliked Adams' petition no matter what its provenance. "Mr. Speaker, the member from Massachusetts would screen himself from the censure of this House because he has not sent his petition from slaves to your table. Sir, he has sent the petition from the free negroes of Fredericksburg, and that is as wrong and insulting to us as if it were from slaves. The Constitution of the United States no more allows the one than the other, and both are equally insulting. . . . Let me tell the gentlemen it is a firm and unconquerable resolution never to surrender one jot or tittle of our constitutional rights upon this subject. We [southerners] have a common interest in this Government, a common title in this capital; it bears the name of the immortal Washington, and he was a Southern man. Shall we, then, ever surrender the one or desert the other? No, never! Never until this fair city is a field of Waterloo and this beautiful Potomac a river of blood."[48] Alford's response reaffirms the sectionalism and personal flavor of Thompson's commentary. Adams' offense cannot be understood in procedural terms; it must be understood as a personal affront to his colleagues from the South. To even discuss the issues involved brought up the desirability of sustaining the Union. The racial strife envisioned by Calhoun appears as sectional strife here. The explicit refusal to compromise "a tittle" forecasts that strife. Alford's prescient reference to the "river of blood" anticipates Bull Run.

The sectional attack invited response in kind. Massachusetts' Caleb Cushing linked the freedoms enumerated by Adams with the nation *and* the North. "We hold them by the dread of arbitrament of battle. We hold them by the concession of a higher and broader charter than all the constitutions in the land—the free donation of the eternal God, when he made us to be men. These, the cardinal principles of human freedom, He has implanted in us and placed them before and behind and around us for our guard and guidance, like the cloud by day and the pillar of fire by night which led the Israelites through the desert. It is a liberty, native, inborn, original, underived, imprescriptible; and acknowledged in the Constitution itself, as preeminently before and above the Constitution. Now, in their denunciations of the North, it is these, the very primordial rights of the universal people of the United States, that gentlemen from the South assail. They strike at the freedom of opinion, of the press, and of speech, out of doors—and the rights of petition and debate in this House."[49] In the context of this comparatively early, albeit indirect, debate over slavery, the sectional difficulties quickly escalated. North and South alike framed the debates as an attack on the national self and phrased their positions in terms that admitted no compromise. As the debate continued, each contended that any movement on the issue would annihilate their respective regions.

Unable or unwilling to act against the former president, the House did eventually condemn a member for presenting anti-slavery petitions. When Joshua Giddings was censured in March 1842, he resigned his seat and returned to his home district in Ohio to stand for re-election. By an overwhelming margin, he was returned to Congress in May.

The petition controversy demonstrates the value of debate in a situation that does not conform to the rules for technical success. The advocates did not remain dispassionate; instead, they increased their hostility at almost every opportunity. The stakes were raised from the rules of the Congress to the privileges of its members to the freedoms of all Americans. Furthermore, the advocates made each argument a point of personal pride. More than mapping nineteenth-century conceits, the debates called attention to the importance of character, of good-faith dealing among persons in rough agreement with one another as the precondition for successful debate. Discussion of substance gave way to procedural maneuvering and *ad hominem* attacks on both sides. Such tactics are best understood not as defects of debate, but rather as explorations of the status of the agreements that make debate possible. This was not a debate in the spirit of peaceable amity so dear to the masters of the young men's debating societies. That these debates were held at all is strong testimony to the power of the form. Politicians who agreed on very little policy could continue to function by observing the roughest dictates of the rules of debate.

The petition debates made clear the battle lines over which slavery would be fought in the context of union. The positions taken by the extremists, abolitionists and slaveholders alike, changed little from 1837 to their apotheosis in the Brownlow–Pryne debate of 1858. The intractability of each position, rendered as it was in terms of self-definition and preservation of a way of life, did not offer much room for compromise.

Southern threats to leave the Union, which were as old as the first volley in the petition debate, were not made good for almost thirty years. Part of the credit for the temporary preservation of the Union must go to the binding influence of the debate platform. In an era when the disputants were uncertain about their willingness to continue as parts of the same nation, they were usually willing to continue to put their arguments. This willingness, though often protested, lasted well past the point when any substantive compromise was possible. That the language in 1837 looked very much like the language in 1858 drives the point home harder. Only after the violent attack on debates per se in Brooks's caning of Sumner on May 22, 1856, did the threats to foreclose debates become too real to ignore and too direct to outmaneuver.

Summary

By erecting a neutral superstructure in which emotional political argument could take place, debate helped conserve the political system. The assumptions underlying the practice of debate are fundamentally lawful, exerting some control over the positions of the advocates and re-emphasizing the agreements bringing legislators to the same forum. Voters exposed to the practice of political debates, in person and in print, were kept abreast of the issues of the day and the habits of mind of those who would be their leaders. Even when debates failed to match the highest standards for the activity, they produced meaningful discussion of issues important to the nation.

Debate served none of these purposes perfectly. As the Civil War made plain, disagreements can transcend the legal and social ties that bind. In the next chapter, we examine the shortcomings of debate in the prebroadcast era.

CHAPTER 3

The Limitations
of American Debate,
1770-1920

Debates have been beset by abusive advocates, fractious crowds, and unbearable tedium. Even when well conducted, they are sometimes difficult to evaluate, yielding results more consistent with the opinions of the judges than the character of the arguments. Participation in debate can cost politicians flexibility and votes.

In this chapter, we discuss the downside of political debating prior to the broadcast age. Debate is limited by audiences, participants, and the form itself. Because it is a contest, often one played for high stakes, debate frequently elicits mere gamesmanship from participants and partisan responses from audiences. Attempts to "win" diminish the opportunities for compromise in the short run and encourage contestants to exaggerate and exploit their differences. Overreliance on debate as a means of resolving problems and building reputations can worsen both.

Not all these problems inhere in the debate form; many stem from the interaction of ambition and opportunity in an adversarial activity. The limitations of debate should be understood as precisely that: boundaries beyond which a useful activity cannot always go.

Audiences Are Not Uniform, nor Do They Behave
as Impartial Judges

In 1813–14, Yale's seniors engaged in more than forty debates on topics ranging from religion to politics to literature. The whole class was present, but the judgments were left to the president of the college, Timothy Dwight. Dwight revealed the "correct" position on every topic debated that year, carefully explaining the reasons for decision and commenting on the debaters' tactics. The contestants were tasked not with winning or losing, but with fully explaining the best arguments favoring one side of the issue at hand.

Few debates were so orderly or easily brought to conclusion. Political debaters could not count on the close attention or academic distance of a Timothy Dwight. Outside courts of law, debates might continue for years without anything approaching a firm judgment. Standards of evaluation have always been and still remain one of the most difficult problems confronting debaters in any forum. They are particularly vexing for those debaters who deal with large, mixed audiences. The difficulty with standards involves disputes over style, jurisdiction, and the refusal of many audiences to move beyond partisan positions in evaluating the results of debate.

Differences in social, economic, and educational status have posed problems for political debaters in America. Debaters must popularize fairly technical arguments or lose the mass appeal, often forcing a choice between the niceties of debate and popular audience attention. The distinctions are manifested in style and tone. During the Jacksonian period, many politicians sacrificed brilliant parliamentary oratory to appeal directly to the people. Martin Van Buren, who engineered the Democrats' success after Jackson's presidency, reasoned that an appeal to the people was always a more effective means of gathering and keeping power. "Those who have wrought great changes in the world never succeeded by gaining over chiefs; but always by exciting the multitude. The first is the resource of intrigue and produces only secondary results, the second is the resort of genius and transforms the face of the universe."[1]

In appealing to the masses, debaters often lost the support of elites. John Quincy Adams was contemptuous of James K. Polk's common style. "He has no wit, no literature, no point of argument, no gracefulness of delivery, no elegance of language, no philosophy, no pathos, no felicitous impromptus; nothing that can constitute an orator, but confidence, fluency and labor."[2] Obviously, Adams' objections did not prevent Polk from becoming prominent in the party. For Adams, a former professor of rhetoric at Harvard University, rhetorical flourishes indicated sound training and a sound mind. In his inaugural lecture for the Boylston Chair, Adams advised young men interested in a political career to "catch from the relicks [*sic*] of ancient oratory those unresisted powers which mould the mind of man to the will of the speaker, and yield the guidance of a nation to the dominion of the voice."[3] The innovations of the popular orators of the nineteenth century were to be despised; only the classical models, "immeasurably superior" to the contemporary, were acceptable. "A subject, which has exhausted the genius of Aristotle, Cicero and Quintillian, can neither require nor admit much additional illustration. To select, combine, and apply their precepts, is the only duty left for their followers of all succeeding times, and to obtain a perfect familiarity with their instructions is to arrive at the mastery of the art."[4] Because in Adams' view, good rhetoric made the state great, "bad" rhetoric did not merely offend; it endangered the well-being of the nation.

The class dynamic was more complex than a question of rich and poor, schooled and unschooled. Style was taken as an indication of political philosophy. Thomas Jefferson, the agrarian idealist who urged speakers to appeal to the simplest folk in society, deplored the excesses in political speech of the 1820s. Like Adams, Jefferson recommended careful study of the ancients, but chose a different selection of togaed talkers. "Antiquity has left us the finest models for imitation," he wrote. "He who studies and imitates them most nearly, will nearest approach the perfection of the art. Among these I should consider the speeches of Livy, Sallust, and Tacitus, as pre-eminent specimens of logic, taste, and that sententious brevity which, using not a word to spare, leaves not a moment for inattention to the hearer." Where Adams chose ornament and force, Jefferson opted for a plain, uncontrived style. "Amplification is the vice of modern oratory. It is an insult to an assembly of reasonable men, disgusting and revolting instead of persuading. Speeches measured by the hour, die with the hour."[5] He felt that elaborate ornament led to elite appeals at the expense of open argument for the whole people.[6]

The disputes over style were complicated by partisan feelings. Adams was not always fond of Daniel Webster. On at least one occasion he found this most eloquent of his contemporaries "boastful, cunning, jesuitical, fawning and insolent."[7] Webster's elegance of expression could not overcome Adams' suspicions about his integrity.

Adams held no patent on partisanship. Debates, particularly those in Congress, were evaluated by members with a stake in the outcome. Opponents rarely conceded arguments on the basis of effective advocacy. Although Webster's success in his confrontation with Hayne was the most memorable of his career, that did not prevent Thomas Hart Benton from dismissing the speech as entirely irrelevant. Benton conceded that Webster had provided a moving encomium on "the love and blessings of Union," filled with felicitous amplification. "It was up to the rule in that particular. But it seemed to me that there was another rule, and a higher, and a precedent one, which it violated. It was the rule of propriety; that rule which requires the fitness of things to be considered; which requires the time, the place, the subject and the audience, to be considered; and condemns the delivery of the argument, and all its flowers, if it fails in congruence to these particulars. I thought the essay upon union and disunion had so failed."[8] Benton was a unionist; his interest in Hayne's position rested in his concern for continuing provision of public lands and the possibility of firming a western-southern coalition to work against northern politicians. This legislative agenda determined his reaction to Webster's speech more directly than anything the "godlike" Daniel may have said. Webster's speech carried the imagination, but not the opposition.

Van Buren's focus on results and Benton's on process speak to fundamental differences in their understandings of debate. For Jefferson, Adams, and Benton the goal of debate was not simply winning the issue. More than a tool for ensuring legislative victories, debate was a means of improving public discourse. Entering into debate, advocates shouldered the burden of speaking well and the risk of losing to a superior position. Skillful debate would better ensure the success of an argument and instruct the people, whichever side might win. Van Buren objected to precisely this inconclusive quality of debate; he wanted his legislative agenda rather than a means of testing it. To pursue debates with the fixed competitive goal of winning or losing is to forfeit the prospect of synthesis arising from a more open competition. Factors not relevant to "victory" become irrelevant, forgotten.

Winning is also an elusive standard. Even today, analysts are hard pressed to call winners and losers in political debates. Popular wisdom is often a poor guide. "[I]t is hard to render a judgment on who won" the Lincoln–Douglas debates, notes rhetorical critic David Zarefsky. "The combatants were closely matched, and many of their argumentative strategies were similar. Each maintained a consistent stance while accusing the other of inconsistency or worse. Each made the greatest possible use of the available evidence, and each was adept at reducing his own burden of proof and increasing his opponent's. Only gross measures of the effects of the debates are available, and they favor Douglas; Forest Whan, for example, notes that, relative to the 1854 vote, Democrats improved their performance over Republicans in all the central Illinois counties in which both men spoke. Certainly the popular judgment that Lincoln routed Douglas must be set aside."[9]

The problem with deciding the Lincoln–Douglas debates is emblematic of judgment in all political debates. Standards are either arbitrary or partisan and effective only if all parties to a debate agree in advance on the criteria for assessment and the jurisdiction of the judges. Such jurisdiction may be fairly clear in a court of law or a college debate, less so in legislative disputes, and very elusive in public appeals. Because debate itself does not compel capitulation, "losers," even if they recognize defeat, have little incentive to concede a loss. When the form does not mandate a final decision, debaters motivated by interests beyond argument itself have every reason to continue to put their claims. In addition to determining which side "won" the case, debates may edify, express minority viewpoints, create the basis for compromise, or open new perspectives on difficult issues.

This problem of evaluation was amplified by the looseness and indirection of much eighteenth- and nineteenth-century debating. Debates were often contrived in print. Newspaper editors would respond to absent advocates as if they were present, mimicking the debate form and distorting the purposes of the opponent. At other times, speeches given in face-to-face debate were excerpted from context to stand on their own, enabling a politician to tap into the drama of debate without granting an opponent the platform. The printed version of Webster's reply to Hayne, carefully edited and distributed in twenty-one editions by May 1830, encouraged voters to accept uncritically Webster's position as the decisive moment in the debates.[10] Hayne and Benton would have argued the point, but their speeches were not circulated as widely. There were sixty-five speeches on Foote's resolution in 1830. Rhetoric theorists Wilbur Samuel Howell and Hoyt Hudson argue that "it is obvious that the true stature of these replies cannot be measured if we treat them as isolated events."[11] Webster's speeches may well have justified the plaudits, but the looseness of the *printed* debate form made the actual performances difficult for most nineteenth-century Americans to evaluate.

Since transcripts and reports of debates had a greater impact on the public than the oral debates themselves, editing them was an influential act. "It is only tradition and old custom, founded on an obsolete state of things, that assigns any value to parliamentary oratory," wrote Nathaniel Hawthorne. "The world has done with it, except as an intellectual pastime. The speeches have no effect till they are converted into newspaper paragraphs; and they had better be composed as such, in the first place, and oratory reserved for churches, courts of law, and public dinner tables."[12] Hawthorne's objections prefigure contemporary concerns that debaters are framing complex ideas as "sound bites" in order to obtain news coverage.

The use of surrogates also obstructed debate's capacity to reveal a candidate's mind at work. Presidential candidates who relied on the oratorical talent of surrogates did not offer voters direct information about themselves. Debates by those standing in for the presidential candidate may have obscured the deficiencies of some mid-century candidates rather than pose realistic choices to the public. William Henry Harrison, for instance, was not a particularly cogent thinker. Abraham Lincoln was. When Lincoln signed on with Harrison's campaign, voters were treated to a lively display that had very little to do with the old general.

On the other hand, by separating the candidate's image from the issues in the campaign, surrogate debating promoted attention to policy. Voters could not become completely absorbed in the character of the absent nominees because they were forced to come to terms with the surrogates standing before them. Though the surrogates sometimes strayed into personal discussions, the effect was more substantive than much of today's political debating.

However, the advantages and disadvantages of surrogacy do not inhere in the debate form. Surrogacy was imposed on debate during the eighteenth and nineteenth centuries. The form was simply adapted to the sensibilities of the age.

Regular Appearance in Debate Could Be Politically Costly

Some political careers, notably Lincoln's, were burnished by debate; others were tarnished. Webster's eloquence drew attention early in his career. His defense of High Federalism while he was still young was seized on by Robert Hayne and others as inconsistent with the unionist positions he adopted later in life. Webster had never joined with the seeming secession of the Hartford Convention, but he had defended the convention against charges of disunionist sentiment. During the War of 1812, he was convinced that the Republican administration had superseded authority and common sense. Arguing against the draft in the House of Representatives, he claimed that "The operation of such measures thus unconstitutional and illegal ought to be prevented by a resort to other measures which are both constitutional and legal. It will be the solemn duty of the state governments to protect their own authority over their own militia and to interpose between their citizens and arbitrary power."[13] His subsequent defense of the union in 1830 struck some as inconsistent. The perceived shift brought charges of opportunism that dogged him throughout his career.

Webster inadvertently encouraged charges of inconsistency in a great many ways. Ambitious for appointive office late in his career, he made no secret of his appetite for the Court of St. James. Some of his maneuvering was seen as an effort to secure that post rather than as part of a life-long political program. Since he was unable to live on his senator's salary, Webster continued his law practice and accepted large sums from New England's mercantile interests as a condition of remaining in office. Although he could take the money legally at the time, the practice was irregular. He was charged with conflict of interest by his colleagues. Many junior legislators took positions that they later regretted, but few were burdened by early prominence in the same way Webster was.

Two other great debaters of the Congress, Clay and Douglas, were similarly hampered by their active legislative careers. Both were unquestionably powerful; both ran for the presidency; both fell short of the mark. Many attribute Douglas' demise to his 1858 senatorial debates with Lincoln. The debates served as the last hurrah for compromise. Attacked from all sides by the factions of a Democratic party unwilling to part with its extremes, Douglas, the author of popular sovereignty, could not win in 1860.

THIS MONUMENT
WAS ERECTED
BY MOSES AND LYDIA SHEPHERD,
AS A TESTIMONY OF RESPECT TO
HENRY CLAY,
THE ELOQUENT DEFENDER OF NATIONAL
RIGHTS AND NATIONAL INDEPENDENCE.

Because the controversies created in congressional debate alienated influential constituencies, few of the nineteenth century's srongest debaters
became president. This monument on the Cumberland Road pays tribute
to Henry Clay, one eloquent aspirant who failed to gain the White House.

Debates Fostered Insult and Violence

Debates were not always seemly affairs. The contestants often descended to bombast, ridicule, and *ad hominem* attack, if not open violence. Audiences were as guilty as the debaters themselves. Speakers, particularly abolitionists, were the victims of violence and murder. Theodore Weld wore his moniker, "the most mobbed man in America," as a badge of courage. Elijah Lovejoy, another abolitionist, was murdered by an angry crowd. Even formal assemblies produced conflict.

The Congress of the United States was not safe from violence spawned by debate. Of many examples, the case involving South Carolina's Preston Brooks and Massachusetts' Charles Sumner is the most notorious. Sumner had just finished a withering attack on those supporting slavery in Kansas, reserving particularly harsh words for Senators Andrew Butler of South Carolina and Stephen Douglas of Illinois. Sumner named Butler a Don Quixote, Douglas his Sancho Panza, and slavery their Dulcinea. He then impugned Butler's honesty and skill in debate. "There was no extravagance of the ancient parliamentary debate which he did not repeat; nor was there any possible deviation from truth which he did not make. . . . But the Senator touches nothing which he does not disfigure—with error, sometimes of principle, sometimes of fact. He shows an incapacity of accuracy, whether in stating the Constitution or in stating the law, whether in the details of statistics or the diversions of scholarship. He cannot open his mouth but out there flies a blunder."[14] Douglas received worse. Speaking directly to Douglas, Sumner said, "The noisome, squat, and nameless animal, to which I now refer, is not a proper model for an American Senator. Will the Senator from Illinois take notice?"[15]

Preston Brooks, a representative from South Carolina and Butler's relative, decided that physical attack was the only possible response to "this personal affair." On May 22, 1856, two days after Sumner's speech, he strode onto the Senate floor. Henry Wilson described the scene.

> My colleague remained in his seat, busily engaged in his public duties. While thus engaged, with pen in hand, and in a position which rendered him utterly incapable of protecting or defending himself, Mr. Preston S. Brooks, a member of the House of Representatives, approached his desk unobserved, and abruptly addressed him. Before he had time to

CHARLES SUMNER

Insults were not unknown in Senate debate, but Massachusetts Senator Charles Sumner exceeded the rules of decorum. He called Stephen Douglas a "noisome, squat, and nameless animal."

utter a single word in reply he received a stunning blow upon the head from a cane in the hands of Mr. Brooks, which made him blind and almost unconscious. Endeavoring, however, to protect himself, in rising from his chair his desk was overthrown; and while in that condition he was beaten upon the head by repeated blows, until he sank upon the floor of the Senate exhausted, unconscious, and covered with his own blood.[16]

SOUTHERN CHIVALRY—CLUBS VERSUS ARGUMENT

Brooks's attack on Sumner transformed northern perceptions of the proslavery position. The violence embodied an assault on constitutional freedoms. (*New York Historical Society*)

The Brooks episode was preceded by several cases of less damaging violence among congressmen. Henry Clay was indirectly responsible for one melee. "[A]fter having replied to a severe personal arraignment of Henry Clay, former Speaker White, without the slightest warning, received a blow in the face. In the fight that followed a pistol was discharged wounding an officer of the police." White's experience was not unique. John Bell, the distinguished speaker and statesman, had a similar experience in the Committee of the Whole (1838). The fisticuffs became so violent that even the chair could not quell it.[17] Thomas Hart Benton once shouted to Senator Butler, who had a talent for encouraging verbal abuse, "There is a lie in his throat, I will cram it down or choke it out." Both men were restrained by colleagues before the first blow.[18]

All these spicy episodes began with hot language, which was much more common than outright violence. The crucible of debate heats the passions, so it is hardly surprising that they frequently boil over in invective and *ad hominem*. Benton's tirades were a personal trademark, embarrassing his supporters and outraging his foes. Henry Foote thought that Benton was "always more eager to crush the opposition than to win it over."[19] The vision of debate as a kind of conflict made such confrontations more likely.

Benton regretted his colleagues' and his own belligerence. After retiring from the Senate, he devoted the last years of his life to compiling and publishing the sixteen-volume *Abridgment of the Debates in Congress, from 1789–1856*. "Benton had more in mind than 'resuscitating the patriotic dead,' though this he certainly tried to do," reports press historian Thomas C. Leonard. "The project was designed to save that 'brotherly Union' by presenting examples of the 'fraternal spirit' of political discourse. 'Controversy will be quieted or terminated,' a Democratic magazine said, in its review of the *Abridgment*, '. . . and a feeling of security and permanence defused throughout the nation.' . . . [T]here is no question that Benton took a strong hand when the record diverged from his theme of harmony."[20] Benton deleted damaging passages and smoothed over differences in his compilation of congressional debate. Leonard explains: "On April 17, 1850, Benton had taken the floor and made reference to 'agitation' recently seen in the South. The *Congressional Globe* then reported that Senator Henry S. Foote of Mississippi spoke to deplore that notion that Southern leaders could be called 'agitators.' Senator Foote added that 'their calumniators, no matter who they may be, will be objects of general loathing and contempt.' Benton rushed from his feet toward Senator Foote, and the Southerner met him with a cocked pistol. 'Let him fire; Stand out of the way, and let the assassin fire,' the Missourian thundered. In the *Abridgment*, Benton silently deleted Foote's critique and their confrontation. He did preserve a remark he had made before Foote spoke earlier in the debate that week: 'Agitating, exciting, and distracting as is the subject, yet we are acting upon it like a calm and deliberate Senate, and I am willing to go home and sleep upon it, and come back tomorrow, and finish it up harmoniously and understandingly to all.' "[21]

Congress did not have a patent on dilatory argument. On the campaign trail, candidates often blustered and threatened one another. Even the aristocratic Daniel Webster, in the log cabin and hard cider campaign of 1840, dramatized the possibility of violence arising from debate. Silas Wright had been following Webster from stop to stop on the campaign, needling the high-living lawyer about his pretensions to humble roots. Webster roared in protest, "The man that calls me an aristocrat—is a LIAR!" He then took advantage of Wright's absence to issue a challenge. Should Wright continue to accuse and then "not come within the reach of my arm, [he] is not only a liar but a coward."[22]

Debates that descend into invective tend to ossify positions and deepen differences. The Brownlow–Pryne debate on abolition, held in Philadelphia in September 1858, is a case in point. Rather than reaching for understanding and benevolence, or even resolution, the debate entrenched positions over the course of the exchange. "Parson" William G. Brownlow, a newspaper editor and Methodist minister from Tennessee, entered the debate with a well-founded reputation for vitriol. His defense of slavery did nothing to damage that image. Abram Pryne, a young abolitionist cleric from New York, managed some colorful language of his own in his demand for immediate emancipation. The polar positions and venomous style of both mark the Brownlow–Pryne debate as a use of the form not to synthesize, but to differentiate.

Brownlow insisted on reading Pryne's attack on slavery as an attack on the South. Pryne disclaimed any sectional interests, and declined to defend the North. Before the debate he wrote to Brownlow, saying, "I shall by no means undertake to defend the North or condemn the South in all things. It is the institution of Slavery and not the South, upon which I make war."[23] Brownlow refused to depersonalize the issue, responding, "We are unable, in the South, to distinguish between a war upon the South and this institution."[24] The use of the war metaphor suggests the recalcitrance of the participants. Both persisted in the rhetoric of armed conflict. Brownlow protested the actions of northern ministers—he might have named Pryne, but did not do so explicitly—who, he claimed, had sent "uncircumcised Philistines of our New England States, into 'bleeding Kansas,' to shoot down the Christian owners of slaves and then to perform religious ceremonies over their dead bodies."[25] Brownlow insisted that any violent agitation against slaveholding constituted an affront to the fundamental rights of the temporal order, and reiterated that those rights were affirmed in the Bible. Pryne claimed that slavery's "only right is to die. I have nothing to do with any schemes for its amelioration or restriction; but, in the name of God and humanity I demand its annihilation."[26]

Historians have noted that the Brownlow–Pryne debate "summarized in a convenient text-book form all the arguments that Southerners and abolitionists had been developing."[27] Brownlow was not the first to defend slavery as a positive good; that position had been argued for years before he took the podium.[28] His response shows not new evidence or claims, but the calcification of old arguments. In this sense, Brownlow–Pryne was less a colloquy than an exhibition of antagonistic postures. The debaters' willingness to see their respective purposes in these terms is reflected in their joint statement prefacing the published version of the contest. "We live under a Government which tolerates liberty of thought, liberty of speech and freedom of the press; and in this expression of our honest views and feelings—differing widely as we do—upon the subject of Domestic Slavery in the United States . . . we are but exercising a right which belongs to every American citizen. . . . The liberal genius of our free institutions, allows to all unrestricted interchange of thought and sentiment; while men's opinions are received or rejected, according as they possess merit or demerit."[29] Neither disputant expected to persuade the other; their positions would be recognized as worthy or contemptible in and of themselves. Such debate is a means of clarifying the character of the opposition, not a vehicle for change.

Debate Can Substitute for Action When Action Is Needed

One of the advantages of debate is that it can absorb passion, providing an institutional alternative to disruption. On the other hand, debate can substitute for productive action on pressing problems. Minority viewpoints are often neglected while elites debate over a "full and proper response." The beguilements of the form blind participants to the practical implications of delay.

Arguing on behalf of the American labor movement in 1871, Wendell Phillips offered a historical perspective on debates that go on too long. He told management's representatives that

> we could discuss as well as you, if you would only give us bread and houses, fair pay and leisure, and opportunities to travel. We could sit and discuss the question for the next fifty years. It's a very easy thing to discuss, for a gentleman in his study, with no anxiety about to-morrow. Why the ladies and gentlemen of the reign of Louis XV and Louis XVI, in France seated in gilded saloons and on Persian carpets, surrounded with luxury, with the products of India, and the curious manufactures of ingenious Lyons and Rheims, discussed the rights of man, and balanced them in dainty phrases, and expressed them in such quaint generalizations that Jefferson borrowed the Declaration of Independence from

their hands. There they sat, balancing and discussing sweetly, making out new theories, and daily erecting a splendid architecture of debate. Till the angry crowd broke open the doors, and ended the discussion in blood. They waited too long, discussed about half a century too long. You see, discussion is very good when a man has bread to eat . . . ; discussion is bad when a class bends under actual oppression. We want immediate action.[30]

The conditions that make debate possible are similar to those that bind societies. Participants and citizens alike must agree not only on outcomes, but also on the means of obtaining decisions.

Debates Were Not Always Open to Minority Points of View

Though debate can protect minority points of view under some circumstances, not all representatives of such views were allowed an audience in nineteenth-century America. Because debate confers social status on participants, elites were reluctant to offer "inferior" groups the equality of the platform. Many free blacks were denied the chance to represent their views against a white opponent. Parson Brownlow explicitly refused to debate with a black, demanding that Abram Pryne prove his color before accepting the challenge. Women were effectively denied the right to public debate prior to the Civil War. The ban extended to all topics, including politics, religion, and reform.

Angelina Grimké was one of the first to challenge the strictures on women. She labeled such restrictions *"a violation of human rights, a rank usurpation of power,* a violent seizure and confiscation of what is sacredly and inalienably hers—thus inflicting upon woman outrageous wrongs, working mischief incalculable in the social circle, and in its influence on the world producing only evil and that continually."[31] Grimké acted on her convictions. In 1835, in Amesbury, Massachusetts, she answered the challenge of two young men to debate on the subject of slavery. The editor of the Amesbury *Morning Courier* was scandalized, refusing to publish the results of the debate. He explained his decision in a letter to his readers. "The character of the white ladies of the South, as well as of the ladies of color, seems to have been discussed, and the editor of the *Courier* was of the opinion that the reputation of his paper, and the morale of its readers, might be injuriously affected by publishing this debate."[32]

Subsequently, Grimké was shut out of halls across New England. At one point, when refused access to the local church, she lectured in a barn. The pastor said that "he would sooner rob a henhouse than hear a woman speaking in public."[33]

Objections to Grimké's public career crested at Pennsylvania Hall on May 16, 1838. An angry mob rioted outside while she denounced slavery within. Grimké incorporated reference to the mob into the speech as evidence of the brutality of pro-slavery sentiment. "What is a mob?" she asked. "What would the breaking of every window be? What would the levelling of this Hall be? What if the mob should now burst in upon us, break up our meeting and commit violence upon our persons—would this be anything compared to what the slaves endure?"[34] The listeners escaped, but the hall suffered. The mob burned Pennsylvania Hall to the ground the next morning.

Even private debates were closed to women. At progressive Oberlin College, an effort to revive the "Ladies Literary Society" was met with hostility.[35] Oberlin did not approve the group until 1874. When rhetoric professor James Thome staged an exhibition debate among female students in 1846, the faculty objected. The "experiment was not repeated."[36]

Catherine Beecher, daughter of Lyman Beecher and a prominent theorist on education and domesticity, insisted that women exceeded their role by debating. "All the power and all the conquests that are lawful to *woman* are those only which appeal to the kindly, generous, peaceful and benevolent principles . . . a woman is to win everything by peace and love; by making *herself* so much respected that to yield to *her* opinions, and to gratify *her* wishes, will be the free-will of the heart." On the other hand, "a *man* may act on society by the collision of intellect, in public debate; *he* may urge his measures by a sense of shame, by fear and by personal interest; *he* may coerce by the combination of public sentiment; *he* may drive by physical force, and *he* does *not* overstep the boundaries of his sphere."[37]

Women began to make headway on the platform only shortly before the Civil War. Speaking at a rump caucus of the "Whole World's Temperance Convention" (called the "Half-World's Convention") in 1853, Antoinette Brown was shouted down by outraged clerics. The reaction was so extreme that many leapt to the defense of women's right to be heard. Brown's biographer Elizabeth Cazden explains: "The Half-World's Convention was a watershed in women's battle for a public voice. People who doubted the wisdom of women participating in public debates were nevertheless appalled at reports of clergymen shouting gross insults at innocent women. In the aftermath of the convention, it was generally conceded that women, even when they took on 'men's' roles, were entitled to be treated with dignity and respect."[38]

As late as 1897, the University of Wisconsin refused to allow female students to represent the school in a debate with the University of Iowa, reasoning that "ladies in that capacity do no credit either to themselves or to co-education in general."[39] Women's debating societies struggled for acceptance on college campuses in the early twentieth century. Their organizations were not only separate from the men's, they also debated different topics. Even after women were accepted for intercollegiate competition, national debate organizations maintained separate resolutions for men and women. The last separate topic was issued in the 1926–27 school year, when women debated "Resolved: That trial by jury should be abolished," and men debated "Resolved: That the essential features of the McNary-Haugen bill be enacted into law."[40] Subsequently, resolutions were issued for co-educational debate.

As a rule-bound activity implicitly committed to institutional order, debate was at best an uneven vehicle for expressing novel social positions in the nineteenth century.

Summary: The Problems with Debate Stem from Expectation and Execution as well as Form

Many of the more significant limitations of debate are not inherent in the form, but flow from debaters' approach to it. Debate is made to answer for a variety of purposes, some of which are inconsistent. On the one hand we turn to debate to impose order on potentially chaotic legislative agendas, on the other we hope that debate will offer a forum for innovation. The first use stresses rule and predictability, the second the generation of solutions. Debate can serve both purposes, but it does not do both well all the time.

Alternatively, debate is relied on as a means of protecting the rights of minorities, ensuring an audience for unpopular positions, and bringing closure to painful, difficult questions. Minorities who "lose" debates will feel slighted by the process. Majorities tied up in "dilatory" debates with advocates able to manipulate the rules

will feel that debate has broken down. Evaluating the success of a
debate depends on the judge's perspective and purpose.

To understand what debate can contribute and what it cannot,
we need to distinguish between the structural qualities of the form
and the purposes for which we use it. Eighteenth- and nineteenth-
century debates provide us with a record of successful and unsuccess-
ful practices, affording an opportunity to evaluate the contributions
and limitations of the debate form apart from the unique pressures
of the broadcast medium in which debate takes place today. Debate's fundamentally oppositional nature and its strict requirements of time and order exert strong pressure to oversimplify arguments and exaggerate the differences between positions. Because
debate instructs through the competition of ideas, winning and
losing is implied. These are pressures on debating, however, not
rigid demands. Debates can be productive without declaring a victor and can present alternatives without reducing multisided issues
to two-sided ones.

Debate is best adapted to deliberation on fairly specific questions.
Broad areas, such as "the economy" or "defense," allow the advocates too much latitude, reducing the direct clash and comparison
arising from focused disputes. The great debates of the nineteenth
century centered on this sort of narrow issue. Lincoln and Douglas
debated the extension of slavery in the territories. Their arguments
led them into a wide-ranging discussion of slavery, but both debaters returned to the central question in each of their speeches.
Even Webster's reply to Hayne—a speech that began on Foote's
resolution and quickly expanded to consider the strength of the
federal system—remained tightly focused on the prerogatives and
responsibilities of government. The comparatively small range of
issues considered improved the depth of the discussion on each one,
a tradition that contrasts sharply with the breadth of today's
political debates. In 1858, two senatorial candidates, Lincoln and
Douglas, met seven times for twenty-one hours of debate on a
single issue. In 1987, twelve presidential hopefuls met once for two
hours to "debate," among other things, the budget deficit, the plight
plight of the homeless, the wisdom of the intermediate-range missile
treaty with the Soviets, Persian Gulf policy, education, and the
balance of trade.

Issues cannot be defined narrowly unless the advocates find
themselves in rough agreement on the basic questions involved.
Charles Sumner's angry philippic, "The Crimes Against Kansas,"

was offered in debate over Kansas' Lecompton Constitution, a topic that might appear sufficiently specific to satisfy debate's requirement for focus. Sumner, however, understood the dispute as an argument over the morality of slavery and slave owners, the condition of law in the slave states, and the practices of the U.S. Congress. Pro-slavery senators preferred a focus on the admission of a territory and the representativeness of its constitution. The disagreements over jurisdiction sparked both personal attacks and violence. Topic is not only a question of definition, but of what the advocates are willing to risk in face-to-face confrontation. The southern senators were willing to risk Kansas, but not slavery itself. When the debate reached the question of slavery per se, they cried foul. Under such circumstances, productive debate cannot proceed. The subsequent positions may be of interest to analysts, but are not useful for policymaking. The differences between positions will be exaggerated rather than minimized as the advocates move into disagreement not only on the present issue, but on the jurisdiction of the authority to which both had previously submitted.

The importance of encouraging direct clash is evident from the different effects of our early debates. The disputes in the Constitutional Convention of 1787, the Webster–Hayne debate, the Lincoln–Douglas debates, and Pryne–Brownlow were all face to face, and all required considerable accountability of the advocates. The direct response to challenges from an opponent reveals an advocate's preparation and habits of mind. Lincoln occasionally mischaracterized Douglas' positions and had to account for his missteps when Douglas pointed them out.[41] Brownlow chivvied Pryne on the Bible's view of slavery; Pryne had to respond, literally, chapter and verse. Debates that did not feature such direct clash produced less thorough comparison of ideas, or at best encouraged opponents to respond to one another selectively. The buffer provided by a press panel and moderator minimizes direct clash in today's debates. This format increases the likelihood that an artful dodger will be able to duck difficult issues.

Injecting greater clash into today's debates is more than a matter of choosing topics and arranging format; it also involves careful consideration of the condition of public argumentation in a given area. Positions that offer discrete solutions to pressing problems—and command a political constituency in the bargain—seem to encourage more clash than do less developed issue areas. For example, competing programs for apportioning representatives to the

Congress, hotly debated at the Constitutional Convention, were specific and claimed political allegiances. Each debated proposal was an arguable proposition *and* the advocates were in rough agreement on the rights and privileges at issue. Intense political debate for the twenty-five years preceding the convention ensured a common vocabulary. The outcome of the convention was at no time a foregone conclusion; even the final plan was in doubt for months following the last day of debate. The questions, however, were clear from the beginning, enabling confrontation, clash, and productive debate.[42] Debating strategies can always be used to subvert efforts to achieve more direct clash when an advocate perceives an advantage in avoiding the harder question; as we argue in the final chapter, contemporary political debates would be improved if we could specify the issues and a structure that invites as well as elicits argumentative engagement.

The broadcast era has changed debates considerably, but not beyond recognition. In the next chapters, we will examine the emergence and evolution of debate on radio and television, paying particular attention to the surviving strengths and weaknesses of the debate form. In the last chapter, we will consider several approaches to preserving the best elements of debate while minimizing the tendencies to obscure or misuse its oppositional format. The legacy of our early debates illustrates that the choice is not a question of format alone, but of education, preparation, intention, and performance.

---◆---

CHAPTER 4

The Impact of Broadcasting
on Debates

As Calvin Coolidge's Secretary of Commerce, Herbert Hoover led the fight for passage of the Federal Radio Act of 1927. Hoover believed that radio would revolutionize "the political debates that underlie political action [by making] us literally one people upon all occasions of general public interest."[1] He was partially correct.

Throughout most of the nineteenth century, surrogates carried the case for a presidential nominee in speeches that made party and issue more central than the candidate's image. Nonetheless, because it was a person, not an aggregate of issues or a party that became president, image played an inevitable role in the broadsides and torches of the campaigns. Although he lived in a fashionable mansion, William Henry Harrison was cast successfully in the 1840 campaign as a log-cabin-dwelling farmer, for example.

Just as direct appeal to voters was considered unbecoming throughout much of the nineteenth century, direct clash with an opponent was deemed indecorous for the first half of the twentieth. Such clash at first was unthinkable to those not yet comfortable with carrying their own case to the voters directly. As politicians became more familiar with self-promotion, political variables continued to rule out general election presidential debates. One candidate always saw greater minuses than pluses in such an endeavor. At no time in the glory days of radio did an incumbent believe it advantageous to engage an opposing party nominee in direct exchange from the same platform. As FDR repeatedly demonstrated, the benefits of wrapping oneself in the presidency were simply too great. So, for example, in 1936 four presidential contenders spoke at Chautauqua, each on a different date. Prohibitionist candidate

D. Leigh Colvin condemned the other parties for catering to the "liquor interests." Socialist Norman Thomas declared that the election hinged on "Socialism versus Capitalism." By contrast, the incumbent, FDR, positioned himself above the fray. Before an immediate audience of twelve thousand and a radio and film audience of thousands more, FDR spoke as only a president could: "We are not isolationists except insofar as we seek to isolate ourselves completely from war. Yet we must remember that so long as war exists on earth there will be some danger that even the nation which most ardently desires peace may be drawn into war." Because of his special status as president, the last three words of FDR's peroration linger in memory. "I have seen war . . . on land and sea," he said. "I have seen blood running from the wounded. I have seen men coughing out their gassed lungs. . . . I have seen cities destroyed. I have seen two hundred limping, exhausted men come out of line—the survivors of a regiment of one thousand. . . . I have seen children starving. . . . I hate war." When he spoke at Chautauqua ten days later Republican nominee Alf Landon accused FDR of using the "machinery of the Federal government to maintain the present Administration in power, and to bring into question the faith of the people in their form of government." Roosevelt had spoken as president, Landon as presidential aspirant. In his attacks on FDR, Landon positioned himself in an arena with fellow candidates Thomas and Colvin. Speaking as president, not as candidate, FDR refused to legitimize those who attacked him. No mention of them passed from his microphone that day. Had FDR elected to debate his opponents he would have granted them the standing that comes of the ability to engage and be engaged. No such legitimacy was gotten by them that fall at Chautauqua. The first incumbent to debate was Gerald Ford, an unelected president behind in the polls.

Even when there was no incumbent, the presumed front-runner then as now had little to gain by legitimizing an opponent in a face-to-face exchange. When William Jennings Bryan took to the stump in 1896 delivering over 600 speeches to voters in twenty-seven states, McKinley's manager, Mark Hanna, dispatched a Republican speaker to follow his trail, rebutting his speeches town by town. Like FDR, McKinley stood above the contest. The structure of the debate suggested that Bryan was opposing the Republican "truth squad" rather than McKinley. Meanwhile, on his front porch seated in a rocking chair, McKinley received delegations of well-wishers at his home in Canton, Ohio, and rocked his way to the presidency.

Incumbents have downgraded their opponents by pairing them with lesser officials as well. In 1972, members of Richard Nixon's cabinet and his vice president responded to Democratic nominee George McGovern's campaign speeches, creating the sense in news coverage that McGovern was contesting with Spiro Agnew or John Mitchell for some office other than the presidency.

Only when both sides see an advantage in debating have debates occurred in the past. Until the broadcast age, the simple facts of constituency and geography dictated that there would not be a comparable advantage for both presidential candidates. In a congressional or senatorial race the district or state was often small enough to enable debaters to reach the natural supporters of both sides. Debates resulted. But what of a national election when one candidate stood to gain before a rural constituency and another from an urban one? Only when the broadcast media made it possible to reach a national audience did this worry fade. Not until 1960 would two nonincumbent major party nominees see debating as mutually advantageous. And then the legitimation given the less experienced, less known senator from Massachusetts prompted his opponent to shun debates in both of his subsequent election bids.

In their effort to institutionalize general election debates, the Republican and Democratic parties hope to remove political calculations from the process. If the debates they offer follow past practice, they will merge traditional debate with three related broadcast forms. The televised debates Americans have watched in previous general elections are a hybrid created by fusing characteristics of the traditional debate, the staged debate, the question-and-answer session, and the press conference. To identify the genus and genesis of broadcast presidential debates, we will devote this chapter to tracing the origin and teasing out the identity of each.

Traditional Debate

The infant medium of radio simply carried to the nation's living rooms the form of debate that had earlier characterized town meetings and the U.S. Congress. In 1928, the League of Women Voters, which had been founded only eight years earlier, broadcast a weekly ten-month series of debates on important issues. Representatives of the political parties, reporters, and editors but not presidential candidates took part in their exchanges.

Theodore Granik's "American Forum of the Air" followed a similar format, pitting two speakers against each other on a topic of national concern. Granik framed the question, introduced the speakers, and interjected questions to clarify confusions or redirect a line of argument that didn't seem to be going anywhere. The arguments were focused; the clash, direct; the form, free flowing. Speakers were not bound by prescribed time limits. Courtesy, a sense of fair play, the fear of a disapproving audience, and the occasional intervention of the moderator guaranteed that each side received a hearing.

In the early broadcast debates, the moderator who handled introductions and transitions and who monitored the clock only occasionally moved in to focus the clash. The print press synopsized and quoted segments of the exchange. This reportorial function raised charges that coverage was ideologically driven. In a press conference with newspaper editors in 1938, FDR complained of reports of a radio debate between Roosevelt opponent Senator Arthur Vandenberg of Michigan and FDR ally Senator Lister Hill of Alabama. Each had spent a half hour of radio time evaluating the Roosevelt relief program. The *New York Sun,* the president protested, had deleted the paragraphs of the AP story that dealt with Hill and run an account that presented only Vandenberg's case. "If you people think that is fair newspaper editing," declared the chief executive, "I do not. Now, you find hundreds of cases of that kind."[2]

Even after press conferences and debates were broadcast live, the charge that the press was distorting political events persisted. By focusing on a single moment from a presidential debate, the television networks shaped and some argued misshaped viewers perceptions of the whole encounter. As reporters moved from reporting to interpreting the outcome of debates, they would be charged as well with reducing campaigns to "games" or "horse races," emphasizing strategy, not the substance of the arguments.

To fend off those who saw redistributing existing radio channels as a means of increasing educational programming, NBC-blue instituted "America's Town Meeting of the Air" and NBC-red gave national time to what to that point had been a local program, "The University of Chicago Round Table."[3] In "America's Town Meeting of the Air," which debuted in March 1935, time limits and audience questions were a standard feature. A forty-minute period was divided in classical debate fashion, with each speaker receiving equal time. The final twenty minutes of the hour were reserved for audience questions. One "meeting" in 1946 debated the question "Should the United States adopt the Baruch report on the international control of atomic energy?" Hanson Baldwin, military editor of the *New York Times,* spoke in favor of adoption; Senator Revercomb, a member of the Senate Military Affairs Committee, opposed it.

By inviting partisans of each party to hear the other side's views as well, "Town Meeting" overcame the selective exposure that otherwise characterized the information seeking of Republicans and Democrats. "If we persist," noted moderator George Denny, "in the practice of Republicans reading only Republican newspapers, listening only to Republican speeches on the radio, attending only Republican political rallies, and mixing socially only with those of congenial views, and if Democrats . . . follow suit, we are sowing the seeds of the destruction of our democracy."[4] The program met its objective. A survey of "Town Meeting" mail revealed that the program prompted family discussion, further reading, and, among 34%, a change of opinion.[5]

To encourage audience participation, a prize was awarded to the listener who asked the best question. "Where is the Atomic Commission to get its Big Stick to enforce the provisions of the Baruch Report?" was the best question asked of Baldwin and Revercomb.

The topics were of national interest. Among them: "Should the United Nations abolish the veto power?" and "Can we have world peace without world law?"[6]

At issue was not the political future of either speaker but rather the cogency of their cases. Concerns about the speaker's "image" make less sense in such an environment. Although the credibility of the speaker inevitably plays some role in our assessment of argument, only when we must simultaneously decide who to entrust with governance *and* who is making the better case do the broader questions of the character and competence of the speaker become central.

Revercomb and Baldwin could as well have been surrogates standing in for one party or another, one candidate or another. After an issue had been defined and argued by those with no electoral interest in the outcome of the debate, a candidate could "take a stand" on that issue. Cases then had a life of their own as they had in the pseudonymous exchanges that constituted the

Federalist Papers. The source of the argument was less relevant than its substance. When carried in print or by surrogates, arguments are not "embodied" the way they are when allied with a candidate.

An impressive performance on such a program could of course fuel presidential prospects. Businessman Wendell Willkie, the 1940 Republican nominee, drew initial attention to his talents with articles in major magazines and praiseworthy performances on "America's Town Meeting of the Air" and "Information Please."

But since the issue before the audience was not whether or not to elect but which side had presented the more cogent case, neither side needed to fear that direct clash would create a backlash. Both were free to try to discredit the ideas being offered by the other; neither had a great incentive to discredit the opposing speaker in the process.

This tradition of debates survives in the series "The Advocates," produced by WGBH in Boston. In 1984, for example, viewers heard the then U.S. Ambassador to the UN Jeane Kirkpatrick and *National Review* publisher William Rusher defend Ronald Reagan's candidacy and Massachusetts Governor Michael Dukakis and Massachusetts Representative Barney Frank defend Walter Mondale's. Here was a level of substance and degree of clash not found in the actual presidential debates of that year.

For five weeks, advisers to Jimmy Carter, Ronald Reagan, and John Anderson were questioned as part of the series. For the session on U.S.–Soviet relations, former NATO commander Alexander Haig took Reagan's side. Carter was represented by a deputy assistant for national security, David Aaron. Image was muted in the equation. "We're trying to give people a good look at how the candidates, through surrogates, want to be perceived and how they stand up when they're asked tough questions on the issues, which doesn't really happen anywhere else," observed the executive producer Peter Cook.[7]

Reviewing a tape of a 1980 "Advocates" debate on energy, *New York Times* critic John Corry concluded that we can have "proper campaign debates on television."[8] "The topic was energy, and how the candidates would ensure its supply. What emerged . . . was a clear feeling about the differences between conservative Republicans and liberal Democrats. Mr. Rusher and Mr. Stockman were even prescient; they told us what would happen in a Reagan Administration: deregulation and an emphasis on leasing public lands.

Viewers who voted for Mr. Reagan knew what they were voting for."

When candidates carry *their own cases* to the public through the forum of debates, clash is minimized and attempts to personalize arguments magnified. Here a speaker has much to lose or gain by the voters' judgment not simply of the case but of its presenter. Factors not relevant to assessing the claims of Lister and Vandenberg came into play. How well was the advocate responding to stress? Did one speaker seem more compassionate and humane? Was one brighter? Better prepared? By aggressively challenging the opponent, a candidate risked appearing unfair, unsporting, contentious, or disagreeable.

Accordingly, the debate in the Oregon primary of 1948 between Stassen and Dewey invited a different mindset from listeners than did the debate between Lister and Vandenberg. The "great debate" between Republican candidates Harold Stassen, ex-governor of Minnesota, and New York Governor Thomas Dewey played a role in the undoing of Stassen's presidential bid. Held May 17, 1948, the debate was carried nationally by ABC, NBC, and Mutual radio to an audience estimated at between 40 and 80 million. One of the largest audiences in radio history had abandoned the "Carnation Contented Hour" and Fred Waring to listen to Stassen and Dewey.

The Republicans' nominee against FDR in 1944 had in 1948 won the New Hampshire primary. Where that primary is now taken very seriously by party professionals and the press, it wasn't then. Stassen took the more important Wisconsin primary and followed that up by winning the preference poll in Nebraska. After victory in Nebraska, Stassen led Dewey in the Gallup Poll. In a major misstep, Stassen then challenged Taft on his home ground in Ohio. Taft won the larger number of delegates there. Without a win in Oregon, Dewey was unlikely to win the nomination. In the Oregon primary, he and Stassen debated one of the few issues to decisively divide their candidacies: Should the Communist party be outlawed?

The issue was an important one. In mid-March, James Reston of the *New York Times* defined the "real fear" as whether we are "going to deal with the real aggression . . . Communist fifth column aggression by infiltration?"[9] The same week a Communist coup added Czechoslovakia to the growing number of Communist-led states, a list that included Yugoslavia, Bulgaria, Rumania, and

Poland. The first Communist blockade of Berlin occurred less than six weeks before the debate.

Stassen and Dewey had taken clear and opposite positions on outlawing the Communist party. In early April, Dewey argued that he wanted to keep the Communists "out in the open where we can beat them." The next day, Stassen stated, "I think the Communist party organization has been clearly shown to be a subversive arm of the foreign policy of the Soviet Union and as such I think it should be outlawed in the United States and all freedom loving countries."[10] On May 3, Dewey devoted a radio speech from Portland to the subject. "I want the people of Oregon and of the United States to know exactly where I stand on this proposal because it goes to the very heart of the qualification of any candidate for office and to the inner nature of the kind of country we want to live in," declared Dewey.

As the debate approached, Stassen increased its decisiveness by charging Dewey with "a soft coddling policy" toward Communists and alleging that Dewey's home state of New York was the U.S. center of Communist intrigue. These charges legitimized Dewey's strong defense and aggressive attack on Stassen's position. Responding to attack is fair play. Initiating the attack carries risk.

Dewey's initial reluctance to debate enables us to focus on the question: Why had it taken so long for a face-to-face clash among a party's contenders to take place? "I usually disapprove of personal debates between Republicans," Dewey explained, "because they tend to weaken and divide our party. However, I consider the proposal to outlaw the Communist party as so dangerous to our freedom and the security of this country that I think a full discussion of it under the auspices of the Multnomah County Republican Committee, using every modern facility of communication, is essential, so that every citizen of the United States may know just what is at stake. The whole future of our free institutions is involved."[11] So long as parties controlled the nomination process, party discipline could keep a contender from an environment in which savaging the opponent was appropriate behavior.

Although, from our vantage point, Dewey defended the more reasonable position, the public didn't see it that way in 1948 when Dewey's position was controversial. Stassen wanted Dewey to support the Mundt–Nixon bill, which in 1950 would pass the Congress to become the Internal Security Act. Still, throughout the debate, Stassen seemed defensive, "tired and somewhat ill-prepared";

Dewey's mind seemed sharper-edged.[12] Where Dewey tossed aside his prepared remarks, Stassen read from a carefully crafted script. Dewey sounded decisive; his convictions lived. "[I]n words long remembered by listeners who forgot other debating points,"[13] Dewey declared: "I am unalterably, wholeheartedly, and unswervingly against any scheme to write laws outlawing people because of their religion, political, social, or economic ideas. I am against it because it is a violation of the Constitution of the United States and of the Bill of Rights, and clearly so. . . . I am against it because I know from a great many years' experience in the enforcement of the law that the proposal wouldn't work, and instead would rapidly advance the cause of Communism in the United States and all over the world. . . . Stripped to its naked essentials, this is nothing but the method of Hitler and Stalin. It is thought control, borrowed from the Japanese war leadership. It is an attempt to beat down ideas with a club. It is a surrender of everything we believe in."[14]

The debate demonstrated the value of focusing on a single issue. The specifics of the Mundt–Nixon bill were explained; the experiences of other countries that had outlawed the Communist party detailed; Mundt was cited to rebut Stassen's interpretation of the bill; and the constitutional ramifications of passage were probed. In rebuttal, Dewey proved precise, his indictments telling. Stassen foundered. Because the debate was able to deal at length and in depth with a clearly defined issue of importance to the public, and because time was allotted for rebuttal, the format invited illumination of the issue and the candidates' stands on it. The candidates' differences on outlawing the Communist party were clarified and defended, their intellects publicly exercised in revealing ways. Dewey won on issue and image and with that the primary and his party's nomination.

The next primary debate demonstrated the disadvantages in moving from the traditional debate form. In what was billed as a "discussion," Democratic contenders Adlai Stevenson and Estes Kefauver met before a national television audience May 21, 1956. The discussion ranged across foreign and domestic policy. A moderator, Quincy Howe, phrased questions and apportioned time. Just as Dewey had expressed hesitance about engaging in a personal encounter, so too did Kefauver. Kefauver, who won the flip of the coin giving him the right to speak first, announced that the campaign must "not degenerate into a mere personal conflict" but should instead be waged on the issues.[15] In the next hour, the two candidates found little about which to disagree.

In the Dewey–Stassen debate, image and competence on an issue joined. But the link is not an inevitable one. The possibility that good looks, a good speaking voice, a commanding presence, or a facility for television or radio could supplant substance raises a first set of questions that we will address in the next chapters: What if anything do debates tell us about the performance in office of the person who will be president? Are some cues about image actually valuable indicators of performance? Can factors irrelevant to effective governance disqualify a candidate in debates? Are there alternative ways to judge the legitimacy of the issue positions of one side or the other?

Traditionally, debates provided an audience with sustained exposure to direct clash over a single issue. As the Stassen–Dewey debate demonstrates, nothing inherent in radio barred such an encounter. A prolonged interchange about a single issue enables even less educated members of an audience to judge the merits of the case in ways foreclosed by monologic speeches. "No ordinary bystander is equipped to analyze the propaganda by which a private interest seeks to associate itself with the disinterested public," noted Walter Lippmann in 1925. "It is a perplexing matter, perhaps the most perplexing in popular government and the bystander's only recourse is to insist upon debate. He will not be able, we may assume, to judge the merits of the arguments. But if he does insist upon full freedom of discussion, the advocates are very likely to expose one another. Open debate may lead to no conclusion and throw no light whatever on the problem or its answer, but it will tend to betray the partisan and the advocate."[16] Such revelation is less probable as the range of issues to be debated multiplies. The Stassen–Dewey debate was the first and last presidential broadcast debate to limit itself to a single issue.

Radio didn't kill traditional debate directly. Instead it massaged into the audience the expectation that the medium would entertain, that its messages would be brief, and that channels could be changed when a program proved boring. Nineteenth-century political debates did not vie for audience attention with circuses, drama, music, sitcoms, and first-run movies. Contemporary debates do.

No longer was the audience captive in a political hall. Now the boring speaker could be replaced by entertainment on the other channel. Or the bored listener could simply turn off the set. "Radio and television broadcasts do permit some debate," observed Lippmann in 1955. "But despite the effort of the companies to let opposing views be heard equally, and to organize programs on which there are opposing speakers, the technical conditions of broadcasting do not favor genuine and productive debate. For the audience, tuning on and tuning off here and there, cannot be counted upon to hear, even in summary form, the essential evidence and main arguments on all the significant sides of a question."[17]

As we noted, in the nineteenth century, debates were a form of entertainment as well as education. We do not mean to suggest, of course, that nineteenth-century audiences were models of sobriety. Davy Crockett recalled, for example, that to draw voters to his speech he had to kill coons, trade them for whiskey, and then treat his would-be audience at the bar. In return, the patrons of the bar patronized his speech. As the available means of distraction increased, speeches and debates in and of themselves held less appeal than they once had. To attract and then hold the fleeing attention of the audience, political speeches grew shorter and were increasingly guised as entertainment.

Where in the nineteenth century, entertainment had lured audiences to speeches, now speech became entertainment. The torch parade of the past century was designed to draw voters to the speeches. Once there, the voters were captives. In the entertainment-saturated environment created by the broadcast media, neither speech nor traditional debate held its former allure. To attract and hold an audience, both now had to entertain. To preempt audience flight, reasoned producers, the program not only had to entertain but its speeches and statements had to be short. From its earliest days, political pundits projected that the new medium would result in abbreviated political speech. In 1924, the candidate who would lose the general election to Calvin Coolidge predicted that radio "will make the long speech impossible or inadvisable . . . the short speech will be the vogue."[18] The pundits were prophetic.

Throughout the 1940s, political content borrowed the form of game shows, radio dramas, and soap operas to entice viewers to embrace one point of view or another. With the Dewey–Stassen debate a noteworthy exception, call-in shows with their built-in audience involvement and political claims camouflaged as entertainment displaced traditional debates. In 1928 the Democrats described their

Where, in the nineteenth century, parades lured audiences, such as this crowd at a Lincoln–Douglas debate, the advent of the broadcast media transformed political speech into entertainment. (*Library of Congress*)

dramatization of Al Smith's life "radio entertainment in its best vein." The program included stage and concert stars. In 1944 Norman Corwin produced a series of brief testimonials for FDR that culminated in a musically backed chorus simulating the sounds of an accelerating train. The "Roosevelt Special" brought the world of entertainment and the world of politics together. Lucille Ball, Tallulah Bankhead, and Irving Berlin were among those who spoke eight- to ten-word endorsements of the incumbent president.[19] In 1948 the Democrats appropriated the form of a quiz show. The question: Who is the candidate? The clue: a period of dead silence. The answer: Governor Dewey, "who says nothing on any issue."[20] The Republicans volleyed with short homey dramatizations. A marriage license clerk asks a couple what they plan to do about the national debt. They would, he reminded them, shoulder a debt of $1017.26. The couple reconsiders marriage. The prospective groom concludes, "Somebody is giving us a dirty deal." The somebody, of course, was the Democratic party.[21]

The 1952 televised speeches of Eisenhower were staged by the New York advertising agency Batten, Barton, Durstine & Osborn. The speech itself would last a bare twenty minutes. The remaining time would be consumed by the arrival and departure of "the hero." Ike would enter from the back of the auditorium and greet the crowd. The crowd would wildly express its enthusiasm. The camera would cut to Mamie in the box. Ike would mount the platform and wave to Mamie. Mamie would smile. The crowd would be quieted only gradually. Then the speech. The five-minute ads that helped elect Ronald Reagan in 1980 were different in degree but not in kind. After stills and filmed footage illustrated the road that had taken Reagan to the nomination, the candidate spoke directly to the voters.

Since the advent of the broadcast media, the length of political messages has decreased steadily. In the election of 1856, Charles Sumner's eighty-page-long "Crimes Against Kansas" speech was reprinted as a campaign document. Almost a million copies were sold. Were we to type out all of Reagan's 1984 broadcast campaign messages, the resulting manuscript would not approach the length of Sumner's single speech. Few could be induced to pay to read or hear any of the rhetoric generated in a modern presidential campaign. But where it required effort to purchase and read Sumner's speech, today much exposure to political information is cost free and effortless. Once political interest correlated with exposure to political messages; now exposure to television correlates with exposure to political messages. Interest in television and interest in campaigns have increased together.[22] Indeed, in one survey, half of those who reported watching political ads indicated that they had been unable to avoid them.[23]

The need to reach the nation through news has altered the nature of political discourse. Where once the stump speech had persuasion of the immediate audience as its goal, it now sets its sights on securing a favorable bite of the evening news. Crowds have become wallpaper; the speech itself, a picture frame, structured with two criteria in mind: eliciting the applause to telegraph its success to the eavesdropping world and encasing the desired newsbites. Where in the nineteenth century a two-hour speech was commonplace, the typical stump speech today averages seventeen minutes.

Survival of the briefest increasingly has become a political imperative. The thirty-minute speeches that reached the nation's Motorolas in the 1940s were standard fare as well in America's first telecast presidential campaign in 1952. By 1956, the five-minute speech as spot was edging out the longer speech. In 1964, the five-minute ad gave way to the sixty-second spot. Then the thirty-second spot appeared on the horizon. With time for little more than a slogan, an assurance, an assertion, and a smile, such ads cost candidates more and delivered less than did their dimly remembered ancestor—the political speech.

Not only are we seeing less of candidates now but when offered longer exposure we opt instead for entertainment. On September 22, 1964, Americans faced a revealing choice. Would they settle into their sofas to watch that embodiment of high culture known as "Petticoat Junction"? Would they savor the sin and seduction of "Peyton Place"? Or would they watch past president Dwight Eisenhower discuss the future of the world with Republican presidential nominee Barry Goldwater? In overwhelming numbers, Americans confessed that in their hearts they preferred the clinches of "Peyton Place" and the comedy of "Petticoat Junction" to political conversation between a person who had been president and one who aspired to be.

The incident was not an aberration. In 1972 over half those interviewed in one survey reported watching the Democratic convention because, with all three networks airing it, there wasn't any other choice.[24] This response prophesied viewer behavior when given a choice in 1979. In November of that year, *Jaws* faced off against Roger Mudd's documentary on presidential aspirant Edward Kennedy. *Jaws* swallowed "Teddy." That pattern repeats itself each time the public chooses prime-time drama over network documentaries and yellowing movies over convention coverage and is reflected in the conclusion that "the higher the level of abstract, issue-oriented, political content," the smaller the likely audience.[25]

Presidential speeches don't fare well either. Reagan's typical speech has attracted a smaller audience than did Carter's. Carter attracted a larger audience than had Ford.[26] And when a candidate does deliver a well-publicized national speech, it is likely to attract favorably disposed partisans whose attitudes are already set.[27] Accordingly, it functioned well for one of the uses McGovern put it to in 1972—raising funds from dedicated partisans—but failed to accomplish his overriding goal of winning converts to his cause.

Our collective preference for sitcoms and sharks would be unalarming if we read the major newspapers, digested position papers, and mulled over books about the issues of the day. Newspaper reading, for instance, plays a primary role in promoting awareness of the issues themselves and the candidates' positions on them.[28] Unlike television viewing, newspaper readership correlates with voters' knowledge of the candidates' positions and with participation in the campaign.[29] And the prime predictor of whether a first-time voter's knowledge of the issues will be accurate is that person's newspaper use.[30] All this would prophesy an increasingly informed electorate were it not that the public is relying more on television for news.[31] As a practical matter, "Television is the preeminent link between national affairs and the national public."[32]

Although reading is hardly a national pastime, in the typical week more people are exposed to newspapers than to network news.[33] But Ann Landers and the scores of the Boston Celtics draw more interest than the congressional deliberations over the contras. Of the 64% who said they read a newspaper, barely a third reported paying a great deal of attention to news about government and politics.[34]

The televised debates of the past two and a half decades have been shaped by the assumption that their audience has a short attention span and is drawn to the event by the prospect of clash. All the devices in television's repertory are unpacked to hold attention. Where radio's political programing drew from the popular genres of that medium, we will suggest that the grammar of the televised presidential debates borrows from television's game shows.

The need to entice an otherwise inattentive audience creates the second set of questions for those who favor more meaty debates: Can the substance of debates be increased without sacrificing the entertainment values that draw otherwise disinterested viewers to watch? Or, alternatively, how can an appetite for political substance be cultivated in an anorexic electorate? Among the means that have been tried are telethons, press conferences, and staged or edited debates created by individuals other than the candidates. Facets of each of these forms appear in general election presidential debates.

The Created, Edited, or Staged Debate

A simulated debate carried by radio in the 1936 campaign previewed the uses news and advertising would make of debate content in future years. Frustrated by their inability to engage Roosevelt on their terms, the Republicans edited segments from his speeches for rebuttal by Senator Arthur Vandenberg. The recording was smuggled into the radio studio from which Vandenberg planned to broadcast. So controversial was this move that twenty-one of the sixty-six stations that had scheduled the political program cut it from the air.

By the mid-1960s, Vandenberg's move would be uncontroversial. In 1964, for example, ads for Goldwater clipped segments from Johnson's speeches which the Republican nominee then challenged.

Editing clips from debates to reinforce key ideas or remind voters of a candidate's performance also became standard political practice. In 1960 Kennedy used televised clips from the first debate; Nixon used radio—each reinforcing the perceptions created by the medium on which he had "won."

The Kennedy campaign took the ability to edit a step further. First, a skillful editor clipped reaction shots in which Nixon was scowling, sweating, smiling, and nodding his approval at Kennedy's points and furtively looking off camera. Then those were intercut into Kennedy's opening statement. Nixon at his worst throughout the entire debate contrasted with Kennedy at his best. Since the shots of Nixon did not occur in Kennedy's statement but elsewhere in the debate, the Republicans cried foul. The Democrats denied any wrong-doing. The press failed to investigate.[35]

As one of us learned when her father inserted a marauding black bear into scenes of her birthday party, editing can rearrange reality. But it can also educate. On November 24, 1953, Edward R. Murrow's "See It Now" aired "Argument at Indianapolis." A group of Indianapolis citizens had rented a hall to organize a local chapter of the American Civil Liberties Union. A famed civil liberties lawyer was scheduled to address the group. Opposing groups including the local chapter of the American Legion forced cancellation of the hall and succeeded in barring the group from several other municipal facilities. Finally a Roman Catholic priest offered the use of his church. The "See It Now" crew intercut the Civil Liberties meeting with an American Legion meeting condemning it. The intercutting constituted a compelling case for the right to express all sides of an issue, an implicit condemnation of those who opposed the right of the Civil Libertarians to meet and organize.

A similar early use of juxtaposition demonstrated what can be learned outside verbal statement about the character of candidates. Another of Murrow's "See It Now" programs showed Senator Robert Taft and Senator Leverett Saltonstall campaigning. Each was shown speaking. At the conclusion of each address the camera tracked the speaker's descent from the podium. Coming on autograph-seeking children at the foot of the platform, Taft swept them aside. Saltonstall approached the same children with interest and briefly engaged them. Murrow overlaid no commentary on the contrasting responses. They required none.

A controversial, important, and uniquely televisual debate occurred when Edward R. Murrow lodged a half-hour indictment against the tactics of Wisconsin Senator and Communist hunter Joseph McCarthy. McCarthy was given equal time to respond. Murrow's analysis used the capacity of television, still an infant medium in March 1954, to indict McCarthy in his own words. "Tonight," Murrow noted at the program's opening, " 'See It Now' devotes its entire half hour to a report on Senator Joseph R. McCarthy, told mainly in his own words and pictures. . . . If the Senator feels that we have done violence to his words or pictures, and desires, so to speak, to answer himself, an opportunity will be afforded him on this program."

Murrow then abutted contradictory statements by the Wisconsin senator. A film segment showed McCarthy cautioning that if the fight against Communism became a fight between the Republican and Democratic parties, one party would be destroyed and "the Republic cannot endure very long under a one-party system." Then a tape of McCarthy's voice said that Democrats bear the "stain of a historic betrayal."

Murrow also challenged McCarthy's facts. The senator was shown informing a witness that the Civil Liberties Union had been listed as a front for the Communist party. "The Attorney General's List does not and never has listed the A.C.L.U. as subversive," added Murrow. "Nor does the F.B.I. or any other Federal government agency." For twenty-two minutes, "See It Now" documented McCarthy's use of innuendo, half-truths, falsehood, and intimidation. The program discredited both McCarthy and his methods.

On April 6, McCarthy responded. The senator labeled Murrow "the leader and the cleverest of the jackal pack which is always found at the throat of anyone who dares to expose individual Communists and traitors," noted that in every country the Communists had to find "glib, clever men like Edward R. Murrow," and claimed that Murrow, by his own admission, "was a member of the I.W.W. . . . a terrorist organization." Documents featuring the word *Communist* were waved. McCarthy closed by resolving that he would not be thwarted by "the Murrows, the Lattimores, the Fodters, *The Daily Worker,* or the Communist Party itself." In his twenty-two minutes, McCarthy had demonstrated anew each of the tactics Murrow had documented and discredited on the earlier broadcast. Murrow had argued and McCarthy had confirmed the dangers embedded in the senator's ideology and tactics. Image and issue had joined to discredit McCarthy and to help lodge *McCarthyism* as a pejorative eponym in the American political vocabulary. Had McCarthy not engaged Murrow in debate before a common audience, and in the process confirmed the charges he was attempting to dispatch, the damage to McCarthy's credibility would have been less severe.

As important for our inquiry is the fact that the "debate" illuminated the characters of both Murrow and McCarthy. Murrow read from a text to ensure that he said exactly what he meant to say. By contrast, McCarthy's countercharges blistered with *ad hominem* attacks. Murrow's tone was measured; by mid-speech McCarthy's had become hyperbolic. Murrow documented claims carefully, citing and showing sources and quoting directly from them. By contrast, McCarthy clothed assertion in such language as "Communist slave masters by the jackal pack" and noted that "if . . . Mr. Murrow is giving comfort to our enemies, he ought not to be brought into the homes—of millions of Americans—by the Columbia Broadcasting System."

Throughout, the senator seemed engaged in the creation of a drama in which truth was subordinated to plot. Murrow concluded that the fault was not really McCarthy's. "He didn't create this situation of fear, he merely exploited it; and rather successfully. Cassius was right. 'The Fault, dear Brutus, is not in our stars, but in ourselves.' " By contrast, McCarthy seemed set on a personal vendetta against Murrow. Verbally and nonverbally, in choice of evidence and phrasing of claims, McCarthy emerged as less trust-worthy and credible than Murrow, a contrast tellingly disclosed by the debate form in which they engaged. More revealing than the claims of either man was how he chose to phrase and document them. On this one occasion at least, the verbal-visual evidence pro-vided by a televised debate yielded insight about two individuals and their positions on a controversial set of issues.

At one level, Murrow was simply doing what all reporters do. By editing together excerpts from any exchange, reporters digest the news. These digests have been indicted for focusing on campaign strategy not substance, a criticism that raises the questions: How, if at all, can news coverage of campaigns, in general, and debates, in particular, better inform voters about what matters or should matter about the substance of bids for the presidency? And what inducements, if any, will encourage voters to learn from the avail-able sources of news and information?

The National Question-and-Answer Session

Broadcasting was expected to change dialogues between speakers and voters into monologues. Gone would be the hecklers, the questioners, the palpable give and take that comes of confronting a breathing, pulsing crowd. In most cases that is in fact what oc-curred. But live radio and television made possible another form of communication—the question-and-answer session between candi-dates and citizens. In 1949, Oregon Senator Wayne Morse took to the radio to answer questions from listeners for an hour and a half. In 1952 Judge Francis Cherry gained an upset victory in the Arkansas gubernatorial primary by taking an entire day's worth of questions, over five thousand of them, in a Little Rock radio studio.

In 1950 Thomas Dewey carried the talkathon to television in his successful run for the New York governorship. For eighteen hours, Dewey answered questions about hospitals, taxes, veterans' benefits, and other topics of state and national concern. "He answered them in awe-inspiring detail," observed one commentator.[36] In 1950, Vice President George Bush's father, Prescott Bush, captured the Connecticut Senate seat of Democrat William Benton with an audience participation program as well.

On May 1, 1952, the League of Women Voters and *Life* magazine co-sponsored a nationally telecast "Democratic and Republican Candidates Forum" moderated by newsperson John Daly. A poll of League members created a pool of questions. Two of these questions were asked of each candidate. After their replies, questions were asked by the audience. Neither Stevenson nor Eisenhower participated. Paul Hoffman stood in for Stevenson. Appearing with him were former Governor W. Averell Harriman, Senator Estes Kefauver, Senator Robert Kerr, former Governor Harold Stassen, and Governor Earl Warren.

Because radio reaches a narrower band of citizens than television, it is an ideal means of reaching subgroups of the audience. In the New York mayoral election of 1965, Republican Congressman John Lindsay conducted a question-and-answer session on election eve on a radio station with high listenership among blacks. Strong support for Lindsay among blacks helped give him the election.

Since audiences are drawn to discussions especially tailored to their interests, televised debates about the concerns of some electoral subgroup can function in some of the same ways as these early uses of radio. So, for example, Pan American University in South Texas hosted a debate among Republican and Democratic presidential contenders in December 1987. With the approach of the Super Tuesday primary, in which the southern states would vote, and Texas a key state, the major presidential hopefuls (minus returnee Gary Hart) participated eagerly in a debate that was carried live in the Hispanic-vote-rich markets of the Rio Grande valley, El Paso, Corpus Christi, Laredo, and San Antonio.

Such recent attempts to involve audiences have shielded the candidates from cranks and eccentrics. But such precautions were not always standard fare. On the eve of the 1960 primary election in West Virginia, Hubert Humphrey took unscreened calls in a television studio. The questions failed to address his central issues; lengthy statements by callers absorbed his dearly bought time; at one point the operator broke in to clear the line for an emergency. "The telethon lost all cohesion," wrote campaign chronicler Theodore White, "proving nothing except that TV is no medium for a poor man."[37]

Humphrey learned his lesson. His election eve telethon in 1968 was supervised by a skilled professional media consultant. Audience call-ins were a part of both the Democrats' and the Republicans' election-eve telethons in 1968. In 1976 Carter reverted to taped questions which he answered from his home in Plains, Georgia.

Facing hostile questioners is a powerful means of defusing an issue. Communication scholars tell us that such confrontation both heightens the credibility of the skillful respondent and invites audience attention. JFK used the questions of the Houston Ministerial Association in September 1960 to dispel fears about his Catholicism. By rebroadcasting his performance in predominantly Catholic areas, Kennedy also boosted his showing among Catholic voters. There is a marked difference between the clarification of issues and the level of education achieved by the Humphrey telethon in West Virginia and the Kennedy question-and-answer session with the Houston ministers. Those who belittle citizens' questions generally draw their evidence from such experiences as Humphrey's; those who advocate citizen questioning point to Kennedy's. When the phones are simply opened to all callers, the ill-informed, those bent on self-promotion, and those intent on political sabotage are given an open line; the personal accountability that comes with physical presence increases responsible questioning.

In 1968, Richard Nixon appeared in regional broadcasts taking questions from citizens' panels. Because the form was in many ways tightly controlled by the Nixon campaign, it provides an interesting test of the ability of ordinary citizens to ask tough questions. Although Joe McGinniss' best-selling *Selling of the President* would have us assume otherwise, the questions were in fact as hard hitting as those fired at candidates in press conferences. Panelists asked, for example, if Nixon would ask Republicans to "support suspension of section 315 to enable a two-way debate with Humphrey and without Wallace, if Nixon were using panel shows to avoid professional interviewers, if civil disobedience could ever be justified, what he meant by 'an honorable end' to the war, whether 'law and order' was a code phrase for racism, should Justice Fortas be confirmed, was there a conspiracy between Nixon and Senator Strom Thurmond to block the confirmation and whether he favored including the Viet Cong in a coalition government."[38]

In the election of 1988, Harvard's John F. Kennedy School of Government confirmed that an audience composed of graduate students and faculty can ask probing, thoughtful questions. By providing access to a public broadcasting audience in key primary states, including Iowa, Massachusetts, and New Hampshire, the forum attracted all the candidates except Vice President Bush. The hourlong question-and-answer sessions were moderated by Marvin Kalb, former television journalist and now director of the Joan Shorenstein Barone Center on the Press, Politics, and Public Policy.

On the assumption that reporters are more knowledgeable and skillful in follow-up questioning and less intimidated by the cameras, the national audience, and the presence of political heavyweights, many prefer that reporters ask questions of the candidates. Since it has been used in each of the televised general election debates, this is a familiar form, although one without a counterpart in the prebroadcast age.

Experiences in telethons raise a third set of questions for those bent on improving presidential debates. Should there be questioners? If so, who? How should they be selected? Since the candidates prefer the buffer provided by questioners, they are a likely element in any discussion of debates. The form to which the presence of reporters hearkens is the radio and television interview show or press conference.

The Presidential Press Conference

The notion that a presidential candidate might be expected to answer the questions of voters was alien to the campaigns of the nineteenth century. Having an incumbent respond directly to the questions of reporters who would then report those answers to the public did not take hold until the Truman presidency. The institutionalization of the presidential press conference set in place assumptions of presidential accountability that carry over into debates.

Throughout the first half of the nineteenth century, citizens learned the policies of presidents by reading their inaugurals, veto messages, state of the union addresses, and farewells. Only gradu-

Similarities between presidential press conferences and debates include use of reporters as questioners and a broad range of addressed topics. In both environments, speakers have shown a talent for ducking tough questions, answering unasked ones, and reciting practiced responses. (*League of Women Voters Education Fund*)

ally, as Jeffrey Tulis has documented,[39] did the notion that the president should speak directly to the people take hold. Candidates for the presidency began carrying their case directly to the public. Woodrow Wilson's presidency marks an important turning point. Where from the time of Jefferson through Teddy Roosevelt, presidents had sent written state of the union messages to Congress, Wilson broke with tradition to deliver his orally. Where most of his predecessors had left campaigning for the presidency to others, Wilson took to the stump on his own behalf. Following TR's practice, Wilson held press briefings. But where TR had limited his conferences to the select few, for the first two years of his presidency Wilson opened them to all reporters. Then, convinced that they were unproductive affairs, Wilson abandoned press conferences. The professional identity of the press was not sufficiently strong or the expectations of the public sufficiently primed to presidential accountability to cause an uproar.

Through a gradual process, the superior-subordinate relationship between president and press gave way to the assumption that they were equals. The notion that the press has a right to access to the president gradually took hold and with it the sense that the function of the press is to act as a check on presidential power. TR had dictated who could and could not have access to the news and on what terms. Reporters who wrote stories he disapproved of were banished. Wilson's press conferences resembled seminars in which a professor lectures pupils, a marked contrast to the rough and tumble give and take we recognize today.[40] Harding reintroduced the press conference but, after a misstatement required a retraction, required that all questions be written out and submitted in advance.

Coolidge added restrictions, among them the stipulations that reporters neither quote nor indicate that they had seen the president and must not mention when a question was ignored.[41] Under the rules laid out by Coolidge, "the correspondents are supposed to present those [presidential] views as if they had dropped from heaven, and are wholly unprotected when, as has happened, Mr. Coolidge finds it expedient to repudiate them."[42] From Wilson through Hoover, a president could not be directly quoted without permission.

During FDR's four terms the press conference, which had from Wilson through Hoover been a sometime thing, was institutionalized. On nearly one thousand occasions from his election until his death, FDR took questions from reporters. FDR's press secretary Stephen Early superintended the rules: reporters could directly quote FDR with permission; specified material could be attributed to FDR but without direct quotations; some material would be given on background—no reference to the White House permitted; "off the record" remarks were not to be repeated even to absent reporters. Although Truman held fewer press conferences per month than FDR, he did embrace FDR's rules and press conference practices.

By FDR's first term, radio had begun to displace print in carrying some sorts of news to the public. It is revealing that the father of the fireside chat used press conferences as a means of transmitting information and influencing how it would be used but did not envision broadcasting the conferences themselves. The press conference was for FDR a means of channeling the flow of information to the press. When FDR wanted to speak to the American people directly, he did so by delivering speeches or fireside chats.

By broadcasting news conferences live, Kennedy altered their function. Here was a means of employing reporters as props through which to transmit a set of unfiltered messages to the public. Here was a way as well of asserting one's competence as president.

But as a means of news gathering, the live broadcast left much to be desired. Where FDR could provide information "on background," a president in a live press conference couldn't. Where FDR could go "off the record" to clarify, in televised press conferences Kennedy and his successors could not. The public press conference was a place in which a president should be circumspect, not fully disclosive. Educating the public cannot be a paramount goal when some information must be withheld for security reasons and when statements must be phrased in ways so as not to exact political damage. To obtain information they once got from the president, reporters now had to cultivate other channels. The notion that the press conference enables the president to present a case to the American people and simultaneously be scrutinized by the press is comparatively recent and one reflected in the commonplaces in which we ordinarily discuss debates. Whether the press conference does either well is a question too seldom asked.

The legitimizing function of the press conference was first recognized by Eisenhower's aides. After his heart attack in 1956, filmed press conferences were employed to demonstrate that he was sound in both mind and body—strong enough to continue as president and worthy of re-election. When shadowed by charges of corruption or hints of scandal, confronting the press becomes a way of setting the issue aside. So, for example, it was in a press conference that Democratic vice presidential nominee Geraldine Ferraro addressed questions about the financial irregularities in her congressional campaigns. When the age issue surfaced in the 1984 Reagan campaign, Reagan's avoidance of press conferences became an item of discussion. Holding a press conference can be a way of confirming that a person is up to the job. Increasingly, this performative function has been the one served by the press conference. Little hard news is generated here. Minimal education is offered. With the assumption that the press conference is a gauge of presidential competence comes a corollary—presumably such a vehicle could expose incompetence as well.

One powerful factor propelling candidates, press, and the public toward press conferences and debates is the disillusionment that followed the revelations of Vietnam and Watergate. Voters sought additional sources of evidence about those who would lead. The "character" of the candidate became more salient. The confrontations debates create seemed one way to test the character of the candidates. In 1968 and 1972 Nixon had conducted carefully choreographed campaigns. The debates of 1976 were consistent with the candidates' avowals that unlike their predecessors they would bring candor, openness, and honesty to government.

With the belief that the press is the fourth estate came the assumption that reporters stand in for the American people, asking the questions we would ask, seeking the information we need. In a country founded on a fear of unchecked power, such an evolution is unsurprising. During Nixon's final press conferences, the function assumed by reporters was lie-detector. One objective of the press became keeping government honest.

Reporters assumed that role more frequently. The press obtained access to the Pentagon Papers and published them; the press confirmed Nixon's complicity in Watergate. Where it had once assumed a subordinate relationship to the president, for a time during Vietnam and Watergate the press seemed to occupy a position of moral superiority. Speaking to the National Press Club in 1978, a former editor of the *Wall Street Journal,* who had begun covering the White House in 1936, noted that in those earlier times "we in the press did not think of ourselves as adversaries, enemies even, of our government."[43] "The relationship between the White House and the news media since 1965," wrote Grossman and Kumar in 1981, "might appear to demonstrate three points: first, that the relationship is characterized by an underlying antagonism; second, that it is subject to dramatic and unpredictable changes; and third, that it is still affected by the traumas of Watergate and Vietnam."[44] The assumption that the press panel belongs in presidential "debates" is one by-product of the assumption that its role is that of watchdog.

The idea of a president answering press questions before a national audience was not on anyone's mind in the infancy of radio. Early radio announcers conveyed "the news" by simply reading newspaper headlines and stories over the air. Weekly news talks by newspaper reporters such as H. V. Kaltenborn followed. In 1933 radio began to interrupt programming with news flashes furnished by the Associated Press. From 1933 to 1935 newspapers fought radio for the right to carry the news. During the "press-radio war," radio could broadcast only thirty-word news bulletins. Broadcast of news "hot off the wire" had to be delayed.

The agreement couldn't last. News was there to be gotten by radio reporters as well as those salaried by newspapers. Networks began creating news staffs of their own. Reporters were stationed in major world capitals. Radio began to carry the voices of world leaders—from Hoover to Hitler—into the nation's living rooms.

With the emergence of news bureaus came the radio documentary as an art form; its narrative gave coherence to world events. On D-Day in 1944 radio reporters carried news from the landing barges and from the Normandy beachhead. Radio carried on-the-spot reports of the Japanese surrender on the U.S.S. *Missouri* in Tokyo Bay. The day in which we would get most of our news by listening and watching rather than reading was on the horizon.

Relying on radio rather than newspapers for information carries a trade-off. "The listener can form his own opinion from the candidate's utterance, before the press or the parties can instruct him," noted Eunice Fuller Barnard in 1924. Where the newspaper will provide balance and correct errors, the broadcast speech will not. By contrast, the reader must trust the accuracy and representativeness of the selections made by the print reporter. So, concludes media scholar Edward Chester, "one must choose between the distortions of an uncorrected speaker and those of a correcting reporter."[45] Ideally, of course, the voter wouldn't have to choose. The press conference and interview shows attempt to give us the best of both worlds.

In 1946 Martha Rountree and Lawrence Spivak inaugurated an unrehearsed radio interview program titled "Meet the Press." There the nation's top reporters asked questions of major national figures. As its contribution to the discussions about presidential debates in 1960, NBC proposed to make available to the candidates eight one-hour sessions of "television's oldest news interview series" "Meet the Press." Had the proposal been accepted, it would not have provided a form markedly different from that in which Kennedy and Nixon actually met.

The extent to which such a format can inhibit direct clash was clear in the debate between Democratic hopefuls Robert Kennedy and Eugene McCarthy before the California primary of 1968. By styling the "debate" a "Special Edition" of the regular program "Issues and Answers," ABC circumvented the requirement that if one candidate is given time, all must be given time. Three ABC correspondents posed questions, and Frank Reynolds moderated. Midway through the program McCarthy complained, "This is not really shaping up as a debate. We're just going to sit around a table and be nice to each other."[46]

In 1951 Harry Truman okayed the recording of his press conferences to enable White House reporters to check the accuracy of their notes. Where FDR had permitted no more than a quoted phrase, by mid-summer of that year, Truman had approved broadcasting portions of his sessions with reporters. Ike permitted telecasting his news conferences. "In the hands of President Eisenhower," commented the New York *Herald Tribune,* "the new form of the press conference is a means of giving information to the public, of bringing the President closer to the people, and enhancing that legitimate authority which is possessed by the Chief Executive as the representative of the entire nation."[47] One of Ike's press conference answers figured prominently in the 1960 presidential campaign. When asked by reporters what Nixon had contributed to the Eisenhower presidency, the former general replied that if given a week he might think of something. The Democrats showcased Ike's response in a radio and a TV ad. In one of the Kennedy–Nixon debates, Nixon was questioned about Ike's answer.

By okaying the filming and broadcasting of his press conferences, Ike hoped to overcome the effects of selective reporting. Upset that reporters had mischaracterized Ike's response to criticism from Senator Joseph McCarthy, White House press secretary James Hagerty noted, "To hell with slanted reporters, we'll go directly to the people who can hear exactly what Pres. [Eisenhower] said without reading warped and slanted stories."[48] By viewing the press conference as a means to communicate directly with the American people, Eisenhower expanded its function. No longer was the press corps a conduit of the news conference; instead, it participated in sending a message from the president to the public.

By telecasting a Citizens for Eisenhower press conference in October during the 1956 campaign, Eisenhower's strategists merged elements of the staged debate, the citizen question-and-answer show, and the press conference. In the broadcast, the president responded to planted questions. Presidential press secretaries succeeded in planting questions at regular press conferences as well, a factor that clearly differentiates press conferences from presidential debates.

Kennedy took press conferences a step further by permitting them to be broadcast live. His presidency also introduced the now familiar pattern: the president opens the press conference with a statement; reporters follow up with questions. Kennedy's first broadcast press conference attracted an audience of 65 million people in 21.5 million homes. These encounters between press and president drew viewers to their sets. The conferences averaged an audience of 18 million. One survey found that 85% of the audience was not engaged in dial flipping but had instead tuned in to hear the press conference.[49]*

Apart from learning that all can be unfair in both love and politics, the press and presidents soon became aware of the limitations of this form of communication. When asked whether he had given any thought to improving the press conference by limiting it to a single subject, Kennedy replied, "I think we do have the problem of moving very quickly from subject to subject and therefore I am sure many of you feel that we are not going into any depth. So I would try to recognize perhaps the correspondent on an issue two or three times in a row, and we could perhaps meet that problem." The problem persisted. As the press conference of October 3, 1964, was ending, a reporter noted, "But Mr. President, we have more questions." Replied Lyndon Johnson, "I'm sure that would be true if I stayed here all day." By limiting answers to brief time periods and minimizing follow-up questions, the presidential broadcast debates magnify this problem. "What bothers me about TV debates," noted panelist Morton Kondracke, "is that they isolate the candidates from real challenge. There is only one follow-up on each subject . . . and candidates are free to practically ignore the questions altogether."[50]

---

* Where the Democrats had doctored Nixon's appearance into one of their ads in 1960, the Republicans returned the favor by misusing a press conference tape of Kennedy in 1963. During the Kentucky gubernatorial campaign, an edited tape created the impression that Kennedy favored interracial marriage. After Kennedy said, "Good afternoon, ladies and gentlemen," the editor deleted twelve lines of comment about civil rights. Adjoined to the opening greeting was the statement, now ripped from context, "I would say that over the long run we are going to have a mix. This will be truly racially, socially, ethnically, geographically. That's really the best way." The Republican gubernatorial candidate lost by a narrow margin.

Broadcasting press conferences made them widely and directly accessible to the public but at a price. Gone was the spontaneity that had marked earlier uses of the form. "By the time President Truman left office, the press conference, which under Roosevelt had been a highly informal—almost casual—affair, mirroring a unique presidential personality, had become an institution."[51] Widespread printing of stenographic transcripts of congressional speeches elicited the same trade-off in the nineteenth century. Members of Congress responded to the fact of publication by delivering prepared scripts.

So carefully do presidents now prepare for press conferences that only rarely does a question catch a president by surprise. The Kennedy staff, for example, anticipated most questions and rehearsed an answer with the president.[52] As we note in the next chapter, the same is true of broadcast presidential debates.

In press conferences, presidents proved skillful at ducking embarrassing questions, answering what they wanted to be asked rather than the question posed, and providing packaged answers. "In general, and most particularly since the advent of live television coverage, the presidential news conference may be characterized less as an exercise in responsive two-way communication between leader and followers than as an exercise in the purposeful manipulation of images and symbols by the various presidents," concluded political scientist Jarol B. Manheim in 1979.[53] The exceptions are noteworthy for attacking the presupposition of mutual respect on which the institution of the press conference has traditionally rested. In a news conference on October 26, 1973, Nixon accused the press of "vicious, distorted reporting" and told CBS correspondent Robert Pierpont that he wasn't angry because "one can only be angry with those he respects." Such moments of spontaneous self-revelation are rare in any public presidential discourse.

A number of presidents have questioned whether the press interview or conference was a forum that ought to elicit spontaneous response. In February 1885 Grover Cleveland dismissed a question about a pending matter of policy by saying, "Young man, that is an issue too big to be brought up in a brief interview that is rapidly drawing to a close."[54] When asked seven days after his inauguration how he planned to deal with inflation, Nixon responded, "I do not believe that policy should be made by off-the-cuff responses in press conferences or any other kinds of conferences."[55] The possibility that a presidential candidate will make an ill-considered recommendation in the heat of a debate and then feel pressed as president to honor it is comparably troubling.

Like debates, press conferences have been criticized for entertaining rather than informing. "One of the most important problems surrounding the Presidential news conference was that its essential purpose—to inform the people—had been subverted," concluded Nixon aide James Keough. "Television had made it too much of a show, calling upon the President to give a performance and encouraging too many reporters to have their moment of glory on camera."[56] Others would argue of the debates that the reporters asked questions designed to elicit "news," not the information the public required.

The Kennedy presidency also gave rise to the personal press conference labeled "A Conversation with the President." "Some of the 'evening with the president' types of meetings held by recent presidents more closely resemble the early press conferences than do the contemporary televised conferences," observes political scientist William Lammers.[57] Bill Lawrence of ABC, Walter Cronkite of CBS, and Eleanor Roosevelt for PBS were among those who participated in broadcast interviews with Kennedy. On December 17, 1962, the networks simultaneously carried a "conversation" among correspondents from each of the networks and the president. Like press conferences, these conversations jumped from topic to topic with minimal follow-up.

But unlike other interviews, press conferences, or debates, the December 17 conversation among the network representatives and Kennedy functioned as a retrospective on what Kennedy had learned in his first two years in office. Kennedy's thoughtful discussion of his mistaken expectations about the powers of a president, his reflections on decision-making style, the mistakes he'd made, and the difficulties in passing a legislative program confirm his press secretary's observation that "never before had the American public had such an intimate glimpse of a President: his personality, his mind at work, his sense of history—and his sense of humor."[58]

Comparing his experience with his expectations, Kennedy said:

Well, I think in the first place the problems are more difficult than I had imagined they were. Secondly, there is a limitation upon the ability of the United States to solve these problems. We are involved now in the Congo in a very difficult situation. We have been unable to secure implementation of the policy which we have supported. We are involved in a good many other areas. We are trying to see if a solution can be found to the struggle between Pakistan and India, with whom we want to maintain friendly relations. Yet they are unable to come to an agreement. There is a limitation, in other words, upon the power of the United States to bring about solutions. I think our people get awfully impatient and maybe fatigued and tired, and saying "We have been carrying this burden for seventeen years; can we lay it down?" We can't lay it down, and I don't see how we are going to lay it down in this century. So that I would say that the problems are more difficult than I had imagined them to be. The responsibilities placed on the United States are greater than I had imagined them to be, and there are greater limitations upon our ability to bring about a favorable result than I had imagined them to be. . . . It is much easier to make speeches than it is to finally make the judgments, because unfortunately your advisers are frequently divided. If you take the wrong course, and on occasion I have, the President bears the burden of the responsibility quite rightly. The advisers may move on to new advice.

Gone are the simplifications of the 1960 debates; present is a sense of the complexities of the office and the person grappling with its requirements.

Although the audiences for them have been minuscule, comparable one-on-one interviews with presidential aspirants have been conducted. In 1976 PBS broadcast such a series moderated by Bill Moyers. His interview with Reagan is a remarkable preview of the style that would characterize that presidency. In December 1987, David Frost opened a thirteen-part series titled "The Next President." The series' sponsor *U.S. News and World Report* published articles based on the interviews. Mutual Broadcasting carried excerpts. The series showcased six Republicans and six Democrats and their wives. Less philosophical than Moyers, Frost's programs served a useful expository function by creating a private sense of the public persons who sought the presidency.

The most direct equivalent of the "conversational" format in a presidential debate occurred in the CBS and NBC primary debates of 1984 among Democratic contenders Gary Hart, Jesse Jackson, and Walter Mondale. In the CBS "debate" moderated by Dan Rather and the NBC encounter supervised by Tom Brokaw, the candidates were seated around a table. Responses were not bound by time limits. The exchanges were free flowing and conversational.

The discussion quickly moved beyond that usually elicited in press conferences and traditional debates. The give and take evinced a spontaneity that has characterized neither other debate formats nor press conferences.

Early primary debates, such as the one that occurred at St. Anselm's College in Manchester, New Hampshire, on February 23, 1984, placed items not central to the front runner's candidacy on the political agenda. In early debates, for example, the issue of female representation on the Democratic ticket became more central than it otherwise would have been. (*League of Women Voters Education Fund*)

HART: Was the money legal or was it illegal as the *Wall Street Journal* and other publications have suggested? It's a serious question in this race.

MONDALE: Once again we see Gary Hart trying to raise a charge that he knows is without substance. Those local committees are authorized by the Federal Election Commission by their rules. . . . Now Gary Hart is leading a charge here that suggests illegality and criminal behavior. I think he ought to take that back. The other day there was an editorial—

HART: I've never said that.

MONDALE: You have said that. The other day there was an editorial in the *Washington Post* saying just what I've said, that to go be-

The unprecedented number of debates in the Democratic primaries of 1984 among Jesse Jackson, Walter Mondale, and Gary Hart enabled Jackson's cash-poor campaign to carry its case to the country without the extensive use of paid advertising that had characterized long-lived primary bids in past elections. (*League of Women Voters Education Fund*)

hind here and suggest anything other than ethical behavior goes beyond the bounds of propriety.

BROKAW: Do you want to look him in the eye and say that you didn't accuse him of criminal activity?

HART: He knows I didn't.

MONDALE: Did you not suggest a possible judicial investigation?

HART: I said that the Reagan Justice Department would be very likely—

MONDALE: Now what do you think that suggests?

BROKAW: Let's just try to get this resolved.

MONDALE: Do you think that's overparking or something?

HART: Mr. Mondale knows that the law, Federal Election Commission laws—and it wasn't my suggestion that this money was illegal, it was other unbiased neutral journals and investigators in this country—has the obligation to carry out the Federal election laws of this country. Those are civil laws as well as criminal. I never said anything about criminal.

The format seemed to energize the candidates; at the same time it invited audience attention. Lost here but present in the one-on-one interviews was the reflective answer, however. In this form of conversation, clash was a decisive variable.

The "conversation" seems to move past the pat answers and evasions of press conferences and broadcast debates. By so doing, it invites the question: Is the paired conversation a viable alternative to the standard general election presidential debate?

Summary: Broadcast "Debates"

The general election debate form is now so ritualized that for most it seems as patterned as a waltz. The moderator introduces. The candidates stand behind podiums. The panel of questioners is seated. Questions will not be timed; answers will be brief. Some provision will exist for rebuttal. Topics will shift drastically from questioner to questioner. Two minutes for farm surpluses. Two minutes for the low level of the campaign. Two minutes for nuclear disarmament.

The common audience, the presence of opposing candidates, the time limits, the right to rebut, and the established rules are vestiges of traditional debate. From the press conferences come the multiple topics, the question-and-answer form, and the use of interrogating reporters. The production techniques and the abbreviated answers are residues of television's grammar, a grammar most evident in the "staged debates." The presence of a studio audience and repeated hints from the panelists suggesting that they see themselves as the deputies of the American people are residues of the telethon.

This strong amalgam that is neither press conference nor debate derives strengths and limitations from each of its ancestral forms. The clash and brevity are expected to attract and hold an audience. Here is a gladiatorial contest in miniature. The questions are expected to elicit a clear sense of person and policy. The presence of both press and opponent is intended to ensure accuracy and unmask special pleading. Critics claim that instead actual clash is minimal and then occurs on simplistic and superficial grounds. Rather than eliciting depth, the format invites sloganeering. Brief answers on a shower of topics create an informational blur. The press panel asks questions designed to elicit news headlines, not information of use to voters. The superficial is rewarded; the substantive, spurned. In the next chapters we address the problems and potential inherent in the anomalous form that has come to be known as the presidential debate.

◆

CHAPTER 5

The Power of Broadcast
Debates

The general election debates of 1988 face two challenges in their efforts to attract viewers. The unprecedented number of debates in the 1988 primaries devalued debate as an activity. From a special event, worthy of unique attention, debates slipped to being a routine part of life, of no special note. Additionally, past debates have fallen below the lofty expectations the press set for them. None of the debates have been "Great."

Still, general election debates command large audiences including many individuals who seek out little other political information during the campaign. Where a mere fifteen thousand heard the typical debate between Lincoln and Douglas, more than a thousand times that number viewed each of the televised presidential debates. Over 60% of the adult population—an average of 77 million individuals—watched the first Kennedy–Nixon debate.[1] Some believe that the viewership for the second and third debates of that year was even higher.[2] Historically, other campaign messages have failed to attract audiences comparable in size to those drawn to the debates. In 1964, for example, no message by either Johnson or Goldwater reached even a quarter the audience that watched the first of the 1960 Kennedy–Nixon debates.[3]

Where six of ten watched in 1960, that number became seven of ten in the first two debates of 1976, dropping back to the 1960 average for the third of the Ford–Carter encounters.[4] More than 120 million viewers saw the 1980 Carter–Reagan debates. But four years later, the numbers were down. In 1984, the general election debates drew 85 million viewers. Even with that drop, the debates reached more viewers than any other single campaign message. But

On October 13, 1960, two candidates separated by three thousand miles participated in the third broadcast presidential debate. Nixon debated from a television studio in Los Angeles; Kennedy, from one in New York. (*Library of Congress*)

the decline is alarming, for alone among the messages of the campaigns the debates have given a large heterogeneous audience the chance to directly compare the major candidates for office.

Not all or even most viewers pay close attention, however. "At most," concluded one set of researchers after the 1976 debates, "about a fourth of the electorate followed the debates quite closely, another fourth paid them little attention, and the remaining half watched some part (but not all) of some (but not all) of the debates."[5] With debates comes campaign interest. Roper surveys indicate that as debates progressed, so too did the electorate's interest in the campaign.[6] The exception occurred in 1976 when the dullness of the first two Ford–Carter debates diminished voter enthusiasm for the third.[7]

In the general election, Americans will sit down for the dinner served by debates; otherwise, we are fast-food addicts. Debates held in the primaries draw smaller audiences. The nationally aired Republican debate held in October 1987 attracted between 8 and 10 million—a fraction of the available viewers. Larger numbers preferred the opening of a safe recovered from the *Titanic*. In the Boston market, which reaches parts of the early primary state of New Hampshire, 3.7% of the 2 million households with televisions tuned to the debates. Twenty-two percent viewed the opening of the safe on another channel.[8] A nationwide poll conducted by the Gallup Organization and the Times Mirror Company in late October and early November of 1987 found that 68% of those surveyed reportedly paid very close attention to news accounts of the rescue of a Texas girl, Jessica McClure, from a well; only 15% said they paid very close attention to news about the Democratic presidential race, and 13% reported close attention to the Republican.[9]

The result is not surprising. In early stages of campaigns only those who would spend their honeymoon at a presidential convention are likely to be paying close attention to politics. As the general election approaches, the attention of the public increases.

The problem posed by the different points at which voters become interested is that many miss the phase in which basic positions are first articulated. By the time these citizens begin to pay equal attention to candidates and children trapped in wells, the press is reporting not the basic positions of the candidates but what is new about their positions. Those who lack the basic information have no ready way of getting it when they need it. For these voters "Jake and the Fatman" symbolizes the early campaign. The prime-time drama about a district attorney ranked 44th in the late November rankings in 1987. But its audience was larger than that for NBC's "debate" among twelve presidential hopefuls. In a light moment of that debate, Vice President George Bush teased that he'd rather be watching "Jake." This level of early inattention to political fare accounts in part for the fact that public affairs programming on PBS often fails to attract even 3% of the viewing public. Ratings for "The MacNeil–Lehrer NewsHour" sometimes are so low that they merit only the Nielsen asterisk, a sign that the audience is too small to be reliably estimated.

Light reading dominates our choice of magazines as well. For every household to which a public affairs magazine is delivered, 100 are receiving *Good Housekeeping*.[10]

Responding to the public's disinclination to absorb serious content delivered in half-hour or hour-long time blocks, political consultants prepare menus filled with thirty- and sixty-second ads. "When the electorate wants fast food," one consultant told us, "it would be suicidal for me to serve up a seven course meal. The day a political speech can compete with 'Dynasty' or even 'Dialing for Dollars' is the day political speeches will return to television. Until then, it's spots they'll watch so it's spots they'll get."

Debates Expand on Information in News and Ads

In campaigns without debates, spot ads and news snippets provide most of our information about those who would lead the nation. In practical terms this reliance on spots and snippets means that we base voting decisions on bites of information averaging a quarter of a minute to a minute in length. And even those granules of information do not receive the concentrated attention of viewers. Many who pick up political information from TV news and ads are passive receivers of inadvertently gotten information. Their casual attention is conducive to awareness but not to a substantive command of information or issues.[11]

Unsurprisingly then, over the past quarter-century, surveys have found repeatedly that even at the most intense point in the campaign, over half of the population cannot identify any one of the congressional or senatorial candidates seeking to represent them.[12] Only one in five can recognize the principles articulated in the Bill of Rights.

The high levels of response to opinion polls create the illusion of a knowledgeable citizenry, an illusion unmasked when one-third of a sample offered an opinion on whether the Public Affairs Act should be repealed. Since it doesn't exist, the act is unlikely to be repealed.[13]

Of course, even the best-paid congressional staffer isn't knowledgeable about each of the thousands of acts passed by Congress. In the modern era, legislation is to political problems what Dr. Sweeney's Lineament and All Purpose Health Aid was to the miscellaneous maladies of the nineteenth century, and often with comparable effect. Repeatedly since 1952, the valuable National Election Study series (NES), which reports public response to a large number of questions about national elections, has found that over two-thirds of the adults in the United States agree that "sometimes politics and government seem so complicated that a person like me can't really understand what is going on." Since 1972, a rising percentage has concluded that government officials don't know what's going on either.

As we will note later, debates function in part to persuade voters that the debating candidates *do know* what's going on in politics and government. In most debates, favorable disposition to both candidates increases, making both winners of sorts. The general lack of comprehension of the intricacies of public policy positions explains the fact that few viewers recognized Ford's statement on Poland in the second debate of 1976 as a blunder. It also accounts for the influence of media personnel and their experts on our conclusions about who "won" or "lost" a debate.

As much as our disciplinary identity would incline us to it, we can't legitimately claim that speeches alone are the solution to all that ails the body politic. Just as news and spots are not necessarily sterile, speeches are not necessarily substantive. It takes less than thirty seconds to say "I will go to Korea" or "I love you." Nothing guarantees that a half-hour speech will say more than that. Indeed, many say less.

However, a snippet cannot disclose a mind at work. Nor can it assume the burden sustained by great public figures from Demosthenes to Churchill. These speakers took the time to trace the history of their ideas and in the process revealed something of how they saw the world. Today, history has little place in public discussion except when selectively marshalled to show that an opposed policy is a mistake. There was an age in which speakers spoke until audiences nodded either in agreement or in sleep. The thirty- and sixty-second units in which denture adhesives and Dodge trucks live out their advertised lives had not yet come to exercise their Procrustean tyranny on messages and audiences' attention spans. When ideas governed length of utterance, speakers could take the time to define their terms, a process that expresses assumptions. In the past, speeches assumed the burden of outlining and scrutinizing policy alternatives, demonstrating a command of the situation, showing an understanding of alternatives, and only then defending the preferred policy. Such statements confirmed that speakers were uttering convictions grounded in thought, evidence, and reasoned assessment of alternatives.[14]

By contrast, most spots argue by hitting and running, slinging a supposedly telling statistic or anecdote under a questionable claim as if it constituted proof. In ad McNuggets, candidates can do little more than assert the godliness of their side and invite assent either because they and the public embrace the same pieties or because the candidate seems trustworthy.

This doesn't mean that viewers don't learn from ads. A number of studies report that audiences gained useful information from them.[15] In an information-poor environment filled with passive receivers of political information, ads perform an important function. The highest information gains produced by ads occur among low-interest voters.[16] Those who are less sophisticated politically and those who can't make up their minds about candidates are the most likely to learn from political spots.[17]

If sustained encounter with political ideas is our goal, then broadcast news provides little more and sometimes less than spot ads. Indeed, some academic analysts believe that there is more issue content in ads than in news,[18] a finding corroborated in a separate study that concluded that television news tells people little about the issues in a campaign.[19] An important distinction comes from political scientist Thomas Patterson, who argues that television news creates clear-cut "campaign issues" that can be digested in thirty seconds but shies away from "policy issues," which require elaboration and lack the dramatic interest that holds viewers.[20] Rather than focusing on the substance of a candidate's message, broadcast news tends to concentrate on the strategy prompting it or its probable effect on the race's outcome.

Whatever the case, neither ads nor news offers sustained encounter with the candidates' ideas. In 1984 the typical spot ad was thirty seconds long; the typical network slice of a presidential candidate's speech, a bare fifteen seconds.

And the electorate doesn't give sustained attention even to those fleeting fragments. Of all types of programming, news receives the lowest level of attention.[21] In the early 1970s one study concluded that among ten types of programming, news was most likely to drive viewers from an operating television set. Only advertising chased more away.[22] When asked to spontaneously recall the stories they've seen, only 5% can.[23] The lowest recall rate occurs when viewers are asked about political analysis and commentary.[24] Not only do average viewers learn little from typical news stories but what information they do acquire is quickly lost to memory.[25] Television news places new information, in the form of vague impressions about the world, in short-term memory, but the information is not available to conscious recall.[26] For news coverage to facilitate what we would typically view as learning, this information must be activated by some other source. Newspaper stories and conversations are among the means of cueing such recall and integrating it into long-term memory. To the extent that debates stimulate conversations about politics, the interaction of the conversation and the short-term memory may increase learning. Such integration may also facilitate action—in the case of an election campaign, of voting.

As an hour- or hour-and-a-half-long message, the debates provide a level of contact with candidates unmatched in spot ads and news segments. The debates offer the longest, most intense view of the candidates available to the electorate. Uninterrupted by ads, uncontaminated by the devices programmers use to ensnare and hold prime-time attention, the debates offer sustained and serious encounters with candidates.

Intense information seeking would not be required if the presidential candidates were all the kids next door grown older. But in a nation of millions, few of us personally know anyone running for president. And increasingly, those who seek that office do so after minimal national exposure in other offices. Where in the early years of the Republic, presidents had often served previously as ambassadors, diplomats, or members of the cabinet, both of our last presidents rose to that office from governorships. Where senators are in a good position to gain national media attention, it is more difficult for a governor to do so. What this means is that prior to Carter, Dukakis, and Reagan's announcements of candidacy, even newsaholics knew little about those who would lead. Moreover, few of us have had direct experience of this person's behavior as a governor. As a result, we start most campaigns trying to match names to faces and named faces to records and promises.

Debates Provide Information Envisioned by Various Theories of Democracy

Political scientists disagree on what voters need to know and correlatively on what sorts of data candidates should provide. Each theory of democracy offers its own notion. Debates provide something of what each of the major theories asks.

*The Electoral-Competition Model: Policy Information and
Party Stands*

One model of populist democracy—the electoral-competition model
—envisions highly informed voters with clear policy preferences and
precise perceptions of party stands. This is the model implicitly
favored by most analysts of presidential debates. Debates are able
to provide viewers with a clearer sense of policy differences than
they had before viewing but are not of themselves able to raise the
ill informed to a command of the campaign that would satisfy those
who view such differentiation as the sine qua non of intelligent
voting.

Still, the educational impact of debates is surprisingly wide. Although the most reliable predictors of debate viewing are political
interest, consumption of televised news, and education,[27] debates
are a source of information for all classes, educational levels, and
races.[28]

The ability of viewers to comment sensibly on the candidates and
their stands on issues increases with debates.[29] Over the same
period, there is no comparable informational gain about issues not
discussed in the debates. A study of Wisconsin voters[30] found that
during the debates the percentage of viewers who could not report
candidate positions declined from 20% to less than 10%. When
viewers are compared to nonviewers, and all other factors including
education are factored out, researchers still find that viewers gain
more information about candidate stands than nonviewers.[31]

By logging the accuracy of citizens' command of candidates' policy positions both at the beginning and end of a debate and comparing the information level of debate viewers and nonviewers, we
can assess the learning produced by debates. When educational
level, partisanship, political interest, and other media use were
controlled in a 1976 study, debate viewers demonstrated a higher
level of learning about size of government, unemployment, military
spending, and inflation. Debate viewers also more accurately perceived the differences between the parties on inflation, unemployment, defense spending, and the size of government.[32]

Of course, debates do reinforce the dispositions of those who have
already decided how to vote. In the typical election, although not
in 1976, about two-thirds of the electorate has decided its November
vote by the end of the party conventions.[33]

The general reinforcing function of debates applies as well to party dispositions. The party with the largest number of adherents, which through 1984 has been the Democratic party, has, as a result, the most to gain. For these voters, debates strengthen existing convictions. For those who are otherwise uninvolved in the campaign, who receive most of their campaign information from the mass media, and who decide how to vote late in the campaign, the debates are an important source of information.

Unlike ads and news, which tend to expose viewers to one or two issues, the debates offer a smorgasbord. Since some issues are more salient than others to each viewer, this variety enables individuals to learn about issues that may be important to them, although not to news agencies or ad consultants. Among the topics treated by debates but not by news or ads were the two tiny islands, Quemoy and Matsu, that attracted so much attention in the 1960 debates; in 1984, Reagan's patterns of church attendance and views of Armageddon received national scrutiny only in the debates.

Debates also may prompt information seeking. The 1976 debates seem to have increased viewers' dispositions to use interpersonal discussion as a means of seeking information about the candidates.[34]

The knowledge provided by general election debates comes at an opportune time. For many, the elections are of little interest until shortly before the first Tuesday in November. A study of the 1976 debates concluded, "[T]hose individuals who watched the debaters exhibited a heightened political awareness at exactly the time when political information is crucial—shortly before an election. In this respect democracy was well served, for without the debates a significant proportion of the electorate would have remained relatively uninformed about the candidates."[35]

Debates also increase the likelihood that a candidate will take specific stands on issues, and will specify the ways in which goals would be reached, a specificity more often wanting in speeches and ads. Since voters can only recognize differences when they are articulated, such specificity is consistent with populist democracy.

Promising all things to all people is a long-lived tactic memorialized by Machiavelli, who recommended that a prince be a great "feigner and dissembler."[36] The move has been recognized by political theorists through the history of campaigning. Indeed, ambiguity may be the mainstay of effective politics. "No man . . . who fully and frankly expressed his real convictions, made manifest exactly the way he felt and thought on public matters, could possibly be elected to any considerable office in the United States," theorized one political scientist.[37] "Given the presently prevailing institutions of the American polity," wrote Harold Lasswell of the 1960 debates, "we must not overlook the possibility that a true debate between presidential candidates would threaten the genius for ambiguity that is essential to the operation of our complex, semi-responsible, relatively democratic system of multi-group coalitions."[38] But what is good for the politician may not be good for the voter who requires the information considered desirable in the populist democracy model.

Rarely is specificity to a candidate's advantage. In a large heterogeneous country filled with many special interest groups, any specific taking of stands is liable to alienate someone.[39] Holding those of dissimilar inclination behind one's candidacy can often be achieved only by a calculated vagueness. Accordingly, we hear ambiguity in Nixon's 1968 plan to end the war in Vietnam. Whether he would "bomb 'em back to the stone age," pull back into enclaves, and then withdraw or end up somewhere in between remained for voters to guess. Since voters are disposed to impose their own positions on the candidates they favor, some heard Nixon promising a dovish end to the war; others, a hawkish one.

The need to retain conservative support while appealing to moderates and independents propelled Ronald Reagan away from specificity in the 1980 campaign. "We were in a delicate position," explained one senior Reagan staff member. "His position on the issues during the primaries was not going to help us any more than it already had. . . . What we did *not* need were lengthy position papers, rigid commitments, long policy commentaries. Our problem was keeping him from getting too specific or too detailed about issues. . . . [O]ur basic thrust . . . was the same—stress his warm and self-assured leadership, keep the organization going, *ignore but not antagonize the Far Right*."[40]

In 1972 and in 1976 two noteworthy instances of specificity undercut campaigns. Throughout the 1972 campaign McGovern was haunted by the specifics included in his Alternative Defense Posture of January 1972. The programmatic details were the straw from which the Nixon campaign built one of its most effective attack ads in the general election. As a hand swept toy planes, ships, and soldiers from a table, an announcer noted: "The McGovern Defense Plans. He would cut the Marines by one-third, the Air Force by one-third; he'd cut Navy personnel by one-fourth; he would cut interceptor planes by one-half, the Navy Fleet by one-half, and carriers from sixteen to six. Senator Hubert Humphrey had this to say about the McGovern proposal . . . 'It isn't cutting into the fat; it isn't just cutting into manpower, it's cutting into the very security of this country,' "[41] As the primaries progressed, McGovern's stands on cutting defense became more ambiguous.

In September 1975, presidential hopeful Ronald Reagan proposed transferring $82.4 billion in federal programs to the states. The Ford campaign invited reporters to focus on this proposal in New Hampshire, a state without a state income tax. The questions and Reagan's inability to answer them damaged his candidacy.

Both of these examples show the dangers specificity poses for candidates. But at the same time, each reveals how poorly thought out these candidates' proposals were. Demanding more of such specificity and obtaining it from all sides in each race would require a level of forethought and planning desirable in a system in which a president is required to submit a budget within three months of the national election.

Candidates view the suggestion that they might deprive anyone of anything with an enthusiasm ordinarily reserved for the bubonic plague. Accordingly, most candidates envision purchasing new programs from the increased economic growth they foresee or from other savings gotten by efficient management. When asked directly what sacrifices they are willing to impose, we see the full extent to which they will duck a response. In 1976, for instance, Ford managed to suggest that the sacrifice he was willing to impose on the American people was a tax cut!

Perhaps specificity is not next to godliness in politics. Detailed promises are useful if they foreshadow actual conduct in office. Clearly that is not always the case. In 1932, FDR pledged both to remove the government from the free-enterprise system and to balance the budget. The Democratic platform underscored the balanced budget pledge. Those who read Richard Nixon's career as a guarantee that he would be an anti-Communist president were surprised to find that it was he who created détente with the Soviets and advanced discussions with the Chinese. His overtures ran counter to the Republican platform of 1968 that opposed recognizing Communist China. "They warned me that if I voted for Barry Goldwater, we'd be in a land war in China," noted one pundit. "I voted for him and look what happened." Contrary to his promises,

Carter failed to balance the budget, reduce inflation, or significantly reduce unemployment.

Despite these dramatic examples of failed promises, candidates do, by and large, work to keep their promises.[42] By inviting specificity, debates aid those engaged in predicting how the behavior of one would-be president might differ in office from another. And, if reporters and the public would come to expect such things as a projected federal budget from candidates, the natural give and take of debates would be more likely to focus on both means and ends than currently is the case.

But like spontaneity, specificity is not unequivocally desirable. Specific promises such as those of Carter and Ford to conduct negotiations in the open impede a president's ability to act in the best interest of the country. By contrast, specifics on how a goal would be accomplished can distinguish a candidate of "blue smoke and mirrors" from the candidate of substance. The country had the right to know in 1968 how Nixon would end the war in Vietnam and how in 1976 and 1980 Carter and Reagan respectively planned to balance the budget. When unrelenting questioning by debate panelist Elizabeth Drew did not produce clear explanations from Carter, the electorate got its first clear hint that Carter's promises might not be matched by performance. By ducking behind the gospel of supply-side economics in 1980, Reagan disclosed his faith in a questionable theory. In both instances, the lines of argument elicited in debates revealed a gulf between a proposed plan and its probable outcome.

Debates also heighten the candidate's responsibility to engage the issues considered central by the other side. In the ads, speeches, and debates of 1960 Kennedy answered the question, "Who can better get the country moving?" Nixon phrased the campaign's central question differently. Capitalizing on Kennedy's comparative lack of foreign policy experience, the vice president asked, "Who better understands what peace demands?" In debates candidates address questions viewed as central by their opponents in an environment in which the electorate can compare the answers. Where in stump speeches candidates tend to indict their opponents, in debate the threat of imminent rebuttal invites a response to charges pending against one's candidacy.[43] In debates, candidates engage both in case building and refutation.

Consequently, debates are able, although they do not always do this, to produce a clarity and specificity otherwise absent in campaign discourse. A content analysis of the 1960 debates revealed that Kennedy and Nixon "made clearer their positions, than they did in other campaign situations."[44] In forums in which the subject matter is candidate controlled, discourse tends to be more vague. Remarks and speeches fall into this category. Press conferences, interviews, question-and-answer sessions, and debates are more likely to elicit specific statements about policy.[45]

After analyzing presidential campaign speeches from 1960 through 1976, political scientist Benjamin Page concluded that the typical campaign speech "may include a reference to one of the handful of important proposals which candidates regularly repeat; it may include some pat phrases alluding to policy, or some minor proposals of an organizational or informational sort; but it does not present the candidates' stands on many policies or in any great detail. The infrequency with which candidates discuss policy is a major factor preventing most Americans from learning what the stands are."[46]

Had there been debates in 1964, Johnson's plans for Vietnam might have been probed. Had there been debates in 1968, Nixon's secret plan to end the war would not have remained secret, and Hubert Humphrey might have broken earlier than he did with Johnson over the conduct of that war. In 1972 debates would have held Nixon accountable for the ongoing pursuit of a war he had promised in 1968 to end as well as for the growing evidence of malfeasance in Watergate.

In debates, candidates also set the standards by which their presidencies will be judged. "The major purpose of an election for president is to choose a leader," noted Carter in the last debate of 1976. "Someone who can analyze the depths of feeling in our country to set a standard for our people to follow, to inspire our people to reach for greatness, to correct our defects, to answer difficult questions, to bind ourselves together in a spirit of unity." By those standards, the president who in his last year of office delivered the so-called malaise speech failed.

Carter projected in the 1976 debates that "we will have a balanced budget by fiscal year 1981." "I keep my promises to the American people" he pledged. That pledge became the basis for a widely aired attack ad sponsored by the National Conservative Political Action Committee in 1980.

Debates Can Preview the Substance of a Presidency

By incubating premises that will produce policy, debates preview the substance as well as the communicative style of the presidency. In Kennedy's statements that "we want" the Cuban people "to be free again" and his hope that one day Cuba "again would be free" we now hear a disposition to approve the Bay of Pigs operation. In Nixon's pledge that "there isn't any question but that the free people of Cuba—the people who want to be free—are going to be supported and that they will attain their freedom" we now hear a revelation that the Bay of Pigs plan existed within the Eisenhower Administration.

The central themes of the Kennedy presidency pervade the 1960 debates where Kennedy repeatedly called for sacrifice and pledged that the country would bear any burden in defense of freedom. Reagan's 1980 claim in the debate with Carter that he would not negotiate with terrorists may have helped invite Reagan's self-damaging lie about the trade of arms for hostages known as Irangate. "I believe that it is high time," said Reagan in 1980, "that the civilized countries of the world made it plain that there is no room worldwide for terrorism; there will be no negotiation with terrorists of any kind." Reagan's public accountability for extricating hostages and punishing terrorists was magnified in the 1984 debates when Morton Kondracke noted: "Mr. President, four years ago you criticized President Carter for ignoring ample warnings that our diplomats in Iran might be taken hostage. Haven't you done exactly the same thing in Lebanon not once but three times, with 300 Americans not hostages but dead. And you vowed swift retaliation against terrorists, but doesn't our lack of response suggest that you're just bluffing?"

Debates Increase Candidates' Responsibility for Their Claims

Debates are important not simply for what they say and show but for the changes in campaigns they have precipitated and the access to the electorate they have provided to those whose candidacies will not survive long enough to receive public inspection at the national party conventions. Debates act as a check on the manipulative instincts of those who would fashion a president from the polled preferences of the electorate. News coverage provides a reality check dictating that ads not create an image dissimilar to that seen nightly on broadcast reports. To an even greater extent than news, debates minimize consultants' instincts to airbrush heroic attributes onto their candidates. To mute the image projected by the first debate of 1984, Reagan could not rely simply on ads or news coverage. Credible performance in a second debate was required. So debates offer an additional environment in which to test the accuracy of the image projected by candidates in more controlled formats.

Debates magnify the accountability of the candidates for the attacks and tactics of their campaigns. In an era in which sophisticated ads dissociate the responsible candidate from anonymously voiced attack ads, the debates force candidates to take responsibility for the assaults committed in their name. This function was illustrated dramatically when in the nationally televised New York Democratic primary debate of 1984 Mondale and Hart engaged in an exchange about the fairness and accuracy of each other's advertising.

HART: There's an ad I understand—Mr. Mondale says he hasn't seen his ads, television ads. I can tell him about one that's running in New Jersey now. It has a pistol. We differ over what kind of national gun control laws there ought to be. Mr. Mondale, because of that difference, has an ad in which a pistol rotates toward the viewer, the chamber turns and the barrel ends up pointed right at the viewer and strongly suggests that I would needlessly endanger people's safety or their lives. He knows that's not the truth, I'm offended by it. I don't think it's healthy for this process. . . .

MONDALE: It was Gary Hart that ran an ad in New York that suggested that I wanted a war in Central America. It's Gary Hart . . . about days of shame, even though he himself had spoken up for our rescue mission in Lebanon. Let's get on to the real issues. . . .

Being forced to face one's opponents in debates also may moderate the stridency of campaign discourse. In a speech at Texas A & M in the primaries of 1984, for example, Gary Hart indicted the past Democratic administration for "the days of shame we all lived through four years ago." America had been, he said, "held hostage to the ayatollahs of the world." Two days later in a debate in Texas, Hart backed down. He hadn't meant to suggest that Mondale had been derelict in duty, said Hart, but only that the country needed to be prepared militarily.

Responsible Party Model: Party Differences
A responsible party model requires only that voters have well-founded party loyalty and a clear sense that a candidate identifies with party. Since FDR, the stands of the two major parties have differed in a number of ways. "On the issues of domestic welfare, Democrats have tended to favor an active federal government, helping citizens with jobs, education, medical care and the like," notes Page. "Republicans have wanted less government spending and lower taxes. On labor-management relations and regulation of the economy, Democrats have allied themselves with labor and Republicans with business."[47] In each of the years in which presidential debates have occurred, such differences have emerged in those encounters. In the 1960 debates voters could learn that, consistent with the philosophies of their parties, Kennedy and Nixon disagreed on federal aid to education, what would be called Medicare, and the minimum wage. Nixon had cast a tie-breaking vote in the Senate against a bill that would have provided federal support for teachers' salaries; Kennedy favored it. Kennedy believed in federal medical insurance for the elderly; Nixon favored existing federal assistance through state programs. Kennedy favored upping the minimum wage to $1.25; Nixon to $1.15. Kennedy favored more federal intervention than Nixon and a greater level of federal spending.

In 1976, the debates also showed differences along party lines. Carter supported and Ford opposed national health insurance, the public sector jobs bill (Humphrey–Hawkins), and tax reform. In 1980, Carter favored and Reagan opposed the Equal Rights Amendment. Reagan favored and Carter opposed the Kemp–Roth tax cuts. In 1984 Mondale promised a tax increase, while Reagan held to a no-increase stance.

By clarifying areas of agreement and disagreement within and between political parties, debates in the primaries also advance the objectives of those who espouse a responsible party model. In September 1987 the Democratic and Republican contenders met in separate forums at the University of North Carolina, Chapel Hill, to debate how to improve American education. Where the Democrats favored increased federal aid to education, the Republicans argued that dollars were not necessarily the answer. The Republican avenues to improving teaching stressed the free market in the form of tuition tax credits or educational vouchers that would permit parents to select the public or private school of their choice. The Democrats looked to forms of federal reinforcement: a longer school term (Biden), rewards for school districts whose students improved (Gephardt), or federal efforts to recruit and educate teachers (Dukakis).

Political party conventions are generally controlled by political activists who tend toward the ideological extremes of their parties. Accordingly, the Democratic platform often expresses ideological positions to the left of the Democratic voters and candidates and the Republican party to the right of its cluster of presidential contenders. Ongoing primary debates in a large field of candidates could provide an impetus for the platform to more closely represent the mainstream of the party. Across primary debates, areas of consensus should emerge. The October 29, 1987, Republican debate on William Buckley's "Firing Line" revealed, for example, that the Republican contenders agreed that they opposed abortion and backed Reagan's Strategic Defense Initiative. They did differ on when the so-called Star Wars program should be deployed. Following Mikhail Gorbachev's visit to the United States, the Democratic candidates banded together in support of the U.S.–Soviet treaty. With the notable exception of George Bush and Robert Dole, the Republican candidates expressed strong reservations. In the absence of debates, the Democratic agreement with Reagan and Republican disagreement might have been less apparent to the press and the electorate.

Not all the recognized areas of intraparty agreement make party heads smile. "G.O.P. candidates agree that deficit must be tackled but offer no plans" proclaimed a headline in the *New York Times* December 22, 1987.[48] And when no Republican candidates accepted an invitation to attend a forum on environmental protection, the five Democrats agreed that "the Republicans, at least during the Reagan era, did not care much about the environment."[49]

The primary debates also provide a party with the chance to test new ideas. Among these in 1988 was drug testing of those who apply for driver's licenses. Additionally, the primary debates may alert the public to problems that do not lend themselves to popular solutions, as did Ernest Hollings' 1984 proposal to reduce the military's reliance on enlistment by the poor by restoring the military draft and Bruce Babbitt's 1988 proposal to reduce the deficit by raising taxes and means-testing the entitlement programs. Proposals tried out in the primaries of one campaign can be refined for reintroduction in the next. A position embraced by the Republican candidates in 1988—attacking the deficit with a budget freeze—was first proposed by Democrat Fritz Hollings in the debates of 1984. The linchpin of Richard Gephardt's 1988 campaign—protectionist trade responses—was advocated in 1984 by Walter Mondale. But the case was telling against domestic content legislation, which Mondale championed in 1984. Backed by the United Auto Workers, the bill would have required that any automobile sold in the United States contain a certain amount of American parts and labor. Four years later, domestic content legislation was not part of Gephardt's trade package.

The responsible party theory presupposes that parties differ, that candidates of one party will behave differently from candidates of another when elected, and that the electorate is willing to trust party identification in voting decisions. The theory is endangered neither by the much discussed decline in party identification nor by diminished party control over candidates who no longer need party help to be elected. Although direct delegate selection in primaries, the availability of federal matching funds, and candidate access to television diminish the hold parties have on candidates, Democratic candidates still differ in identifiable ways from Republicans. And those differences continue to matter even to voters who tell pollsters that they are Independents.

From 1945 to the mid-1960s, voters tended to think of themselves as Republicans or Democrats. Then citizens began to call themselves Independents. Ticket-splitting rose. This change would be cause for concern if these were traditional independents—less interested, less informed, less grounded in information when voting, and less likely to vote. Advocates of the responsible party model take comfort in recent scholarship that has revealed a partisan dimension to some independents. When first questioned, the so-called partisan independents label themselves independents; when queried further, however, they indicate a preference for one or the other party. These voters "express a keener interest in politics and public affairs, know more, vote more frequently, and participate more avidly in campaigns than do pure Independents."[50] In 1980, 35%

of the electorate labeled itself independent. Of that 35% however, 21% were partisan independents.[51] So for the electorate at large, party remains a useful, predictive classification.

Utilitarian Theories: Crediting and Blaming
The utilitarian theories require even less of voters. If government should provide the greatest good for the greatest number, then a simple sense of popular well-being is sufficient to determine whether the incumbent is worthy of re-election. Voters carry into the voting booth their sense of the well-being of the daily lives of those who make up the community. This sense is shored up by an awareness of how much more a new car, college tuition, or a pound of hamburger costs than it did before the incumbent took office. When a neighbor is drafted to fight in a war, the leave-taking communicates a political reality more credible than any ad, speech, or news clip. If most people are satisfied that the country is better off than before, as they were in the fall of 1984, the incumbent is re-elected. If most are unhappy and the aspirant offers a credible hope of change, as in 1980, we vote to "throw the incumbent out."

This doesn't mean that we translate our own economic well-being directly into voting behavior. Where political scientists once held that voters were motivated by their own personal economic health, recent studies have challenged that conclusion. There is a tie between voting and voters' perceptions of economic conditions in the country *as a whole* but not a clear link between voting and peoples' perceptions of how well off they are personally.[52]

The fact that we do hold politicians accountable for our sense of the country's well-being can be an albatross or an amulet for incumbents. Since they will be blamed for conditions that may not be of their own making, why, they might well reason, should they not take credit for any good that has occurred whether by their doing or not during their term in office?

At some basic level, there is no real cause for concern over the inability of people in the street to identify who is on what side of an abstract issue or to specify the details of "Humphrey–Hawkins" or "Simpson–Mazoli." Insofar as debates offer the strongest case the candidates can make for one interpretation of the country's well-being or another, they enable voters to test the legitimacy of their own diagnoses. Since all change is not remedial and the incumbent is not necessarily responsible for the perceived erosion in the country's fortunes, information beyond the price of cars and cat food is useful as well. Debates provide such information.

Even in the absence of debates, however, voters do seem able to gather information and draw intelligent conclusions about matters of importance to them. "In 1960, for example," notes political analyst Stephen Hess, "Nixon received 58 percent of the Negro vote in Atlanta; in 1964 Goldwater received less than 1 percent of that vote. Many of those voters may not have known the substance of the Civil Rights Act of 1964, many may not have known that Goldwater voted against it. But their massive vote-shift suggests that they had a firm notion of which candidate was most sympathetic to their interests. In the words of V. O. Key, '[V]oters are not fools.' "[53] So the Republic will not be lost for want of debates.

Character Theories: Who Is the Person Who Would Lead?

Character theories recognize that voters don't vote for issues but for people, in some cases people who espouse certain stands on issues. This realization has led some, such as James David Barber, to advise voters to scrutinize a candidate's character.[54] Selection of a "benevolent leader"[55] requires information different from that privileged by other theories of democracy. While political scientists seek links between character and presidential behavior, voters continue to make voting decisions based on their sense of the person seeking their votes.

"[V]oters who pay attention to the personal characteristics of candidates should not be dismissed as irrational," argues political scientist Benjamin Page. "While the ambiguity of candidates makes it costly to find out in any detail exactly what policies they stand for, information about personal characteristics is relatively cheap and abundant: it can be drawn from memory of candidates' past experiences, from observations of major campaign decisions, and from scrutiny of performances in TV newsclips and televised debates, speeches and interviews."[56] Page examines three clusters of attributes important in assessing the benevolence of a leader: knowledge, experience, and competence; warmth, activity, and strength; and candor, dignity, and stability.[57]

Barber's predictions of the behaviors of President Richard Nixon prompted careful attention to his distinctions between energy levels (active and passive) and emotional outlook (positive and negative) of presidential candidates. Active positives, argued Barber, are most likely to pursue result-oriented action; active negatives will hold tenaciously to failing policies. The active positive was Barber's ideal. Jimmy Carter was supposed to be an active positive.

What issue-fixated academics think voters need to know may be a function of the educational process that values consumption of print, detachment, an ability to codify and classify, and a rational model of thought and decision making. Meanwhile, advocates of a character model find support in actual voter behavior. During the 1980 presidential campaign Darrell West monitored audience responses to speeches. He found that the audiences applauded nonpolicy appeals rather than policy ones. Candidates were more likely to elicit signs of reinforcement when they expressed general goals or discussed their own values and qualities.[58] So what can we know of the character of the candidates, and how, through the communication provided by the debates, can we know it?

Trait-based explanations of voting tell us what we say we look for. When asked what they liked and disliked about the presidential contenders, approximately one-fourth of the American public has reported such personal traits as warmth, honesty, or intelligence.[59] Among the traits routinely appearing in assessments of presidential hopefuls are competence and integrity. Of the two, competence generally carries the greater weight.[60] Specific historical circumstances, such as Watergate, can shift our focus to integrity, however. Although the relationship may follow an inverted U curve, we also expect presidents to be knowledgeable.[61] Leaders should be brighter than followers, but not too much brighter. So, for example, the only president with a PhD received only 40% of the vote in 1912 and less than half of the total popular vote four years later. We also know that voters say that an ideal president will not be "power hungry."[62]

Regardless of the set of character traits analyzed, debates can enable a candidate to pass the threshold test that asks, Is one or the other acceptable as president? In 1960 and 1980 the debates put to rest reservations that enabled their winners to assume the White House.

But, if debates are to reveal a candidate's competence, intelligence, integrity, or warmth, they must show something other than the crafted construct of image-makers and speech writers. And here we confront a problem. The candidates' relentless rehearsals give lie to the claim made by moderator Frank McGee at the end of the second Kennedy–Nixon debate that "neither the questions from

Kennedy's skillful response to questions and artful use of humor in the debates of 1960 previewed his press conference behavior as president. (*Library of Congress*)

the reporters nor the answers you heard from Senator John Kennedy or Vice President Richard Nixon were rehearsed."

Still, although many of the candidates' answers are canned, the very fact of rehearsal provides valuable evidence. Indeed, many of the debates' supposedly spontaneous gaffes were preplanned. The extent of Carter's inability to adapt to a contemporary audience is evident in the revelation that his allusion to his daughter's fears about nuclear proliferation, an allusion considered damaging both by his supporters and opponents, was the product of forethought and defied the advice of his aides. "The President had told us in the debate practice that afternoon about his conversation with Amy," recalled Carter aide Hamilton Jordan,[63] "saying that the response of the little girl was a way to personalize the real concern of the American people about nuclear war. Maybe he should work it into the debate? We all argued against it." Nor was the most fateful gaffe of modern debate, Ford's liberation of Poland, inadvertent. As his preparatory notes revealed, that was a claim to which Ford had given thought and in which he believed.

The supposedly spontaneous moment in which Reagan dispatched Carter in their 1980 debate was choreographed as well. Reagan dexterously parried what he viewed as Carter's recurrent distortions of his record by saying, "There you go again . . . ," a line that, according to Reagan watcher Lou Cannon, possessed "all the careful spontaneity of a minuet."[64] When the debates reflect the answers sculpted by the candidates' advisers, that too is revealing. To the extent that those who prepare the candidates for the debates shape the subsequent presidency, the patterns of thought, recurring lines of argument, and pervasive presuppositions residing in a candidate's answers prefigure a presidency. Only in a sustained encounter are such patterns apparent, however.

And as the clock edges toward the half-hour mark, the likelihood diminishes that a candidate is merely speaking someone else's subjects and verbs. Even if the answers are prepackaged, they are likely to have been processed through the candidate's own categories of thought and linguistic reflexes. The fact that candidates cannot foresee all possible questions or memorize all possible answers means, then, that debates provide otherwise elusive clues about the communicative tendencies of the person who would be president.

Across the debates we begin to hear patterns and reflexive moves that characterize one speaker more so than another. In the interstices of sentences reside information about the habits of mind of the person who would be president. In one set of debates, for example, a single candidate said:

The present bureaucratic structure of the federal government is a mess. And if I'm elected that's gonna be a top priority of mine to completely revise the structure of the federal government, to make it economical, efficient, purposeful and manageable for a change.

My opponent quite often puts forward a program just as a public relations stunt, and never tries to put it through the Congress by working with the Congress.

We are no longer respected.

There has been absolutely no progress made toward a new SALT agreement. He has learned the date of the expiration of SALT I, apparently.

As a nuclear engineer myself . . .

There was a time when there was hope for those who were poor and downtrodden and who were elderly or who were ill or who were in minority groups, but that time has been gone.

And now the federal government has become the world's greatest slum landlord.

And we've got 35% unemployment rate in many areas of this country among construction workers. And Mr. Ford hasn't done anything about it. And I think this shows a callous indifference to the families that have suffered so much.

The monographs that have pondered Carter's self-aggrandizing tendencies and hyperbolic bent could as readily have pivoted on the evidence contained in these fragments from the Carter–Ford debates.

In the debates we see candidates unprotected by speech writers. In that state some otherwise unapparent dispositions show through. Occasionally, George Bush's thoughts are so saturated in adjectives that they raise the question: Why does Bush enthuse so when the competence of his boss is called into question? Doth the gentleman protest too much? "I don't think you can go assigning blame. The President, of course, is the best I've ever seen of accepting that. He's been wonderful about it in absolutely everything that happens." "I wish everyone could have seen that one. The President, giving the facts to Gromyko in all of these nuclear—nuclear meetings—excellent. Right on top of that subject matter. And I'll bet you that Gromyko went back to the Soviet Union saying, 'Hey, listen. This President is calling the shots. We'd better move.' " "In one respect, Vice President Bush dismayed even his well-wishers," editorialized the *New York Times.* "So exuberant was he in his determination to tell the Reagan–Bush story that he often bubbled over into gush."[65]

In the debates we hear as well statements that will become mainstays of such Nixon parodists as Rich Little: "Let me make one thing clear." And we note Nixon's tendency to simultaneously assert and deny that he intends to posit a self-indulgent claim or gratuitous attack. "I know Senator Kennedy suggested in his speech at Cleveland yesterday that that committee had not been particularly effective. I would only suggest that while we do not take the credit for it—I would not presume to—that since that committee has been formed the price line has been held very well within the United States."

Some of the evidence we gain is nonverbal. Political scientists tell us that "when candidates for political office are shown on the television screen, audiences tend to use the pictures to judge the candidates' personality traits such as competence, integrity, leadership, and empathy."[66] Among the nonverbal data ripe for voter gleaning were Gerald Ford and Jimmy Carter retaining their wooden postures through twenty-seven minutes of silence as technicians rushed to repair a malfunctioning sound system; Carter speaking in deferential tones in his first debate as if he were in awe either of Ford or the presidency; Ronald Reagan striding comfortably across stage to shake a startled incumbent president's hand; Geraldine Ferraro maintaining eye contact with her hastily jotted notes rather than with the camera.

Of course, it is possible to control some nonverbal behavior. But a candidate able to effectively counterfeit such cues in the debates may well do the same in the White House. At one level, it doesn't really matter if Ronald Reagan is personally affable when dining with friends at the ranch. The affability previewed in the debates forecast his public behavior as president well. At another level, however, psychologists have found few able to counterpoint an emotion or be without "leaking" some disconfirming nonverbal cues.[67] Even when facial movements are controlled, body movements or the tone of voice often betray the attempted deception.[68] When a speaker's nonverbal cues conflict or depart from social norms, the audience becomes wary.

Debates Reveal Communicative Competence and Habits of Mind

The extent to which the debates presage the communicative patterns of a presidency is evident in our ability to identify the presidential aspirants who uttered the following statements:

> As a matter of fact, twenty-five percent of the total tax deductions go for only one percent of the richest people in this country. And over fifty percent of the tax credits go for the fourteen percent of the richest people in this country. When _____ first became president _____, the first thing he did in October, was to ask for a four point seven billion dollar increase in taxes on our people in the midst of the heaviest recession since the Great Depression of the 1940s. In January of _____ he asked for a tax change, a five point six billion dollar increase on low and middle income private individuals, a six and a half billion dollar decrease on the corporations and the special interests. And December of _____ he vetoed the roughly eighteen to twenty billion dollar tax reduction bill that had been passed by the Congress, and then he came back later on in January of this year and he did advocate a ten billion dollar tax reduction, but it would be offset by a six billion dollar increase, this coming January, in deductions for Social Security payments and for unemployment compensation.[67]

> I wish he could have been with me when I sat with a group of teenagers who were black and who were telling me about their unemployment problems. And that it was the minimum wage that had done away with the jobs that they once could get. And indeed, every time it has increased you will find there is an increase in minority unemployment among young people. And therefore I have been in favor of a separate minimum for them.

Not only do the debates forecast Carter's simultaneous fondness for exaggeration and detail and Reagan's habitual move from a single illustration to a generalization but they also provide comparative data on the argumentative dispositions of candidates.

When making comparable claims, Carter's hyperbolic bent contrasts with JFK's restraint. Where Kennedy contended that "our power and prestige in the last eight years has declined," Carter argued that "our country is not strong anymore, we're not respected anymore." The extent to which Dole's acerbic attacks overstepped accepted boundaries of political discourse is clear in a comparison between the debate rhetoric of Nixon and Dole. Nixon noted that "there were three Democratic presidents who led us into war." But, he quickly added, "I do not mean by that one party is a war party and the other party is a peace party." By contrast, Dole asserted that the pardon by Ford of Nixon is "not a very good issue any more than the war in Vietnam would be, or World War Two, or World War One, or the War in Korea, all Democrat wars, all in this century. I figured up the other day, if we added up the killed and wounded, in Democrat wars in this century it would be about one point six million Americans, enough to fill the city of Detroit."

So too are the communicative strengths of candidates revealed. Reagan's self-effacing humor, his genial ability to disarm, and his capacity to reassure account for his victory in the debate with Carter and for much of his personal popularity as president. Kennedy's humor served him well both in the debates and in the presidency. By telling Richard Nixon and the Republican party to go to hell, former president Harry Truman became a presence in the Kennedy–Nixon debates. Kennedy's dexterous dismissal of a request that he apologize on behalf of the Democratic party shifted responsibility to Mrs. Truman. "I really don't think there's anything that I could say to President Truman that's going to cause him, at the age of seventy-six, to change his particular speaking manner. Perhaps Mrs. Truman can, but I don't think I can." The move prefigured Kennedy's use of humor to deflect unwanted questions at press conferences.

Since the president is the only elected spokesperson of all people, rhetorical skill should not be undervalued. FDR succeeded where Carter failed, in part, because one was an effective communicator and the other was not. Rallying the support of Congress and the public requires persuasive skill some have lacked. JFK's proficient use of public and private channels of communication in the Cuban Missile Crisis enabled both sides to edge back from the brink of war. When the shuttle *Challenger* exploded, taking with it the first teacher in space, Ronald Reagan was able to contain the trauma by speaking reassuringly to the watching children of the nation.

In the debates, Kennedy's talent for educating without patronizing is plain. Answering the question, Why does the government pay the farmer for not producing? Kennedy says:

> The farmer plants in the spring and harvests in the fall. There are hundreds of thousands of them. They really don't, they're not able to control their market very well. They bring their crops in or their livestock in, many of them about the same time. They have only a few purchasers . . . that buy their milk or their hogs—a few large companies in many

cases—and therefore the farmer is not in a position to bargain very effectively in the market place. I think the experience of the twenties has shown what a free market could do to agriculture. And if the agricultural economy collapses, then the economy of the rest of the United States sooner or later will collapse. The farmers are the number one market for the automobile industry of the United States. The automobile industry is the number one market for steel. So if the farmers' economy continues to decline as sharply as it has in recent years, then I think you would have a recession in the rest of the country. So I think the case for government intervention is a good one. . . . Secondly, my objection to present farm policy is that there are no effective controls to bring supply and demand into better balance.

Patterns of communication not as readily seen in other formats have been revealed by debates as well. In the snippets of time and space allotted reporters, it is difficult to showcase an instance of fundamental candidate incoherence. Only by hearing Ford's entire summation in his first debate and Reagan's in his last could viewers come to question the ability of these two presidents to cogently develop their own ideas.

Reagan began his closing statement in 1984 with an indication that he was not in sharp mental shape. "The question before you comes down to this: Do you want to see America return to the policies of weakness of the last four years?" He then recalls an assignment of years past to write a letter for insertion in a time capsule. He was thinking about it, he recalled, as he drove down the California coast. "And I found myself wondering what it would be like for someone . . . wondering if someone, a hundred years from now, would be driving down that highway, and if they would see this same thing." He then contemplated "what a job I had with that letter. I would be writing a letter to people who know everything there is to know about us. We know nothing about them. They would know all our problems. They would know how we solved them and whether our solution was beneficial to them down through the years or whether it hurt them. They would also know that we lived in a world with terrible weapons. . . . They will know whether we used these weapons or not." Here Reagan raised the disturbing possibility that he believes that future generations could survive a nuclear war.

"Well, what they will say about us a hundred years from now depends on how we keep our rendezvous with destiny," Reagan continues. "You know, I am grateful to all of you for giving me the opportunity to serve you. . . . George Bush—who I think is one of the finest vice presidents this country has ever had—George Bush and I have criss-crossed the country, and we've had, in these last few months, a wonderful experience. We have met young people. We have met your sons and daughters." At that point the moderator interrupts. Reagan's time is up. Any editing would have looked like an act of sabotage. Few news outlets can or will take four minutes of news time or the equivalent space to demonstrate candidates lost within their own messages.

From the debates we learn that some candidates are ready, indeed eager, to impugn the motives of their opponents where others assume that the nominee of the other party is a person of integrity, good intentions, and good will. Some—specifically Carter and Dole—are more mean spirited than others. By contrast, in 1960 Nixon repeatedly credits Kennedy with honorable motives. A low point occurred in the primary debates of 1984 when Senator Ernest Hollings snapped at Reubin Askew, "You listen. You've got a tic in your ear too." Askew suffers an involuntary muscle contraction—a facial tic. Hollings' remark seemed cruel, a violation of the conversational norm that dictates that a person's infirmities not be ridiculed.

Some are more disposed than others to ally otherwise unrelated topics, to produce non sequiturs. The thought of George Meany seems to invite or at least elicit sarcasm from Dole:

> And I get a little tired of Governor Carter's anti-business attitude. I know they get great support, monetary support, from George Meany. In fact I've been suggesting that George Meany was probably Senator Mondale's makeup man—he may or may not have been, they did a good job. But I think it's time for the American people to understand that this is a very serious election.

> Well, I'd say as far as the League of Women Voters are concerned, you can look at that two ways—either I was wrong half the time or they were wrong half the time. And I think, knowing the League of Women Voters, I think I'll take my interpretation. But with reference to—and they—'cause they—very fine, but they tend to be a little bit liberal. Now, George Meany, he wants the right-to-work law repealed in Texas, in my state.

Some, like Ford, use evidence to sustain a claim. Others, like Carter, employ evidence to demonstrate a command of evidence. Non-incumbents seem more disposed to lard their remarks with almanac-like detail. The tendency is less marked in Carter's performance in 1980 than 1976, for example.

The Freudian slip has played a role in debates as well. In his debate with Mondale, Republican vice presidential nominee Robert Dole implies that Ford has not provided leadership. "It's an honor and a privilege to have known President Ford for sixteen years, as I said at the outset. He's a man of unparalleled decency and honesty and courage. He's a man we can be proud of; he's gonna give us that leadership that America needs. . . ." And between the lines, we hear the possibility that Mondale sees more areas of disagreement than agreement with his running mate when he says, "I made it clear to him [Carter] that I was not interested in serving in a role that was ceremonial, or serving in a role where if I really felt deeply about something I was prevented from saying so. . . . And during this campaign on three separate occasions where I agreed with mis—disagreed with Mr. Carter, I've said so in the course of this campaign." In her debate with Bush, as in her acceptance speech at the convention, Geraldine Ferraro states that she is running for president.

Debates Foreshadow Presidential Strengths and Weaknesses

Reagan's casual command of facts and his rambling closing statement in the last debate of 1984 are consistent with an insufficient grasp of the issues and details on the table at the Reykjavik summit and with his failure to monitor the intrigues revealed in the Tower Commission Report. Carter's fondness for hyperbole haunted him when newscasts replayed his extravagant praise of the Shah of Iran after the hostage taking. His obsession with detail prefigures a presidency without an overarching theme.

In negotiations with heads of state, in discussions with political leaders, or in extemporaneous statements and speeches, the ability to suppress the inappropriate remark before it is uttered is a virtue. The debates reveal that some candidates monitor their own expressions, adjusting thoughts in midsentence; others speak without hearing the meanings issuing from their statements. Nixon does not hear the possible indictment of his wife in his statement that "America cannot stand pat. We can't stand pat for the reason that we're in a race, as I've indicated. We can't stand pat because it is essential with the conflict that we have around the world that we not just hold our own, that we just not keep freedom for ourselves." Nor does Ford seem conscious that he is condemning what most take to be an advantage of the American system when he says that "our children have been the victims of mass education." Ford also implies that the country's monetary policy is sound despite him not because of him when he says: "The chairman of the Federal Reserve Board should be independent. Fortunately, he has been during Democratic as well as Republican administrations. As a result in the last two years we have had a responsible monetary policy." At the end of his 1980 debate with Ronald Reagan, incumbent Jimmy Carter may have been divining the outcome of the election when he thanked "the people of Cleveland and Ohio for being such hospitable hosts during these last few hours in my life." Nor did Ronald Reagan apparently hear self-criticism when in the summation of the October 21, 1984, debate with Mondale, he asked: "Do you want to see America return to the policies of weakness of the last four years?" In the first presidential debate of that year he had noted, "I pose a threat to several hundred people if I go to church."

Some statements may have been crafted to appear unplanned. In a debate in October 1987, Alexander Haig slipped a long-lived indictment of Vice President George Bush into a discussion of a meeting the two had on arms control several years before. "I never heard a wimp out of you," noted Haig. After the debate, Haig, "who is known for his unusual locutions, insisted his use of the word 'wimp' had been a matter of 'Haig-speak.' "[69]

In one of the 1960 debates, Richard Nixon caught himself before he completed his pledge to get rid of farmers. "If a Negro baby is born—and this is true also of Puerto Ricans and Mexicans in some of our cities," noted Kennedy in the first Kennedy–Nixon debate, "he has about one-half as much chance to get through high school as a white baby." Realizing that babies don't get through high school, Kennedy adjusts the next sentence. "He has about one-half as much chance to get through college as a white *(pause)* student." In one of the primary debates of 1984, Mondale too corrected mid-gaffe. "I told you what I was going to do to get those deficits down and educate the next generation. Those aren't special interest groups. I said I'm going to stand up for special—uh—for—against special interests, and I'm going to support Social Security and Medicare."[70] In February 1988, Gary Hart, whose liaison with a young woman had raised questions about his character, added a moment of inadvertent humor to the *Dallas Morning News* debate when he said, "The road to Hell is paved with bad . . . er . . . good intentions."

In a time surfeiting in speech writers, a speaker's self-awareness of the words spoken also may provide an indicator of the extent to which a speaker is processing the thoughts spoken. Interestingly, the candidates who usually caught such slips, as did Nixon, were those more disposed to play a role in creating their own speeches. By contrast, the candidates who speak nonsensical or self-indicting words, seemingly unaware of their meaning, as did Ford and Reagan, were the presidents more reliant on the talents of professional wordsmiths.

Debaters reveal by omission as well as commission. In the Williamsburg debate, Ford either cannot remember or chooses to suppress the name of the Supreme Court Justice he fought throughout the 1950s to impeach. "I believe, however, a comment ought to be made about the direction of the Burger Court vis à vis the court that preceded it." "When Mr. Ford . . . forgot or avoided mentioning the name of Earl Warren, the late Chief Justice of the United States, titters of amusement rippled through the audience," noted the *New York Times*.[71]

Some answers set off warning signals. Responding to a question about Truman's swearing, the person who would add "expletive deleted" to the national vocabulary edges toward self-serving, self-righteousness that, replayed in the wake of Watergate, would indict this earlier feigned indignation. "I see mothers holding their babies up," he said, "so that they can see a man who might be president of the United States. I know Senator Kennedy sees them too. It makes you realize that whoever is president is going to be a man that all the children of America will either look up to, or will look down to. And I can only say that I'm very proud that President Eisenhower restored dignity and decency and, frankly, good language to the conduct of the presidency of the United States. And I only hope that, should I win this election, that I could approach President Eisenhower in maintaining the dignity of the office."

In 1976 Dole dismissed the debates saying that he would rather have spent the time devoted to preparing for them on campaigning. Most people, he averred, would have preferred to watch Friday night high school football rather than a vice presidential debate.[72] Dole's lack of preparation gives us the chance to assess the value of the spontaneity so much sought by analysts of presidential debates. In Dole's answers are sarcasm, gratuitous humor, and, more often than customary in political discourse, an impugning of his opponents' integrity.

I think tonight may be sort of a fun evening.

I don't know much about Governor Carter. I've tried to find out. I know he's very ambitious. I know he wants to be president. He's been running for three years.

I understand from Bobby Smith, who's supposed to be the ag expert in the Carter campaign . . .

It just seems to me that some of those who lust for power are not really concerned about the people.

Well I might say at the outset I haven't always agreed with President Ford and I've voted to override on occasion—but not every time, as my counterpart has. I think President Ford and hindsight's very good, particularly when you're on the ticket. And my hindsight is, the president's been very courageous.

Well Senator Mondale could tell 'em that because he votes for every piece of spending legislation that comes down the pike . . . unless it's in the area of defense, and then he votes for every budget cut.

Governor Carter won't tell us who he's gonna to put in the cabinet. He probably doesn't know. I think it's kinda nice to be at peace in the world.

I voted for the Watergate investigation. My opponent was absent—which is—we're all absent sometimes, but he's absent more than others. . . . I've always said that the night Watergate happened was my night off, so you can't hook me for that.

Well, first I wish to thank the panel for their indulgence and of course all those in the viewing audience who may still be with us. I really hope—and I haven't prepared any final statement in advance—I really hope you were listening and we were able to tell you who's concerned about the American people.

Of all the candidates who have debated, Dole uses the most colloquial language as well, a tendency that combines with his caustic humor and snide personal attacks to assault the dignity of the office he seeks. More than a decade later, Dole's run for the 1988 nomination required him to bury the hatchet he had wielded in 1976. "They told me to go for the jugular," he joked. "I did. My own."[73]

Dole's disposition to *ad hominem* is disconcerting in one who, as president, would be required to be president of Democrats, Republicans, and Independents alike. Does this tell us anything of importance about prospective president Bob Dole? One clear conclusion is that an unprepared speaker is more disposed than a prepared one to say things later regretted. But are Dole's flubs a product of nervousness and hence unlikely to recur in the shelter of the Oval Office? Are they the visceral defenses mounted by a handicapped person as a means of survival? Do they manifest a dangerous tendency to shoot from the lip? An inability to work productively with members of the opposing party?

As Senate majority leader, Dole worked well with both parties, a fact not forecast by his use of personal attack. In the Senate, both before and after his run with Ford, Dole did his homework. The lapse in preparation in the debate did not capsulize a casual attitude toward important responsibility.

Without question, the 1976 vice presidential debate with Walter Mondale damaged Dole's presidential prospects. But was the reaction to Dole fair? Did it presage dangerous presidential behavior? These questions are not readily answered. But the language of the 1976 debate did forecast Dole's sharp responses when attacked in the primaries of 1988.

Unquestionably, Dole's lack of preparedness showed poor political judgment. Indeed, the fact of careful practice before a debate may betoken a public caution indispensable in successful conduct of the office. In this respect, the practiced nonspontaneity of debates may be one of their useful contributions to the body politic. By reminding candidates of the dangers inherent in the off-the-cuff remark, the ill-considered phrase, debates may sober their public behavior as president. After the debate debacle of 1976, Dole approached subsequent debates well prepared.

There is the possibility as well that the lack of preparedness suggested an inability to trust others with preparing briefing papers, an unwillingness to delegate work to subordinates. Such a disposition, unnoticeable in the 1976 campaign, which was run by the Ford team, was apparent in Dole's presidential run.

Debates Reveal Alternative Views of Reality

Extended pieces of communication reveal the speaker's view of the world more readily than snippets of ads or news can. In the Carter–Reagan debate of 1980 we hear Carter's assumption that the world is a complex place filled with exigencies over which a president cannot exercise much influence. Here Carter sounds much like Ford did in the 1976 debates. By contrast, Reagan envisions a responsible president acting decisively in a world that can be governed by straightforward, simple principles. The change in Reagan's world view is less marked between 1980 and 1984.

In Reagan's treatment of Lebanon in the debate of 1984 we hear an instance in which the world has acted on him rather than he on the world. Where Mondale believes the deaths in the bombing were the by-product of a mistaken U.S. policy, Reagan blames the terrorists and the situation there. They offer dramatically different versions of history. For Mondale, inadequate protection of U.S. forces resulted in the deaths; Reagan believes we had done all that we could to safeguard them. Mondale sees the outcome as emboldened terrorists; Reagan, as increased security and a testament to U.S. determination to do what is right.

The facts that the candidates marshal and the ways in which they interpret them are revealing as well. Both Carter and Reagan offered versions of their elected pasts that differed from the historical record. Reagan suffered amnesia about the circumstances surrounding signing the most liberal abortion bill in the country as governor. Carter insisted that he had cut the size of state government in Georgia when available data revealed the opposite.

Debates Benefit the Candidates

Debates Increase Candidate Preparation for Office

By luring the candidates into intensive study of national and world affairs, the debates benefit the candidates and the electorate in an additional way. Conscious of the presence of a national and an international audience that includes citizens of over one hundred nations, aware that their every word will be scrutinized by press and opponents, candidates do their homework. The process is careful and intensive. No other campaign time is as assiduously protected for study and reflection. Even candidacies built on new ideas, cogently argued, require a leather-palmed candidate able to cheerfully endure endless hand shaking and cursed with a capacity to repeat stock phrases with an air of feigned spontaneity.

Campaigns more accurately test the digestive tracts of the candidates and their ability to survive constant travel on minimal sleep than presidential talents. Because, as Nixon's experience in the first debate of 1960 established, the stakes are too high for candidates to stay on the campaign trail, the debates require the nominees to break from the mind-numbing rituals of campaigning to consider the complexities of the world and confront the strengths of their opponents' positions and the weaknesses of their own. Had Eisenhower debated Stevenson in 1956, we doubt that in 1957 he would have demonstrated a gross lack of familiarity with his own Civil Rights Bill.

Sheltered within the cocoon of the campaign, applauded by perfervid partisans, and briefed to respond in stock ways to standard questions, candidates are not necessarily forced to assess the cogency of their own convictions or their ability to defend them against plausible well-argued alternatives.

In preparation for debates, the candidate will not only hear the other side, but hear it phrased pointedly, argued forcefully, and documented relentlessly—in some cases more relentlessly than in the actual debate. "Prior to the first debate," writes JKF's aide Ted Sorensen, "we reduced to cards and reviewed for hours the facts and figures on every domestic issue, every Kennedy charge and every Nixon counter-charge. We threw at the Senator all the tough and touchy questions we could devise."[74] "For five solid hours that afternoon," recalled Nixon of the same debate, "I read through the digested materials which my staff had prepared, on every issue that might conceivably be raised during the course of the debate."[75] "During the week before the first debate," noted Gerald Ford, "I studied a briefing book on his [Carter's] record. I reviewed positions I'd taken myself on every conceivable issue, and I watched reruns of the Nixon–Kennedy debates. . . . For the Philadelphia debate, my aides positioned me behind a lectern, turned on the spotlights and fired the toughest questions they could find."[76] By alluding in one of the debates of 1976 to the involvement of hundreds of experts in his preparation for the debates, Carter made both his hyperbolic bent and the fact of extensive preparation plain. In 1980, Ronald Reagan heard John Anderson's views previewed in a mock preparatory debate with former Anderson aide David Stockman.

The prophylactic effect of debates is felt as well when candidates fashion public stands in anticipation of questioning before a national audience. Those who hint at secret plans to end wars and balance budgets are aware that before a national and international audience the debate panel will press for details, attempt to unmask ruses, and challenge inconsistencies.

Debates Provide Opportunity to Underscore the Criteria by which Presidency Will Be Assessed

Kennedy focused on domestic issues; Nixon, on foreign policy. Carter invited a repudiation of everything Ford had done; Ford promised to stay the course. Reagan asked if we were better off than we were four years ago. Carter hinted that he had not been the president he had hoped to be but suggested that, if given another chance, he'd do better. Reagan asked again if we were better off in 1984 than we had been in 1980. Mondale warned that both he and Reagan would raise taxes but insisted that unlike Reagan he had had the courage to tell the American people the truth about their future.

But beyond these general expectations, the debates embed the criteria by which each candidate expects the next term to be assessed. By electing one over the other, the electorate is tacitly accepting one set of criteria over an alternative. In the second debate of 1984, Mondale insistently implanted the notion that the president must command detail. "The bottom line of national strength is that the President must be in command. He must lead. And when a President doesn't know that submarine missiles aren't recallable, says that 70% of our strategic forces are conventional, discovers three years into his administration that our arms control efforts have failed because he didn't know Soviet missiles were on land, these are the things a president must know to command. A president is called the Commander in Chief. He is called that because he is supposed to be in charge of the facts and run our government and strengthen our nation." By employing his ability to amiably reassure, Reagan managed to dispatch concerns about his command of the office. Mondale's insistent tack coupled with Reagan's faltering performance in the first debate made him more vulnerable, however, to widespread public belief that his lack of control over the White House precipitated Irangate.

Debates Invite National Acceptance of a Person Who May Become President under Trying Circumstances

When they occur, vice presidential debates legitimize the person who in three of the last eight presidencies has been catapulted into the highest office in the land. In general, vice presidential candidates are little noted in spot ads and seldom remembered in network news. Ferraro played a small role in Mondale's ads in 1984; Dole had played none in the broadcast ads for Ford in 1976. Because she was the first woman nominated vice president from a major party and because her financial entanglements raised serious issues, Ferraro captured an unusual amount of media attention. Coverage of other vice presidential candidates in the age of television has been minuscule.

In the traumatic hours and days after a presidential assassination, death, or resignation, it is particularly important that world leaders have confidence in the competence of the new occupant of the Oval Office. Since most of the debates have bolstered the electorate's respect for both candidates, the presence of vice presidential debates also minimizes the trauma of an unexpected presidential transition at home. As important, the preparation required for a debate ensures that the vice presidential candidates have spent time familiarizing themselves with the central issues of the country, a familiarity we cannot otherwise presuppose. Additionally, the debates provide exposure for those likely to seek election in the future.

Debates Reduce the Cost of Reaching Audiences

The campaign's checkbooks benefit as well. In the primaries where the candidates' capacity to raise money is as crucial as their ability to spend it wisely, the fact of frequent debates can sustain an important but cash-poor candidacy. Without the debates of the 1984 Democratic primaries, for example, the candidacy of Jesse Jackson would have withered. Lacking the money to mount costly ad campaigns in state after state, Jackson sustained his shoestring campaign with his articulate performances in the debates and on his talent for capturing free news time. The debates helped Gary Hart's 1984 bid as well. In late January 1984, Raymond Strother, Hart's advertising director, observed that the three-hour debate broadcast from Dartmouth College "was an opportunity to be heard and seen that we haven't been able to afford in paid media."[77]

The primary debates also enable the interested electorate to hear those who will not be able to raise the money and garner the votes that spell survival in the primaries. In 1984, Fritz Hollings, George McGovern, and Alan Cranston offered important alternatives, worthy of national attention—attention afforded them in the early primary debates. The same was the case for Alexander Haig, Pierre DuPont, and Bruce Babbitt in 1988.

The federal financing of the presidential general election guarantees each major party candidate an equal opportunity to reach the electorate. Prior to such financing, debates had the potential to compensate for inadequate funding. Had Nixon accepted Humphrey's challenge to debate in 1968, the insolvent Democrat's inability to purchase air time in late October would have been less consequential. Indeed, the absence of messages from Humphrey during that critical period may have cost him the election. As the election approached, Humphrey was closing rapidly on Nixon in the polls. Nixon won the presidency that year by a margin of one vote per precinct.

Even after campaign financing, debates assist the candidates by requiring less expenditure for ad time to reach large audiences.

Debates Benefit Campaign Watchers

Debates Mirror Changes in Campaigns

Because debates reflect campaign trends, journalists, historians, and other varieties of academic and nonacademic voyeurs can find in them evidence of how campaigns are changing and how they are remaining the same. Both ads and debates, for example, reflect a shift in the substance of campaigns. The deceptions that accompanied the U.S. involvement in the Vietnam war and the fears attendant on Watergate and Irangate invite public scrutiny of the habits of mind, style of leadership, and personal dispositions of those who aspire to the title Commander in Chief. Americans report that their votes are more influenced by the character of the candidates than by their stands on issues. Accordingly, both ads and the questions and answers of debates have focused increasingly on the personal beliefs and communicative competence of the candidates. The questions posed in 1984 included: "[W]ould you describe your religious beliefs, noting particularly whether you consider yourself a born-again Christian, and explain how these beliefs affect your presidential decisions?" "I'm exploring for your personal views of abortion, and specifically how you would want them applied as public policy. First . . . do you consider abortion murder or a sin?" "Given that you have been in public office for so many years, what accounts for the failure of your message to get through?" There are few comparable questions in the debates of 1960.

In the debates, we see evidence of the demise of substantive speeches and their displacement by spot ads. In response to a question on nuclear weapons control, Nixon in 1960 told the debate audience that a major speech he was to deliver the following week would elaborate his position. In the 1960 debates, the candidates reminded us that elaborations of their briefly expressed debate positions could be found in their speeches on the government's role in strikes, on the role of labor unions, on the standing of the United States in the world community, and on the specifics of farm policy. Both Kennedy and Nixon predicated their answers on a careful reading of the opponent's policy speeches.

By contrast, in the debates of the past decade and a half, the candidates took issue with the claims in each other's ads and news clips. So, for example, when asked what responsibility he accepted for the low level of the campaign, Carter pledged not that the substance of his speeches would change but rather that "during the next ten days the American people will not see the Carter campaign running television advertisements and newspaper advertisements based on a personal attack on President Ford's character." Similarly, in 1984 Reagan reduced Mondale's claim to strong leadership to a Democratic ad showing the former vice president standing on the deck of the U.S.S. *Nimitz*. If Mondale had his way, noted Reagan, there would have been no *Nimitz*. "He was against it." Ads, not speeches, were a reference point for the Democrats in 1984, as well. "[T]hings are not as great as the Administration is wanting us to believe in their television commercials," contended vice presidential nominee Geraldine Ferraro in her debate with Vice President George Bush. So where in 1960 candidates related their answers to a world writ large in speeches, in more recent debates they synchronized their answers with one writ small in ads. In the early debates, candidates took issue with what their opponents had said in speeches; in more recent debates, candidates focused on the misrepresentations in their opponents' ads.

During the campaign, says Ford in the concluding statement of the last debate, "you've seen a lot of television shows, a lot of bumper stickers and a great many slogans of one kind or another. But these are not the things that count." Oddly, he then moves to a non sequitur: "What counts is that the country celebrated its 200th

birthday on July fourth." One question in the 1976 debates is
framed in terms of an ad claiming that Ford has quietly done
the job for black Americans.

The use of ads as a point of reference in an uncertain world
reached its high point in the debate in Atlanta in March 1984 when
Walter Mondale appropriated the claim of a hamburger chain to
question the substance of Gary Hart's new ideas. "When I hear
your new ideas, I'm reminded of that ad, 'Where's the beef?' " observed the former vice president.

Debates Aid in Assessing the Campaign

Not only do debates help us see changes in campaign practices but
they prove useful in assessing a campaign itself. Debates enable
us to test whether or not the thread provided by the campaign slogan is part of a tapestry. Ads digest the essence of a campaign to
a slogan. Although there were worlds of meaning whispered in
"Nixon/Lodge: They Understand what Peace Demands," and "Kennedy: Leadership for the Sixties," those worlds were two-dimen-
sional assertions, not arguments, until given color, texture, nuance,
and complexity in the speeches and debates of the 1960 campaign.

Where ads compress a complex of ideas into a central theme, debates elaborate a candidate's central claim. In the process, they
demonstrate the essential coherence of a campaign. In 1980 Reagan's ads and debate message coincided. "Are you better off now
than you were four years ago?" both asked. The consistency be-
spoke a fundamental coherence to the Reagan effort.

By focusing on some issues rather than others, even when that
requires answering unasked questions, the candidates betray their
sense of the concerns central to the electorate and to their success
in the campaign. So, for example, "in 1960, there were no questions
on health and welfare and in 1976, there was no question on law, but
candidates spoke to those issues. Questions on education comprised
one-fifth of the total words spoken by correspondents in 1960's first
debate, but candidates' education responses made up only 4% of
all their words."[78]

We have noted the things debates accomplish without asking
what for many is the critical question: Do they change votes? So
complex is the interaction among an individual's past, personal
preference, various channels of communication, levels of information, and voting that tracking the relationship between debates and

votes is difficult. Those who have approached the task have produced dissimilar results. Although the first debate of 1976 "did produce a better informed electorate . . . [it] had almost no impact on voting intentions," concluded Abramowitz. But Chaffee's study of the 1976 debates found that "the predictability of the vote from the person's vote intention prior to the debates was *highest among the Non-Viewers and lowest among the Regular Viewers*."[79] We do know that debates don't very often convert partisans on one side to the other, a finding consistent with research that suggests that conversion is seldom accomplished by exposure to any single act of communication.[80]

Present research methods circumscribe our ability to detect influence, forcing us, in the main, to rely on personal reports. The process is complicated by the number of factors other than debates, many of them difficult to control, that could play into a voting decision. Moreover, we have yet to study in detail those groups most susceptible to influence. In 1960, the results were so close that debates may well have been decisive.

Summary

Debates benefit the electorate by revealing candidates' communicative competence and habits of mind, by augmenting the candidates' accountability, by acting as a check on candidate manipulation, and by increasing the candidates' preparation for office. Candidates benefit from the cost-free exposure and by being able to hold opponents responsible for their campaign rhetoric. In a world in which sharks and sitcoms lure voters from political substance, a world in which spot ads and news snippets masquerade as significant political fare, a world in which most citizens believe that it is better to receive information than to seek it, debates are a blessing.

But, as we argue in the next chapter, the promise of debates has yet to be fully realized. In an ideal world, candidates would provide thoughtful, revealing answers that reflect their own sense of self and of the country. Panelists would invite answers at least as useful to the electorate as to the headline writer and copy editor.

CHAPTER 6

The Problems
of Broadcast Debates

"Two hundred years ago, five William and Mary students met at nearby Raleigh Tavern, to form Phi Beta Kappa, a fraternity designed, they wrote, to search out and dispel the clouds of falsehood by debating without reserve the issues of the day," recalled Barbara Walters in her opening statement at the third Ford–Carter debate, held in Williamsburg on October 22, 1976. "In that spirit of debate, without reserve, to dispel the clouds of falsehood, gentlemen, let us proceed." To accomplish this noble objective, candidates were given up to two and a half minutes to answer each question. The other candidate then had two minutes to respond. Each was allowed three minutes for a closing statement. In an effort to forestall failures past, Walters added, "As was initially agreed to by both candidates, the answers should be responsive to the particular questions." But do broadcast debates address the issues of the day, dispelling falsehood without reserve and answering the proffered questions along the way? Can they? Should they?

In this chapter we examine the shadows that fall between the potential of debates and the broadcast reality. We begin by asking what ideal debates would tell us about a presidential candidate. Rather than parsing the political universe into "issues" and "images," we would suggest that the electorate would be well served by knowing: (1) What the candidate considers the most pressing problems confronting the country and how he or she plans to respond to them. (2) Whether the candidate can communicate competently about complex issues in private and do so clearly and effectively to the nation as well. (3) Whether the person will see that the laws are faithfully executed and set an appropriate moral tone for the nation. (4) How, if at all, the job of president will change those answers we have received to earlier questions. How would the candidate respond to the unexpected?

Debates Could More Effectively Reveal Pressing Problems and Proposed Solutions

The brevity of debate answers, the irrelevance of the posed questions, the nature of the question-answer form, the absence of substantive news coverage, and the unfamiliarity of the electorate with the complexities of issues make it difficult for candidates to engage each other intelligently on their substantive disagreements. At the same time, it is not always in the candidates' interest to reveal differences.

Debates Suffer from Compression

From their inception, broadcast presidential debates have borne the characterizing imprint of television on politics: ideas must be trimmed to fit the Procrustean demands of pre-set time limits. And as television moved from infancy to adolescence, the size of the bed it provided for sustained discourse decreased. Accordingly, the debate speeches of the general election of 1984 were half the length of those in the 1960 debates. In 1984, Mondale was given two and a half minutes to answer the questions "Do you accept the conventional wisdom that Eastern Europe is a Soviet sphere of influence? And, if you do, what could a Mondale Administration realistically do to help the people of Eastern Europe achieve the human rights that were guaranteed to them as a result of the Helsinki Accords?" The NBC debate of the 1987 season reduced candidates' answers to a mere minute.

The first president to debate shares with the most recent the view that limitations inhere in the existing debate format. Kennedy noted, for example, that "it might have been better to have had a somewhat freer give-and-take, and an opportunity for Mr. Nixon and myself to develop our thoughts more fully on some of the major and more complex problems."[1] "Having participated in a number of debates myself," observed Ronald Reagan in 1986,

"I believe it is also necessary to take into account the limitations of television as a medium for conveying the complexity of the political process."[2]

The sacrifices occasioned by abbreviation are significant. In brief snippets we are less likely to get past sloganeering to substance, past the canned response to thoughtful expressions of conviction.

In response to Mondale's query "Where's the beef?," Gary Hart inadvertently demonstrated the extent to which the brevity that is a hallmark of presidential debate is inhospitable to developed discourse about policy and susceptible to sloganeering. "Vice President Mondale cleverly has picked up the slogan from a fast food chain and tried to suggest that there are no ideas or issues when he knows full well that they are in the form of a book, in the form of strategy and position papers—quite detailed, quite elaborate. The fact of the matter is that other candidates or the press or whomever really isn't interested quite often in what industrial policies are, what those detailed ideas are." In a forum that rewards a capacity to digest, a slogan drawn from an ad can raise a question that cannot be answered in the abbreviated time provided by the debates, news clips, or ads. In his ads, Hart was reduced to cradling a copy of the book to assert its existence. His new ideas had been captured in the medium of the old order—print. They did not lend themselves to the capsulization required by television. They did not subject themselves to the dramatization of Clara Peller and her microscopic hamburger. They did not invite the attention of an audience that watches but does not read. The Wendy's ad was entertaining, memorable, and brief. Hart's counterclaim was boring, abstract, and entombed in print. Whether or not the book was meaty, high or low in cholesterol, Mondale effectively fried Hart's chances with "Where's the beef?"

When required to speak in brief snippets, candidates are rewarded for simplification and ambiguity rather than complex responses and specificity. In morselized statements, candidates sacrifice the ability to take on their opponents' positions in a fair fashion. Abbreviated answers provide road signs for the knowledgeable rather than a map for the uninformed. Short answers also create the illusion that problems are amenable to simple solutions and at the same time suggest that the obligations of a citizenry can be discharged by listening to such a recitation.

Statements in debates have gotten shorter and shorter because those responsible for them have assumed that it otherwise would be difficult to hold the attention of the audience that preferred *Jaws* to "Teddy." An ideal debate format would maintain a national audience while providing longer and more substantive answers.

We could, of course, get more depth from the shorter answers by focusing an entire debate on a single topic rather than a broad topic area such as foreign or domestic policy. In elections in which a few central questions seem pivotal to the people, the press, and the political scientists it might be possible to isolate such questions. What should the U.S. policy be in Vietnam? was one such question in 1972, as was "law and order" in 1968. Should the budget deficit be reduced and if so how? is a pivotal question in 1988, as is the value of Reagan's Strategic Defense Initiative. But rarely does any question work to the equal advantage of each side; so by focusing on specific questions, we might discourage candidate participation in debates.

The Question-and-Answer Format Is Not Conducive to Substantive Debate

As we noted in Chapter 4, in the process of trying to draw together the advantages of various forms, the current debate format has also appropriated many of their weaknesses. As presently constituted, the structure places irreconcilable demands on the candidates. They are expected, for example, to both engage each other and speak to the mass audience. As every presidential debate has demonstrated, it is difficult to do both. Nixon chose to engage Kennedy in their first debate, repeatedly summarizing Kennedy's points and addressing his arguments. In the process, he lost the opportunities Kennedy seized to play to the folks at home. By so doing, the vice president won as a debater and lost as a would-be president.

Similarly, candidates are told to both answer the posed questions and debate the opponent. "Most of all, the format needs drastic overhaul because its basic flaw is fatal to the idea and practice of debate," concluded rhetoric scholars Lloyd Bitzer and Theodore Rueter after an exhaustive analysis of the 1976 debates.[3] "Ford and Carter were required by the format to answer, but they were expected to debate. They did engage in some debate, but usually only by rebelling against the system—leaving a question inadequately answered in order to engage each other. The only remedy for this is radical alteration through shifting either to a clear version of a 'question and answer' format that permits no combat or to a clear 'debate' format that frees candidates from the obligation to answer questions."

Traditional debate entails two-sided examination of a single focused question. The Stassen–Dewey debate on whether the Communist party should be outlawed pivots, for instance, on a single proposition. Most of the questions asked in presidential debates do not. When germane to only one candidate, the question minimizes the likelihood of any direct clash. "The candidates developed argumentative support for affirmation and denial of *the same proposition* in only twenty-two debate rounds," concluded Bitzer and Rueter of the 1976 debates. "An examination of the rounds shows that propositions of debate were established more often by the candidates than by the panelists." And then, "neither the candidates nor the debate audience usually knew what proposition was at issue until the rejoinder speaker offered his response."[4] So, for example, moderator Frank Reynolds asked about the use and safety of nuclear energy. "Now . . . there seems to be a clear difference between you and the president on the use of nuclear power plants, which you say you would use as a last priority. Why, sir? Are they unsafe?" In his answer to Reynolds, Carter offered the proposition that the United States has no national energy policy. "[T]he energy policy of our nation is one that has not yet been established under this administration. I think that almost every other developed nation in the world has an energy policy except us." Ford responded not to Reynolds' question but to Carter's proposition. "In January of 1975 I submitted to the Congress and to the American people the first comprehensive energy program recommended by any president. It called for an increase in the production of energy in the United States. It called for conservation measures." With viewers' appetites whetted for a response from Carter, a new questioner was given his turn, and the course of the discussion veered to unemployment. Had energy policy been one of three or four topics treated by the debate, we might have gotten beyond Carter's charge that there was no policy and Ford's assertion that there was.

The more extended speech format and direct confrontation characteristic of nineteenth-century debates afforded the sustained analysis missing in our current contests. Lincoln and Douglas demanded—and received—elaborate responses to the questions and challenges they issued. When Douglas thought that Lincoln dissembled, he quoted the rail-splitter at length. Lincoln was forced to respond not only to a charge, but to the refinements and specifications of charges developed throughout the campaign.

Where actual differences do exist, the debates may not make them clear. As we noted earlier, candidates stand to gain little and lose much by being specific. So, for example, a *New York Times* editorial eloquently indicted Walter Mondale and Ronald Reagan for their failure to identify their differences on a number of key issues in their second 1984 debate:

> Mr. Reagan believes that all recent Presidents engaged in "unilateral disarmament" that left the Russians "superior." He is determined to achieve superiority for the United States instead, either by unilateral buildup or, if the Russians can be frightened enough, with their agreement. He seeks superiority not only in offensive weapons, which deter attack by threatening a holocaust. To try to make America invulnerable, he would also break out of treaties forbidding defensive weapons. Eventually he'd offer this defense technology to the Russians if they'd accept "real" disarmament.
>
> Mr. Mondale thinks nuclear superiority is unattainable, indeed meaningless, and therefore finds the arms race pointless, dangerous. He concedes that he foresees no alternative to deterring attack with the threat of mutual devastation. We would return to seeking agreements that guarantee retaliatory "parity"—the certainty that either side could destroy the other no matter which attacks first. He would not pursue defensive weapons because no effective ones are in sight—and because just trying would only stimulate a race for new, overpowering offensive weapons.
>
> There you are: rival positions easily stated. But did either man even come close to framing the issue in that honest fashion? No. And why not? Apparently because Mr. Reagan was afraid to be shown up as indifferent to negotiation while Mr. Mondale was afraid to show himself as panting for Soviet acquiescence. Their mutual name-calling not only replaced serious debate but prevented it.[5]

We are not inclined to rescue the 1984 candidates' reputations as debaters, but consider the name calling far less troublesome than the short time and diminished emphasis on response characteristic of contemporary presidential debate. Name calling is only problematic when it displaces argument, as it is inclined to do when the time is severely limited. Hayne and Webster called one another names without ruining their debates. Insults and euphemisms emerged as important indications of the differences between the two debaters and the positions they represented. The more generous amounts of speaking time demanded direct attention to the substance of the disputes and the implications for national policy.

Debates Don't Address the Right Questions

In every general election debate from 1960 through 1984, reporters have served as questioners. Their presence is justified by their experience as interviewers, their knowledge of politics, their comfort with television, and their disinclination to be intimidated by the prospect of asking tough questions of an incumbent or would-be president.

As important is the fact that the candidates don't want to debate without the buffer the panel provides. In every debate, the toughest questions have not been asked by one candidate of the other but by a panelist. When given the chance to question their opponents, candidates, fearful of the backlash a tough question might invite, often play softball. So, when asked what was the most outrageous thing Mr. Reagan had said in their first debate, Walter Mondale replied that he was "going to use" his time "a little differently. I'm going to give the President some credit. I think the president has done some things to raise the sense of spirit, morale, good feeling in this country. He is entitled to credit for that. What I think we need, however, is not just congratulating ourselves, but challenging ourselves to get on with the business of dealing with America's problems.

"I think in education, when he lectured the country about the importance of discipline. I didn't like it at first, but I think it helped a little bit. But now we need both that kind of discipline, and the resources, and the consistent leadership that allows this country to catch up in education and science and training. I like President Reagan. This is not personal. These are deep differences about our future and that's the basis of my campaign."

When Geraldine Ferraro was asked what question she would most like to ask her opponent about foreign policy, she replied, "Oh, I don't . . . I don't have a single-most question. I guess the concern that I have is a concern not only as the vice-presidential candidate, but as a citizen of this country. My concern is that we are not doing anything to stop the arms race." Bush was even more oblique.

To the same question he responded, "I have . . . I have none I'd like to ask of her. But I'd sure like to use the time—talk about the World Series, or something of that nature. Let me put it this way. I don't have any questions. We are so different from the . . . The Reagan–Bush administration is so different from the Carter–Mondale administration that the American people are going to have the clearest choice . . ."

Candidates are more comfortable hearing their own attacks raised by reporters. Accordingly, it was a panelist, not Ronald Reagan, who recalled that "the President, Mr. Mondale, has called you 'whining and vacillating'—among the more charitable phrases, 'weak' I believe. . . . [H]e has made the point that you have not repudiated some of the semi-diplomatic activity of Reverend Jackson, particularly in Central America." No such harsh words or direct charges passed from the incumbent's lips in the debate.

Despite its advantages, the empaneling of reporters poses problems. Since reporters have been following the campaign since New Hampshire's first snowfall more than a year before, they are more knowledgeable about the candidates' stands than most of the electorate. Questions designed to elicit news do not invite the level of basic information on candidate positions and differences that the less educated viewer would find most useful. In 1984, for example, Mondale was asked "to address the question of nuclear strategy." "The formal document is very arcane," noted the questioner, "but I'm going to ask you to deal with it anyway. Do you believe in MAD—mutual assured destruction, mutual deterrence—as it has been practiced for the last generation?"

One might reasonably argue that press focus on campaign strategy in day-to-day reporting accounts for the second major charge made against reporters as panelists: they are preoccupied with questions about politics and campaigning, not the presidency and governance. In the debate before the 1984 California primary, for example, moderator Tom Brokaw asked whether Jackson had made a deal over delegates with Hart, whether if Mondale won it would be a victory of backroom politics, whether Hart knew the rules going into the campaign, whether Hart would ask for a formal Justice Department investigation of Mondale's so-called tainted delegates, whether the press now makes it too difficult for someone to enter politics, and whether Mondale considered one of his ads fair.

News Coverage Does Not Focus on the Substance of Debates

In 1984 both *Time* and *Newsweek* delayed publication dates by 24 hours to carry accounts of the final Mondale–Reagan debate. The headlines dramatically illustrated the concern that analysts have about press reports of debates. The covers read: "Who Won and Why?"

The sports and battle metaphors through which reporters see and report campaigns have been much criticized by academics, politicians, and newspersons themselves. Too often, for reporters the story is who's winning and losing and how they're playing the game. Were the anthropologists of a future age to divine the goal of our electoral system from news reports about it, they might well conclude that the candidates' aim was being good campaigners and the goal of the media to educate the viewers as campaign consultants. The focus on polls, strategy, techniques, and wins and losses makes sense in a football game where week after week players engage a variety of opponents in the same game to win the right to test the best in a final contest. The relationship between campaigning and governing is more oblique. Nor does much campaign coverage prepare a voter to determine who should lead the country. Is the best tactician the best president? Do the polls reflect the substance of the candidates? Too often reporters ask, "Of what significance is this act or statement for the campaign" rather than for the body politic.

Early nineteenth-century political debaters such as John Quincy Adams bound these questions up in their concern for style. Adams paid attention to composition as the hallmark of mind. The powerful orator was the politician in command of the wisdom needed to govern. His comments on his colleagues covered the substance of the claims as revealed by the language in which they were enveloped as well as the transitory questions of who won and who lost an argument. By focusing on who won, contemporary analysts neglect the historical nexus of debate and intellectual ability.

Although those who cover campaigns bemoan the brevity, superficiality, and manipulative nature of spot ads, telecasters routinely reduce debates to the equivalent. By focusing on some single supposedly decisive moment, news coverage downplays the substance of debates and magnifies their identity as gladiatorial bouts or vaudeville acts. There was more to the Carter–Reagan debate of 1980 than "There you go again" and more to the first Mondale–

Reagan debate of 1984 than Mondale's resurrection of that statement. If post-debate commentary focused on the substance of the exchange—the important similarities and differences expressed—rather than on the strategy, outcome, and potentially fatal gaffes, the viewing public would be better served.

Instead, the debates have adopted some of the stylistic features of game shows. Media analysts Susan Drucker and Janice Platt Hunold see parallels in the ways in which both presidential debates and game shows campaign for their product, build enthusiasm in the studio audience, prepare the candidates, use the panelists and emcee, invoke the constraints of time, employ risk and competition, use cutting and editing, and wrap up the show.[6]

By focusing on who won and who lost rather than on the positions revealed and clarified, press coverage also reinforces the view that elections are "horse races," not processes of preparing the electorate for informed decision making. This focus reflects campaign coverage in general. Half the campaign stories make no mention of policy; more than eight out of ten discuss the question of "horse race."[7] Indeed, in 1976, "voters found much more concentration on the issues they said interested them if they watched the debates rather than attending to subsequent press reports."[8]

This phenomenon prompted media scholar Steven Chaffee to conclude, "Paradoxically, then, the debates themselves brought out issue content but they also stimulated press activity that obscured that information by heavy emphasis on the outcomes rather than the content of the debates." This finding would be cause for minimal concern if the public judged debates in their own right. Instead, a growing body of data suggests that the voters' shifting perception of the candidate's success in a debate is shaped not by actual debate performance but by the media call of who won or lost.[9] The media verdict is most influential on those with the least political information and weakest party ties, a volatile group, decisive in close elections and in need of substantive information.

In 1984; television news provided "a solid base for making assessments of the candidates' personal and professional traits and skills." As noted by political scholar Doris Graber, however, policy skills and negative traits received little pictorial support, while "most messages about character traits and campaign skills, and most positive messages in general, were supported by pictures."[10] Insofar as pictures enhance message impact, this use of visuals decreased the power of the policy discussion that did occur.

Reporters would not have to abandon the language of "winning" and "losing" to increase the substance of their assessments of debates. They would instead displace evaluation of the political implications of the candidates' performance with visually amplified analyses of how well each defined the problems, provided reasoned analyses of alternative solutions, educed evidence to sustain one or the other view, and articulated their positions to the voters.

After Nixon's poor appearance in the first debate, campaigners canonized the rule: Blessed are those who appear presidential for they shall inherit the White House. The aftermath of Gerald Ford's liberation of Poland in the second debate of 1976 added a second rule to the consultants' debate primer: Blessed are those who control the spin on debate commentary for they shall attend the inaugural ball. The filter provided by press commentary is a powerful determinant of the public's perception of the debates themselves. The studies monitoring the reactions of voters during the second debate showed no citizen alarm at Ford's statement about Poland. This was also true of those surveyed immediately after the debate's end. The seismographs did not spike until television commentary labeled Ford's statement a gaffe and speculated about its effect on the race. Those interviewed a week after the debate were more likely to think that Carter won and to mention Ford's remark as a factor in their conclusion. The change was too rapid to attribute it to interpersonal information seeking. Nor is it probable that the political elite transmitted its opinion through personal channels to the less informed. The only plausible explanation is that viewers' assessment of the debate was influenced by media analysis.[11]

What the fates had given, they had taken away. Post-debate commentary after the first debate of 1976 had favored Ford, a favor reflected in an electorate whose impression of Ford's competence increased in the days following the debate.

The homogeneity of campaign coverage contributes to the impact of post-debate analysis. Studies of news magazines, news dailies, the AP, and the national television networks find remarkable similarity in their reporting of candidates and campaigns.[12] Although increasingly "girls" have joined boys on the bus, the pack journalism that Timothy Crouse[13] found on the campaign trail in 1972[14] still survives. And the vocabulary through which the pack sees the world surfeits with game plans, strategies, wins, and losses but suffers speechlessness when invited to describe argument and evidence. By so doing, the media deny the public an important part of what it says it wants from debates. The most common reason voters use for watching debates is determining where the candidates stand on the issues.

Framing politics as a game transcends the lens and pens of the reporters. Academic discussions have their share of "contests" and "game plans." And candidates see themselves as embattled gamesters, as well. When Vice President Bush commented after his debate with Geraldine Ferraro that he'd "kicked a little ass," a Reagan campaign official excused the "crack as part of the 'macho game' of politics."[15] Democrats are every bit as gamey as Republicans. In the June 1984 California debate Mondale noted:

> Now it's the end of the fourth inning, they're 21–0 behind and they say well, some of us got more first downs than others, therefore let us win. You said you're a little confused by what happened. You shouldn't be because that has been going on for over 100 years. When you get toward the end of the game and people are substantially behind, which is the case, two or three things happen. First, they try to change the rules so that they win. And secondly, they start working together as Gary Hart and Reverend Jackson are combining their forces.

Debates Give More to the Information Rich than to the Information Poor

The rhetorical exchanges known as presidential debates make the most sense to those already knowledgeable and the least to those most in need of information.[16] Not only are reporters' questions occasionally unnecessarily technical, but when contradictory accounts of events, acts, and discourse are offered, nothing in the existing format provides a neutral voice able to tell the confused viewer which if either is accurate. What, for example, is a viewer to make of the following exchanges between Mondale and Hart in the March 1984 debate in Atlanta?

MR. HART: In the almost 10 years in the Senate I've cast 5,000 or 6,000 votes. Vice President Mondale in his campaign pulled out about half a dozen of those to attack me showing that I'm not for this and not for that. I'll give you one example. One of those was a vote on O.S.H.A. Now Vice President Mondale knows full well that I am absolutely as committed to a safe work place as he is. The vote was this, and it illustrates the point and the

difference. It was to exempt from certain paperwork requirements small businesses in this country who had 10 or fewer em-
ployees and farmers who employed fewer than five people. It
was that burdensome bureaucracy and paperwork that drove the
Democrats out of office in the 70's.

Now I think we can have a safe work place for people on
farms and in factories without driving small business people and
family farmers off their land or out of their businesses.

MR. MONDALE: I saw that vote, but I've never mentioned it. The
one I talked about is where, unlike Senator Nunn and Senator
Chiles and others, you refused to vote a windfall profits tax,
which, if you'd been successful, would have given big oil $250
billion.

MR. HART: There you go again.

MR. MONDALE: I am going straight ahead here. Secondly, I've talked
about your $10-a-barrel tax. That is the worst idea in this cam-
paign.

MR. HART: It was a Carter–Mondale initiative.

MR. MONDALE: Oh no. I have nothing to do with that. That's the
worst idea. Carter's not for it. Nobody except you are for it, and
you're not talking about it anymore, it's so bad.

MR. HART: Oh yes I am.

MR. MONDALE: A half a million people . . .

MR. HART: Right away.

MR. MONDALE: A half a million lose their jobs. America will become
the highest cost producing area in the country. Talk about intru-
sion and destruction of jobs and entrepreneurship and position
in international trade, this is a disaster, and I don't think you
thought it through.

MR. HART: Well, Mr. Mondale . . .

MR. MONDALE: I don't believe you really . . .

MR. HART: Let me respond. Let me respond.

MR. CHANCELLOR: You either have a choice, it seems to me, and I'm
sorry but the clock is inexorable . . . of having a chance to say
what you want to say at the end or squeezing it there at the very
end and so Senator could you just say it in 25 words or less than
that.

MR. HART: Less than that. I voted for a Carter–Mondale tariff on
imported oil and I was only one of about 15 Senators that had
the courage to support this Administration. And the second
thing is, I proposed a windfall profits tax of 100 percent on old

oil owned by the big oil companies in this country and that goes beyond the Carter–Mondale . . .

MR. MONDALE: This is a complete distortion of what he did.

MR. HART: It is not a distortion.

MR. MONDALE: When we needed you, you were wrong.

MR. HART: No, that's not right.

MR. MONDALE: That is correct.

When debaters presuppose a context not commanded by the average viewer, exchanges become meaningless in informational terms. Unless carefully directed, the conversation also bypasses the audience. At their worst, conversations join two or more experienced discussants in an intimate exchange, eliciting technical language and abbreviated references to complex topics. Disagreements are more likely to be focused in personal terms.

In both cases, *readers* will benefit from the arbitration provided by informed outsiders; *viewers* seldom will. But since readers are more likely to be well informed to begin with, this check in the system does not markedly increase the informational level of the electorate. And in an additional irony, debates encourage the electorate to rely on television for public information when print has proven a more reliable educative form.

The dispute between Reagan and Mondale over whether Reagan believed that nuclear armed missiles could be recalled is illustrative. In the debate Mondale alleged, as he had in his stump speeches, that Reagan was so poorly informed about arms control that he thought that "submarine missiles are recallable." Since Mondale's case against Reagan pivoted on the claim that Reagan lacked the command of the office necessary for effective governance, this was an important claim. In the debate, Reagan responded that that charge was "absolutely false. . . . I never conceived of such a thing. I never said any such thing." Unless viewers recalled the press conference of May 13, 1982, in which Reagan had made the claim, they had no way to know who was telling the truth. Their judgment had to rest on the image created by each in the act of asserting the truth of his position. Readers of the *New York Times* learned the morning after the debate that "there is no way to recall a nuclear-armed missile once launched. . . . In answer to a [press conference] question on what should be included in an agreement on strategic arms reduction, [Reagan] said that 'nothing is excluded,' but that ballistic missiles were the 'most destabilizing weapons, the one that

In the 1984 debate a strong showing by Democratic nominee Walter Mondale and a fumbling performance by the incumbent president raised the question "Was Reagan up to the job of president?" In their second debate, the electorate concluded that the answer was "Yes," a judgment warranted by Reagan's humorous response to a question about his ability to govern. (*League of Women Voters Education Fund*)

is most frightening to most people.' He then noted that a land-based missile, once launched has 'no recall,' and can hit the target in a matter of minutes.

"He went on to say: 'Those that are carried in bombers, those that are carried in ships of one kind or another, or submersibles, you are dealing there with a conventional type of weapon or instrument, and those instruments can be intercepted. They can be recalled if there has been a miscalculation. And so they don't have the same, I think, psychological effect that the presence of those other ones that, once launched, that's it; they're on their way, and there's no preventing, no stopping them.' Mr. Reagan and his aides have maintained that he was talking about the planes and submarines, not about missiles in flight."[17]

Reagan had used a similar move to dismiss a claim by Carter in the 1980 debate. Carter alleged that "when Governor Reagan has been asked about that, he makes the very disturbing comment that non-proliferation, or the control of the spread of nuclear weapons, is none of our business." Reagan responded: "I would like to correct a misstatement of fact by the President. I have never made the statement that he suggested about nuclear proliferation." The next evening ABC news aired footage showing that Reagan had made the claim, although not in the convoluted language employed by Carter.

The problem of relying on subsequent newscasts and print reports for such information, of course, is that these channels of communication attract a much smaller, more knowledgeable audience than do the general election debates. Even if the audiences were comparable, the follow-up reports occur as much as a full day after the confusing argument in the debate.

The ability of viewers to decide who is telling the truth is minimized as well by the debates' ban on visual aids. If the debates permitted the use of tape to document past statements, candidates or panelists might actually replay controversial claims. Viewers could then decide for themselves which candidate, if either, was accurately representing what was said. As we argue in the next chapter, this concept also would set in the campaign a disincentive for hyperbole and misstatement before partisan crowds. Had Edward R. Murrow been limited to the presidential debate form, his report on McCarthy would have lost most of its power, a power gotten by showing the senator making controversial allegations.

Television offers us the chance to improve accountability in debates while reducing the time debaters have to spend establishing facts about positions. A good portion of the earlier Lincoln–Douglas debates was devoted to determining the Republican party platform and Lincoln's stand on it. The debate on the equality of slaves was vigorous when joined, but it took the candidates a long while to establish their positions. Videotaped clips of the sort used to preface discussions on ABC's "Nightline" could minimize this sort of unproductive charge and counter-charge on factual issues and positions issued, increasing accountability and allowing more attention to the rationale.

Debates also increase the personalization of politics, minimizing the anchorage traditionally provided by party. This would be of concern only to tenure-seeking political scientists were it not that a committee of party activists and political scientists was correct when in 1977 it warned that the political party system "is in serious danger of destruction. Without parties there can be no organized and coherent politics." Meeting in the 1980s, the Committee on the Constitutional System offered a comparable conclusion: The "decline of party loyalty and cohesion at all levels of the political system" is a cause of "the failures and weaknesses in governmental performance."[18] As advocates of the "responsible party" model of democracy argue, long-lived identifiable parties also ease the complexity of the voter's task. If candidates adopt traditional party positions, then the voter needs to be familiar only with the ways in which the candidate differs from party. Learning the identity of a stable party is an easier task than learning who the partyless independents actually are and the causes for which they stand.

Some hypothesize that more clearly articulated party identities would increase voter turnout. Since the United States hovers near the bottom when its voter turnout is compared to that of other developed countries, concern about this issue is pervasive. In 1984, for example, 44.8% of the citizens of voting age opted to let others decide whether Walter Mondale or Ronald Reagan would inhabit the White House in 1985. Political scientist Walter Dean Burnham estimates that "about 38 percent of American citizens are 'core' or regular voters for major national and state office; another 17 percent or so are marginals who come to the polls only when stimulated by the dramas of presidential campaign politics; and 45 percent are more or less habitual nonvoters."[19]

Surrogate debaters stimulated party enthusiasm in the nineteenth century. Because prominent advocates who were not presidential candidates stumped in favor of party platforms, parties were proven deeper than their presidential choices and intimately involved in the electoral process. Without some sort of surrogate debating, parties are inevitably hidden behind their candidates.

Since the more educated are more likely to vote and the less educated less likely, one might argue that the comparatively low voter turnout protects the country from ill-informed voting. But to the extent that voting is the way a group is heard in a democracy, patterns of nonvoting mean that the poor, blacks, Hispanics, and those who do not own homes speak in muffled voices and depressed numbers in the voting booth.

Clearly defined, long-lived parties whose sponsorship of a candidate is a signal of a desire to achieve defined ends in a defined way make it easier for poorly educated voters to vote their own self-interest in an intelligent way. In the jargon of political science, "the relative disappearance of partisan teams in campaigns and their replacement by personalistic and imagistic appeals to voters creates conditions that make individual utility calculations difficult, if not impossible."[20] Fearful of the power of demagogues over the ill-informed, the Founders restricted the franchise to propertied white males and entrusted the final selection to carefully chosen pillars of the community—the electors of the electoral college. Since that time, powerful democratic rhetoric has instilled premises challenged publicly at some professional risk.

Debates Could More Effectively Reveal the Public and Private Competence of the Candidate as a Communicator

Yearly the swallows return to Capistrano; with them every fourth year comes the observation by one or another distinguished historian that some of our best loved and most venerated past presidents would not have survived a televised campaign. Washington would not have won a "great" televised debate, noted Henry Steele Commager in 1960.[21] So intimidated by speaking was the author of the Declaration of Independence that as our third president he avoided speaking occasions with a vengeance. The tall, ungainly, gaunt, sunken-faced Lincoln would have been cast for a role in "The Munsters" more readily than as president. And on television, the bespectacled TR would have looked more silly than stately.

But if the underlying assumption of these nay debaters is correct, the flash-fried exposure of news would have scorched such candidacies long before they would have reached debates. There is reason to question the unelectability of our great presidents in a television age, however. The first candidate elected in a televised campaign and the earlier general and hero we remember as the "father of the country" are more similar than different. Eisenhower's credentials were, after all, as general and hero, not speaker or matinee idol. Moreover, the moment of wit that cinched the second 1984 debate for Reagan was feeble compared to that routinely served by Lincoln, whose talent for the telling anecdote would have set well in news bites. Jefferson's knack for the resonant, memorable phrase is a media consultant's dream. And TR's mastery of the pseudoevent—from San Juan Hill on—would have quickly made him a media favorite. Moreover, if there is a form of campaign communication able to reward the thoughtful, structured, bold, articulate answer, it is the debate. Finally, those who conclude that the greatest presidents of centuries past lacked charisma might ask what evidence suggests that Johnson, Nixon, Ford, or Carter was possessed of that elusive gift.

Debates Do Not Presage an Ability to Deal with Communicative Complexity

The ability to deal well with complex communication is a mark of the successful president. In an international crisis, the president who can see the world from the other side, array a vast range of alternatives, and respond creatively will succeed in avoiding hostilities. Political analysts Suedfeld and Tetlock[22] compared the international communications exchanged during crises that led to war in 1914 and 1950 and those that were solved without violence in 1911, 1948, and 1962. When the complexity of the international diplomatic messages was low, the crisis was more likely to lead to war. Those conflicts resolved without war evidenced an increase in communicative complexity as the crisis moved toward resolution. Those that moved toward war showed a decrease in complexity. In the Cuban Missile Crisis, a highly sophisticated communication strategy that included ignoring one letter and responding instead to another prevented possible nuclear confrontation between the superpowers. An ideal debate format would reveal whether a candidate is capable of processing and generating appropriately complex communication.[23]

Debates Prefigure Presidential Skill in Public Communication
but Reveal Little Else Relevant to the Presidency

In the last chapter we argued that debates demonstrate whether a candidate is an effective public communicator; they also reveal patterns that will characterize the person's rhetoric in office. In an age in which communicating with the public is a central presidential role, this is not an insignificant contribution. Still, other important aspects of presidential leadership seem poorly forecast by debates.

"The drama of the situation was mostly specious, or at least had an extremely ambiguous relevance to the main (but forgotten) issue: which participant was better qualified for the Presidency," wrote cultural critic Daniel Boorstin of the 1960 debates. "Of course, a man's ability, while standing under kleig lights, without notes, to answer in two and a half minutes a question kept secret until that moment, had only the most dubious relevance—if at all— to his qualifications to make deliberate Presidential decisions of long-standing public questions after being instructed by a corps of advisors."[24]

Debates fail to elicit or provide a means of evaluating some of the skills central to conduct in office including an ability to ask significant questions, a talent for securing sound advice, a disposition to act judiciously, and a capacity to compromise without violating conscience or basic social principles. "[T]he ability to stimulate a bureaucratic apparatus to bring forth alternatives while no doubt related to an ability to imagine alternatives in the first place, requires a large panoply of talents and disciplines that are not so easily revealed by the debate format," observes political scientist Nelson Polsby. "The capacity to pick correctly among the alternatives, to understand the reasons for picking one alternative and not another, the capacity to see whether the selected alternative is being pursued by a government agency—these managerial talents are quite inexpressible through debate. It is rather like judging the ability of a comedian to get good results from his writers by watching him ad-lib a routine."[25]

Yet efforts to bring the real world to the debates can prove destructive. Candidates consistently refuse to answer hypothetical questions because such questions lock them into a choice between fulfilling abstract promises in specific circumstances or lying to the public. Hypothetical questions by definition ignore the niceties of

In the first debate of 1960, Nixon's televised image undercut the cogency of his argument. The marked contrast between the visual image he projected in that debate and in the three subsequent debates raised the question: To what extent do factors irrelevant to governance impinge on our evaluation of presidential debates? (*Library of Congress*)

context. Answering them risks placing unwise constraints on future presidential action.

Debates' Pictures May Speak the Wrong Words

Since viewers are more disposed to respond to the impression created by a televised message than its substance, by the pictures it conveys rather than the words, those who are naturally telegenic have an advantage not related to their competence or command of the issues. Unfortunately, voters sometimes leap from personal appearance of a candidate to a judgment about that person's ability to lead.[26] Bruce Babbitt's poor TV performance proved costly in the first presidential debate of 1987. Those who have "lost" debates find comfort although not incumbency in this fact. So, the night after his 1980 debate with Reagan, Carter wrote, "In the debate itself it was hard to judge the general demeanor that was projected to the viewers. Reagan was, 'Aw, shucks, this and that. I'm a grandfather, and . . . I love peace,' etc. He had his memorized lines, and he pushes a button and they come out. Apparently made a better impression on the TV audience than I did."[27]

The recollection of the shadowy, shifty-eyed Nixon projected in the first debate of 1960 has forced the attention of consultants on appearance in debates. Before deciding to issue the challenge to debate in 1976, Ford's advisers asked themselves how he'd look on a debate stage. "We also considered the experience of Kennedy and Nixon in the 1960 debates," recalls Ford aide Dick Cheney. "To the extent that physical and stylistic factors were important in public perceptions of who would 'win' or 'lose' the debates, we believed our candidate would come off well. The President's physical size and presence presented none of the negatively perceived characteristics which had supposedly caused Nixon to lose the first debate to Kennedy in 1960."[28]

We can be seriously misled by the nonverbal communication on which television dotes and to which we almost involuntarily gravitate. In the first presidential debate of 1960, Nixon—pale from a hospital stay and perspiring under the hot studio lights—evinced cues that can, but do not necessarily, signal stress. By giving him a sinister look, the beard apparent under his poorly made-up translucent skin complicated matters further. Nixon glanced repeatedly at a clock just off stage. In a bearded, pale, perspiring candidate, this invited the inappropriate inference that Nixon was shifty-eyed.

Additionally, the freshly painted set had dried to a color lighter than that anticipated by Nixon's consultants. Consequently the gray suit he wore blended into the background, blurring his image. Finally, an injury to his knee as he alighted his limousine caused him pain. By shifting weight from that knee to the podium he minimized the pain, but at high cost. During his hospital stay, he had lost weight. His suit, as a result, was a bit large for him. As he leaned on the podium for support, the suit shifted forward on one shoulder, suggesting that he had, perhaps, purchased it second hand or borrowed it from a friend. In a fitted blue suit, his face sun-tanned, Kennedy looked more decisive than his pale, ill-suited, eye-shifting opponent. Although some indict its small sample size, one survey found that those who heard the first debate on radio thought Nixon the winner, where those who saw it on television gave the debate to Kennedy. Even that first presidential debate reveals the candidates' consciousness of the picture they were creating. Dogged by the charge that he was too inexperienced to lead the nation, Kennedy looked resolute. At one point he caught a glimpse of himself on the studio monitor and reacted by assuming a determined expression. As Nixon spoke, Kennedy took notes as if in anticipation of rebuttal. To minimize his youthful look, Kennedy trimmed his bushy hair.

By contrast, Nixon sought to overcome the notion that he was cold and forbidding. Where nary a smile crosses Kennedy's lips, Nixon smiles and nods warmly. It is one such moment of visually communicated "warmth" that was intercut by the Democrats into a Kennedy ad designed to suggest that Nixon agreed with Kennedy on key points. Republicans charged duplicity. The Democrats denied it. Reporters never bothered to check the film to determine who was telling the truth.[29] And where the make-up failed to adequately mask his beard, Nixon had one other facial cue under control. To mute the menacing look that comes when stark black eyebrows slash across a pale forehead, the vice president trimmed them.

The problems posed by make-up did not end with Lazy-Shave. In the fall 1987 "Firing Line" Republican debate, make-up artists shadowed pink cherubic cheeks onto Robert Dole. In the 1976 vice presidential debate, Dole had joked that Walter Mondale's make-up seemed to have been applied by George Meany. In 1987, Dole would have been better served by the level of skill that in 1976 had camouflaged the bags under Mondale's eyes.

Aware of the power of television, candidates jockey for visual

In reaction shots in the first debate, Kennedy deliberately assumed a resolute posture and earnest expression. By contrast, Nixon appeared shifty-eyed and tired. (*Library of Congress*)

advantage in pre-debate negotiations. In 1960, for example, Kennedy's and Nixon's advisers played out the great thermostat war in the television studio in which one of the debates was held. To minimize their candidate's tendency to perspire, Nixon's advisers dropped the temperature; to increase the likelihood that Nixon would be flooded in sweat and to create a climate more comfortable for their candidate, whose unrevealed Addison's disease meant that he was easily chilled, Kennedy's advisers hiked the temperature up.[30]

Throughout this century the taller of the two major party candidates has been the safer bet to win the election. In an election in which that wager would have been a losing one, the shorter candidate, Jimmy Carter, did all that television and orthotics permitted to appear taller. To minimize Ford's advantage, Carter reportedly wore lifts in his shoes during the debates. Additionally, since Ford was three and a half inches taller than Carter, the negotiators agreed in 1976 to the "belt buckle rule." Ford's lectern intersected his torso two and a half inches above his belt; Carter's, one and one-half inches above his. The distances were derived by measuring the inches between the floor and the taller candidate's belt buckle[31] and then splitting the difference.

Those who think such things are silly might ask how they responded to the awareness that 1988 Democratic prospect Michael Dukakis was substantially shorter than the candidates on either side of him in the NBC December 1987 debate. As the camera panned candidates who were being introduced by anchor, Tom Brokaw, it dropped noticeably between Bruce Babbitt and Michael Dukakis and then jumped back up to include Jesse Jackson.

Advisers have also taken care that negative stereotypes not be inadvertently reinforced. To ensure that Ford would not repeat a comedy routine by Chevy Chase, who delighted "Saturday Night Live" viewers with an imitation of Ford tripping down stairs, entangling himself in his phone cords, and falling off chairs, Ford's advisers insisted the water glass on each podium be secured with a brace.

The maneuvering continued in 1984 when "aides said even the lectern angle of eye-contact had been negotiated in advance to minimize the chance for a stare-down or a tell-tale self-doubting blink of an eye as the two veterans faced off in the hall."[32]

Such caution is reassuring for it minimizes the likelihood that irrelevant nonverbal cues will interfere with our judgment of the candidates.

Debates Could More Effectively Reveal the Character of the Candidate

The awareness that two presidents, one from each party, had lied about our conduct of the war in Vietnam coupled with the revelations of Watergate to prompt the press and public to focus attention on the private person who aspired to be president. After the promises of Ford and Carter failed to translate into performance, the distrust of public rhetoric grew. For a brief time, public confidence was restored by the Reagan presidency. In 1984 the country voted its belief that it was in fact better off than it had been four years before. Then the "morning in America" of Reagan's 1984 ads turned for some to mourning. The Iran-Contra hearings and the Tower Commission Report revealed that Reagan was not all that the public image promised him to be. With the stock markét fall came additional public concern that promises do not necessarily translate into long-term performance. At issue then are two characteristics: competence and what the authors of the *Federalist Papers* called virtue or character. In their ads, candidates asserted that they possessed both. Yet verifying the actual presence of these elusive phenomena proved difficult.

Nixon's debates with Kennedy and then his gubernatorial debates with Pat Brown shelter no hint of a disposition to deceive or act beyond the law. Only in his campaign against Helen Gahagan Douglas, a contest that by 1960 was ancient history, did Nixon's tactics approximate those of Watergate. And then the foreshadowing could be found not in debates but in posters and stump speeches.

The one instance in which we know that a debater deliberately lied in what he perceived to be the interests of the country occurred in 1960. Since it was not revealed until well after Kennedy's election and since it was then disclosed by the candidate, its presence in the history of debates does not provide us with a cue useful in an immediate voting decision.

In the fourth debate of 1960, Kennedy favored U.S. involvement in the overthrow of Castro in Cuba. In *Six Crises* Nixon explained his options:

> One course would be simply to state that what Kennedy was advocating
> as a new policy was already being done, had been adopted as a policy as
> a result of my direct support, and that Kennedy was endangering the

security of the whole operation by his public statement. But this would be, for me, an utterly irresponsible act: it would disclose a secret operation and completely destroy its effectiveness.

There was only one thing I could do. The covert operation had to be protected at all costs. I must not even suggest by implication that the United States was rendering aid to rebel forces in and out of Cuba. In fact, I must go to the other extreme: I must attack the Kennedy proposal to provide such aid as wrong and irresponsible because it would violate our treaty commitments.[33]

Nixon's cover was also problematic. After the Bay of Pigs took place, world leaders could point to an articulate rejection of U.S. policy in the words of a sitting vice president. The candidate caught in a security dilemma cannot count on serving the national interest by attacking secret policies.

In the spontaneity that debates were thought to provide, some saw the hope that the person would be revealed. Such hopes were in the main unrealistic.

In 1976 Jimmy Carter and Gerald Ford shattered the illusion that debates are exercises in spontaneous adaptation when for twenty-seven eternal minutes they froze mannequin-like on the debate stage as repair crews sought out and repaired the cause of a malfunction in the sound system. An alien interpreting our culture through a videotape of that debate justifiably might conclude that during the quarter-century of television's dominance of politics, those who wished to be president evolved to a state in which speech was possible only when amplified and movement only with speech. The Malinowskis of that millennium might conjecture that our presidential campaigns also tested a candidate's self-possession. At moments when they least expected it, candidates were required to sustain long periods of silent scrutiny by the assembled nation.

Debates are not Edenic communicative forms. Fig leaves and half-eaten apples abound. After the fourth debate of 1960, critic Max Ascoli observed that in such settings the "protagonists are bound to behave like two talking univac machines, each conditioned to recite a pre-taped message in answer to a foreseeable challenge from the other."[34]

So, for example, Carter aide Stuart Eizenstat reported in 1976 that his group had almost 100% success in guessing which questions would be asked. "Then we tried in the briefing material to give him a model answer in a well-organized fashion."[35] We can almost hear the wheels grinding as Carter recalls the structure he has committed to memory from the briefing book. Within his answer to the question Why does he consider nuclear power plants unsafe? Carter states: "There ought to be a full-time atomic energy specialist, independent of the power company in the control room, full time, twenty four hours a day, to shut down a plant if an abnormality develops. These kinds of procedures, along with evacuation procedures, adequate insurance, ought to be initiated." Then in the abbreviated style of a briefing page, he concludes: "So, shift from oil to coal, emphasize research and development on coal use and also on solar power, strict conservation measures, not yield every time that the special interest groups put pressure on the president like this administration has done, and use atomic energy only as a last resort with the strictest possible safety precautions."

Their Darwinian instincts honed, candidates have developed the ability to evade tough questions and repeat stock answers. "[O]n every domestic issue," wrote David Stockman of Reagan's preparation for the Reagan–Anderson debate, "the staff kept leading him back to a pat answer. Chrysler? It's a symptom of Carter's failed economy. Farm subsidies? More Carter failure. Aid to the cities? Still more Carter failure."[36]

The effectiveness of this process of self-protection may account in part for the finding that most presidential debates don't markedly alter the electorate's perceptions of the candidates. When perception does change, that change generally favors the less well-known candidate, Kennedy in the first debate of 1960 and Reagan in the debates of 1980. Since the first debate draws the most viewers and exercises the most control over the candidate's image, newcomers who fare poorly there, as did Carter in 1976, sacrifice their chance to polish their image.

Candidates seem more preoccupied with seeming competent than with responding to questions with relevant, accurate detail. In 1960, Kennedy's debate performance would suggest that he regarded the ability to recite facts, whether of relevance to the question or not, as a central criterion to be met by one who would be president. "Not even a trained political observer could keep up with the crossfire of fact and counter-fact, of the rapid references to Rockefeller Reports, Lehman amendments, prestige analyses, GNP, and a potpourri of other so-called facts," noted Douglass Cater after the 1960 debates. "Or was the knack of merely seeming well informed what counted with the viewer?"[37] Recurring in the candidates' confessions about their preparation for debates is the notion of cramming. "I had crammed my head with facts and figures in answer to more than a hundred questions which my staff suggested might be raised in the field of domestic affairs," recalled Nixon of the first debate of 1960.[38] We hear hints of this bias toward fact for fact's sake in Carter aide Stuart Eizenstat's recollection that it was crucial that his candidate, a challenger who had not before held federal office, "convince people that he had a grasp of the issues. So it was important that he know a great deal of facts, a lot about programs, and the like."[39]

But this flaw is not unique to debates. In 1960 both the stump speeches and the debates substituted fact flaunting for analysis. Indeed, one researcher found that practice more prevalent in speeches than in the debates of that year.[40]

Those who view command of fact as a prerequisite for holding the presidency are alarmed by the number of times in the course of each debate that a candidate has misused or misstated data. The 1976 debates "afforded the two candidates opportunity to make more misrepresentations, false claims, calculated appeals and empty promises than probably ever were offered so directly to a long-suffering electorate," noted columnist Tom Wicker.[41] Although the United States had backed the previous regime until its demise, Ford credited his administration with the emergence of democracy in Portugal, for example. Those who see effective management and sensible use of advisers as more important in a president than fact hoarding take no comfort in the misinformation candidates have spouted in debates.

Despite Ellsworth's finding that in the debates of 1960 the candidates "devote[d] more time to giving statements of position, offering evidence for their positions, and giving reasoned arguments to support them" than they did in speeches, the argument, evidence, and reasoning found in debates are far from ideal. "Their argument was shallow, often defective in reasoning and evidence," noted rhetoric scholars Lloyd Bitzer and Theodore Reuter of the 1976 debates, "and seldom went beyond the commonplaces uttered for the stump."[42]

Debates Could More Effectively Reveal the Extent to which the Candidate Will Grow in the Job

Rather than exposing whether and how a candidate will grow in the job, debates may reinforce tendencies undesirable in one who would govern.

Debates Reward Some Behaviors Undesirable in a President

Debates foster habits that one would hope would not be reflected in a presidency, including a willingness to offer solutions instantaneously, an ability to simplify complex problems, and a talent for casting the world in Manichean terms. At their worst, debates invite candidates to make distinctions where only shades of difference exist and encourage simplifications that credit neither the candidates nor their audience. When seeking an office that daily requires subtle thinking and nuanced distinctions, a form of discourse that either invites or elicits glib slogan-using should be scrutinized with care. Few are exempt from these tendencies:

> *Mondale:* Mr. Dole has probably the worst record in favor of loopholes of any senator in the United States Senate. Mr. Ford has one of the worst records in favor of tax loopholes in the history of the House of Representatives. I have one of the best records of tax reform in the United States Senate.

> *Mondale:* He [Carter] will not destroy the housing program for senior citizens as this Republican administration has done.

> *Dole:* He [Mondale] votes for every piece of spending legislation that comes down the pike . . . unless it's in the area of defense, and then he votes for every budget cut.

> *Carter:* The present tax structure is a disgrace to this country; it's just a welfare program for the rich.

> *Reagan:* The Soviet Union has been engaged in the biggest military buildup in the history of man at the same time that we tried the policy of unilateral disarmament.

In debates, candidates rarely credit opponents with anything worthwhile. So, for example, Carter repeatedly allies Ford with anything unfavorable about the Nixon administration. But when he comes to praise the opening of China it is "we," not Nixon or the Republicans who are given the credit.

In 1980, Ronald Reagan's amiable manner dismissed fears that as president he would destroy Social Security or prove trigger-happy. In a decisive moment in the debate, he dispatched attacks by the incumbent president with the charge "There you go again." Carter's hyperbolic assaults on Reagan were undercut more effectively by Reagan's demeanor than by his argument. (*League of Women Voters Education Fund*)

And debates can lead presidential candidates to promise policies that as president they should not deliver. In 1976, for example, both Ford and Carter abjured secret presidential decision making.

Moreover, when an incumbent debates, sensitive national security information is put at risk, a factor that may invite a president to lie. So, after the final presidential debate of 1960, columnist James Reston breathed a sigh of relief. "[I]t may not be in the national interest," he noted, "to get into strategic plans for dealing with Cuba, Quemoy, and Matsu on a presentation of this kind."[43] In 1986 former President Richard Nixon wrote the Twentieth Century Taskforce on presidential debates that "under no circumstances should Presidential candidates debate each other during wartime. It would have been highly irresponsible for Franklin D. Roosevelt to have debated Tom Dewey in 1944. And a very serious question could be raised as to whether it would have served the national interest for him to have debated Willkie in 1940 in view of the danger that Roosevelt's highly sensitive secret negotiations with the British might have been exposed and caused not only enormous controversy at home but also, even more troublesome, given aid and comfort to Hitler."[44] Indeed, in 1972 Nixon had used just such an argument to explain why he would not debate McGovern. A president was not in a position to reveal all that he knew on an issue, noted the chief executive.

Summary

Part of the problem pervading discussion of debates is the public expectation that they are a self-sufficient multivitamin with iron. We expect more than any form could possibly deliver. There is only so much that can be accomplished in an hour and a half or two hours. Selecting one form over another involves inevitable trade-offs. How presidential debates could better display the style and substance of the previewed presidency and the person who aspires to craft it is the question we turn to in our last chapter.

♦

CHAPTER 7

The Promise of Debates

Not since Nixon and Humphrey in 1968 have both major parties nominated non-incumbents for the presidency as they have in 1988. Unadvantaged and unencumbered by a record of White House decision making, both candidates are likely to see self-interest served in the exposure and legitimacy offered by debates. And should one or the other be inclined to demur, the expectations created in the public and press by the debates of 1976, 1980, and 1984 will invite words that carry powerful inducements—including *fairness* and *accountability*—and words that convey painful penalties—including *cowardice*. We expect skies to be blue. We expect brides to wear white. And since the last three incumbents have debated, we expect presidential candidates to debate. Moreover, the two major parties have agreed on the dates of four 1988 general election debates. So arm-twisting provides an additional incentive. What this means is that 1988 is likely to go down in history as the year that presidential debates became as certain as taxes and . . . taxes.

The debates of 1988 offer an immediate opportunity to reconsider the flawed format of their predecessors. Even if fashioned by angels and executed by saints, debates cannot reveal all that we would like to know about those aspiring to lead. Nor can they function as the political equivalent of *Everything You Always Wanted to Know about Sex but Were Afraid to Ask*. An alternative format will not propel millions more to the polls or thousands more to devour substantive books about issues. *Playboy* will continue to outsell *The New Republic* and *The National Review*. And free association will still prompt many to guess that Dole is a pineapple company, DuPont a chemical company, and Babbitt a character some teacher once mentioned in English class. In charting a course for improvement, we must not overburden the form. As one of our grandmothers was fond of noting, "You can't get blood from a turnip. But you can get a decent soup."

Before asking the composition of the broth, we might productively summarize the problems televised presidential debates pose for the confrontation, timing, participants, propositions, and judging of a traditional debate.

Confrontation

Moderated debates and press panels minimize confrontation in two respects. First, even though everyone may appear in the same place at the same time, the candidates no longer confront one another directly. Panelists, usually members of the press, sometimes pose questions that can only be answered by one of the debaters. Even when the questions do address disagreements, the debaters are rarely able to provide more than oblique responses to an opponent's position. Moderators often prevent clashes. When in a February 1988 Democratic primary debate Michael Dukakis objected to Albert Gore's characterization of his gubernatorial record, moderator Roger Mudd quashed the argument, assuring the governor that he would get his "chance" later.[1]

A second problem with clash in the contemporary format is the character of the exchanges that emerge between candidates and reporters. When they challenge candidates in interruptions and follow-ups, the locus of confrontation shifts from politician-politician to questioner-politician. Voters find out not how a candidate responds to a political opponent, but how the candidate responds to a third point of view that may have little to do with either of the candidates. Such information may be interesting, but it inevitably complicates the clash.

Equal and Adequate Time

Debate values an advocate's ability to distill complex material into manageable blocks of time. Such a facility is valuable until the time pressures become so intense that slogans displace arguments. In televised debates, candidates are asked to perform miracles of compression, explaining complex positions on major issues in less than a minute. The Brown–Black Coalition debates of January 1988, one of the few to offer direct candidate confrontation, required that questions be put in fifteen seconds, answers made in forty-five.[2]

This breakneck pace contrasts sharply with that of the nineteenth century when debaters often continued arguments for days. Daniel Webster delivered his famous reply to Hayne over two days. In 1858, Abraham Lincoln and Stephen Douglas met for seven debates of three hours each, and those twenty-one hours were all devoted to the extension of slavery to the territories. Today's debates may cover multiple topics in a single meeting, allowing proportionally less time for the development of any one issue. In one day of debating, Lincoln and Douglas could each count on ninety minutes to develop a position, sharing their time with no one. Today's debaters will probably be limited to two hours that will be parceled out among the moderator, the questioners, and the candidates.

The need for more time is obvious; however, American audiences accustomed to the half-hour sitcom are unlikely to sit for hours as candidates detail their positions on television. Long speeches are not only taxing, but expensive, especially if more than two candidates join in debate. Solutions to the time crunch must take account of the episodic character of television programming and respond to the viewing habits of the modern audience.

Matched Contestants

Matching contestants in presidential debating is difficult. The idea of a match begs the very questions that debates are supposed to help answer. The different opinions about what the nation needs in a leader, the diverse kinds of evidence offered by representatives of competing political factions, and the tendency of audiences to think that their favored candidates "win," regardless of academic debate standards, make the notion of matched contestants difficult to describe, let alone produce.

A Stated Proposition

Presidential debates do not revolve around specific propositions or even single topics. Candidates participating in a panel discussion are asked to address a host of unrelated issues from tax policy to arms control to campaign strategy. Topics shift with the questioner and the minute. Though they can make informed guesses as to the likely issue areas, candidates are not generally allowed to know specifically what will be discussed before actually hearing the questions.

Without a stated proposition, debates lose their focus. Issues fragment without a controlling claim to marshal the smaller pieces of information. As a result, the ideas offered in debate may not be directly or clearly competitive with one another. In one Republican primary debate in January 1988, the candidates presented different ideas about the stability and desirability of the Social Security system. George Bush defended the soundness of the system. Robert Dole said that when the system had been threatened, he and other members of Congress arranged a rescue package. Pete DuPont and Pat Robertson indicted the system as fatally flawed and said that an alternative would be needed soon. Jack Kemp noted that the soundness of the system was attributable to general economic trends, not Dole's "rescue" package. The lack of a single proposition confused the exchange, making any sort of resolution difficult.

Stated propositions would invite more coherent debates, but such focused contests bear some costs as well. First, propositional debate limits the breadth of issue coverage in favor of deeper treatments. Although useful when training, inquiry, and edification are the goals, it is of less benefit when trying to assess the qualities of a would-be president. To hear candidates cover the range of issues they would be likely to face in office, many propositional debates would be required.

Second, and more important, propositional debate is geared to the examination of issues, not candidates. In the Social Security exchange, the debaters might have been able to carry on a reasonable debate about the proposition "The United States' Social Security system should be retained in its present form." Bush and Dole would have argued variations on the affirmative; DuPont and Robertson would have taken the negative. It is unlikely, however, that any one candidate would have been happy simply to win that argument. They wanted to make points about leadership and vision, neither of which fit neatly into this version of the propositional format.

A Judge's Decision

The emphasis on wins and losses limits unnecessarily the role of debating in presidential elections. Debate under such circumstances need not be a zero-sum game. In addition to rendering a victor, debates can produce information, new perspectives on a candidate's personal qualities, increased respect for all the participants, and an improved sense of the alternatives for addressing policy problems. These are not, by and large, the elements of political debating that receive press attention. They are nonetheless important contributions of debate that escape the narrow competitive focus usually applied to the activity.

In addressing the diverse American electorate, candidates must appeal not only to the formal argumentative prejudices of elites, but to popular passions as well. Ronald Reagan's "I paid for this microphone, Mr. Green" remains the definitive statement of the 1980 debates.[3] Such moments reveal personal character more vividly than any collection of policy statements ever can. Character concerns, beyond rules governing the distortion of evidence and deportment, are not treated in the formal judging standards. If anything, such concerns are suppressed; the judge must vote for the more ably presented case while despising the presenter. The nation does not and could not tolerate such a standard in arguments over presidential politics. Character concerns will continue to play a large role in the evaluation of presidential debates, a role that will resist codification in the same way a perfect list of presidential qualities eludes political bosses.

The Framework for Change

If asked, educators and theorists of persuasion would lay down a few simple principles that account for the inability of the presidential debates to change attitudes markedly or drastically raise the knowledge level of the moderately interested or poorly informed. Exposure to any single piece of communication rarely produces attitude change. A more likely consequence is reinforcement of existing beliefs. Those who are best informed to begin with will get the most from exposure to postcards signaling stands on issues. Moreover, learning is in part a function of motivation. Those who have been ill disposed to concentrate on politics are unlikely suddenly to devote all their energy to a ninety-minute learning experience. And even when motivation spikes attention, new vocabulary needs time to sink in. Definitions must be embedded. Time is required to get past surface meanings to substance. Through it all, as advertisers who bombard us with the same jingle know, redundancy is correlated with retention. Accepting these precepts as a form of received wisdom, we recommend that we overhaul our concept of campaigns to include planned speeches, debates, "conversations," and press conferences; alter the format of the general election debates and institute party sponsorship of them; invite alternative press practices; and experiment with alternative forms and formats in the primaries.

Overhaul Our Concept of Campaign Communication

To increase the electorate's understanding of the issues, the candidates, and the campaign, we recommend that candidates, press, and public conceive of the election as a campaign composed of a series of distinct but equally important communicative events. No single event can capsulize the wide range of information pertinent to the quadrennial elections, let alone the considerable political agenda discharged between presidential races. The first events would precede the general election by years. Earlier we argued that the electorate was better served when even less educated voters could distinguish between the two major parties and assume that the party's nominee embraced most of what the party stood for. Throughout the book we have claimed that educating voters on the intricacies of issues is better accomplished when it can be separated from questions about the talents and temperaments of the nominees. We have noted as well the advantage in having someone other than news-driven reporters set the agenda for debates.

To frame the electoral agenda, invite education about issues, and provide incentives for parties to sculpt and communicate clear identities, we embrace the proposal offered in 1973 by former FCC director Newton Minow and his associates that "between elections, the national committee of the opposition party, the national committee of the president's party, and the commercial and public television networks should together develop a plan to present live debates—'The National Debates'—between spokesmen for the two major parties with agreed topics and formats quarterly each year (but only twice in federal election years). All debates should be scheduled during prime time and broadcast simultaneously by all networks. This proposal should be carried out voluntarily by the parties and networks rather than be required by legislation."[4] Ads and news coverage would direct public attention to these events as would actual broadcast on all major channels at prime times scheduled well in advance.

Our goal during the general election itself would be to create in the electorate a hunger for political information akin to the addictive lure of the Superbowl and to invite voters to satisfy that need by viewing the acceptance speeches at conventions, one set of Labor Day speeches, three debates, a set of press conferences, and a pair of election eve programs. If an audience as large as that drawn to the Redskins and the Broncos is beyond reasonable expectation, the body politic would still be better off than it presently is if an audience of the size drawn to the televised Kentucky Derby could be attracted. By making these waystations topics of national discussion—as debates now are—we invite increased consumption of the print media that best preview, explain, and contextualize them. But where debates are a sometime thing, ill suited to developing a habit of news seeking, the predictable, recurring pattern forecast here could provide an incentive for information seeking. Meanwhile, of course, the sheer availability of press coverage would make it likely that a reader would chance on a discussion of them en route to the sports page.

Acceptance speeches at party conventions would explain how the candidate relates to the party's tradition and identity and would rally partisans behind that cause. In the calmer, more reflective environment of a prime-time speech to the nation, in back-to-back half hours, each candidate would articulate the issues central to the country and forecast those means of addressing them that would be developed in the campaign and defended in the debates. Spot advertising could then reinforce and dramatize these themes without substituting for a systematic treatment of them. In at least three ninety-minute debates sponsored by the parties, the candidates would address these issues at length and in depth. One debate would partially mimic the Lincoln–Douglas form; the second, a conversational form. The third debate would follow any format on which the two candidates could agree. If they failed to agree, the format would repeat that of the first debate.

We would also institute a general election press conference for each major party candidate. The night after the third debate, each candidate would hold a one-hour nationally televised press conference. Reporters credentialed to the White House would act as questioners. The press conference would focus on follow-up questions raised and not resolved by the debates. Finally, on election eve, each candidate would spend one hour in any way he or she considers appropriate summarizing the similarities and differences between the candidates and their visions of the future.

This proposal invites voters to devote eight and one-half hours beyond the conventions to focused analysis of the merits of the candidates and their ideas—less time than that given to holiday football or the World Series. Exposure to spot ads and news coverage could then build on a knowledge base deepened elsewhere.

Alter the Format of the General Election Debates

Abandon the Press Panel for a Form of Direct Confrontation Similar to Lincoln–Douglas

The first debate would consist of a moderator and the two candidates. Each would open with an eight-minute statement followed by six-minute segments for restatement and rebuttal and two time slots of four minutes each for elaboration. The moderator would intervene only if the candidates veered from the agreed-on topic. This is a twentieth-century equivalent of the Lincoln–Douglas format. Lincoln, not a panel of journalists, posed the questions for Douglas and vice versa.

Only the candidates favor the buffer provided by a press panel. When the field had narrowed to three candidates in 1984, both CBS and NBC adopted the conversational format in their primary debates. Dick Wald of ABC, who coordinated talks between the networks and the Reagan and Mondale camps in 1984, articulated the networks' ideal: "network presentation would create a 'direct confrontation' between the candidates, to allow the greatest room for them to expose their views and differences."[5]

The League of Women Voters, which sponsored the general election debates of 1976, 1980, and 1984, favors elimination of the panel,[6] but has repeatedly succumbed to candidate pressure to interpose press representatives nonetheless. Many who have served as panelists oppose that format as well. Five of the eleven panelists who responded to a survey suggested that debates could be improved by eliminating the panel.[7] They are joined by influential players from the reportorial community. "[O]ne skilled moderator is all the provocation that's required," noted a *New York Times* editorial in September 1984.[8]

Eliminating the panel would reduce the focus on the politics of the campaign and minimize as well the invitation to produce "news." It also would remove reporters from the story they are covering. Whenever reporters do the job of panelists, observes David Broder, "we inject ourselves into the campaign . . . and become players, not observers."[9] Gone too would be multiple questions disguised as one, the mini-speeches that have been incorporated into some panel questions, the hostile question, the one-sided question, and the possibility that the press will divert public attention from the substance of governance to the politics of the campaign.

Focus on a Limited Number of Topics

By focusing on topics, questions appropriately answered only by one candidate will be eliminated, as will multiple queries guised as a single question and questions that unfairly advantage or disadvantage one candidate.

Candidates favor panels for the buffer they provide. Reporters, not the candidates, ask the tough questions of the opponent. Nominees also favor the predictable questions and the ability provided by that format to deliver set speeches and avoid engaging the opponent. By concentrating on a limited number of topics, we would offer the candidates a different sort of predictability.

In the general election, the parties' nominees would focus on the topics addressed in the party debates. Addressing a single topic—such as ways of controlling inflation, or an incumbent's policies toward the Soviet Union—would minimize the candidates' ability to obscure their positions, unfairly attack their opponents, and misstate evidence. The risks in repeating the same statement in different words would rise.

The means of selecting the topics exist. The national polls regularly report which issues the electorate considers most important. In 1976 the Public Agenda Foundation even conducted special polls to determine the topics voters wanted to see discussed in the campaign and apprised the public and candidates of its findings.[10]

If the candidates devoted their Labor Day speeches to topics other than those debated in the nonelection-year party debates, the last of the three debates would focus on two previously undebated topics the candidates consider most central. Each candidate would be permitted to name one of the two topics to be analyzed in the last two-hour block of time. The focus on a single topic would increase the coherence of debates. Where now topic areas career wildly, minimizing education and encouraging sloganeering, sustained inquiry would be promoted by a more limited focus.

Debates Should Center on "Modified Propositions"
Much of the strength of nineteenth-century American debates derived from sustained attention to single propositions. Not until a topic had been much discussed were such clear propositions framed. But once framed, with alternative positions identified, each was well tested in the forum created by classical debate. By displacing single propositions with flurries of questions from interrogating panelists, modern presidential debates have sacrificed the ability to reveal comparative strengths of competing positions, a comparison inevitable in traditional debate. At the same time, contemporary debates have strangled their ability to educate an audience that could, in the sustained clash of a traditional propositionally based debate, come to understand the nuances of an issue as well as its implications.

Consensus was reached or divisions clarified and audiences both elite and popular informed by debates that addressed such focused questions as whether slavery should be sanctioned in the new territories or whether opponents of slavery should be permitted to present petitions from constituents to the Congress. Some were as particular as "Should Andrew Johnson be removed from the presidency under the impeachment clause of the Constitution?" Others were as broad as whether states have the authority to abrogate federal dictates they consider repugnant. Where the impeachment debates concerned Johnson's specific conduct in office, at issue in Hayne–Webster was the general nature of the relationship between the states and the Union. The difference in topic masks the similarity in the form of the debates. Each debate was contested over some single proposed action or class of actions.

In the modified propositional debate, candidates would address themselves to propositionally focused topic areas rather than resolutions embodying a single solution. Where the intercollegiate debate model would require a proposition, such as weapons developed under the Strategic Defense Initiative should be deployed, the modified format would ask, How should the United States protect itself from nuclear attack? The second version does not specify a single solution and invite contest over it but rather asks candidates to articulate their philosophies and solutions and compare them to their opponents'. Education on differences between the candidates and their positions on the issue, rather than in the issue per se, should remain the central task of presidential debates.

A Conversational Format Should Be Instituted
Alongside the Traditional Form
The second debate would be followed by the conversational format employed by the networks in the 1984 primaries. Seated at a table, the two candidates would discuss the topic; the moderator would introduce questions, focus discussion, and arbitrate feuds. This format was used successfully in the Houston primary debate of 1980 and the Rather and Brokaw moderated debates in the 1984 primaries.

The CBS debate was aired from the Low Library at Columbia University just before the 1984 New York primary. The NBC debate originated in a Burbank studio and was broadcast shortly before the New Jersey and California primaries. "These dignified but lively debates went well," recalled Brokaw. "The single moderator format facilitated a coherent, continuous line of questioning. The candidates were easily encouraged to comment on or respond to statements by one of the other candidates. A great many issues were covered in some detail. All the candidates and their managers expressed admiration for the format and gratitude for the opportunity."[11]

The risk in the Lincoln–Douglas form is twofold. By lengthening candidates' statements, the form limits the total number of responses by each. Conditioned by decades of television as entertainment, accustomed to rapid action and waves of visual stimuli, the marginally interested viewer might respond by fleeing to another channel. No intervening panel and moderator can ride herd on the candidate who transforms the debate into a series of set speeches. To hold such candidates accountable, we have built a conversational form and a press conference into our projected campaign.

When the goal of classical debate involves determining which of two sides can marshal the stronger case, and when the audience is already knowledgeable about the issue, the form serves well. In American politics, congressional debates, including Hayne–Webster and the Petition debates, were conducted before an informed Congress. Debates before the Supreme Court presuppose a disinterested and educated panel of judges. In both cases, the immediate audience is able to identify misrepresentation and to hold those who would violate expectations accountable. But in contemporary elections, the audience is neither disinterested nor well informed. The presence of a neutral, knowledgeable authority is thus required. The general election presidential debates have suffered from the absence of that authority.

We would introduce this authority in two ways. First, a prominent journalist or academic would moderate a "conversation" with the two major party candidates. We would also ask broadcast reporters to adopt from their print press cousins the role of post-debate adjudicator.

Although the classical debate format invites clash, it provides no means of enforcing it. In their efforts to be most things to most people, candidates have become adept at ignoring touchy issues, ducking tough questions, and couching controversial positions in calculated ambiguity. Additionally, some candidates have refused to legitimize their opponents by acknowledging the existence of the attacks that are being levied at them. With this strategy, for example, Edward Kennedy successfully dispatched Eddie McCormack in the Massachusetts Senate race of 1962. The conversational form denies a candidate such shelter, a fact dramatically illustrated in the February 23, 1984, Democratic primary debate when Barbara Walters probed Jesse Jackson's attitudes toward the U.S. Jewish community.

WALTERS: Much of your press coverage this week has dealt with charges that you are anti-Semitic, and you have charged that Jewish groups are hounding you. You are accused by the *Washington Post* as referring to New York Jews as "hymies," and you have said that you cannot recall saying that. But on September 28, 1979, the *New York Times* reported your having said, and I quote, "I'm sick and tired about hearing constantly about the Holocaust. The Jews don't have a monopoly on suffering." That same month, on the program "60 Minutes," in speaking of terrorist attacks, you put the PLO and Israel in the same basket. Let's try to clear some of this up and give you an opportunity to answer. Is it unreasonable to think that such statements might be interpreted as being anti-Israel and anti-Semitic?

JACKSON: That's unfortunate, really. I'm convinced that, first of all, we ought to put this matter in context, have a major dialogue with leaders, and then put the matter to rest and move on to the higher agenda of social justice. I am not anti-Semitic. It is unfortunate that there is this continuous struggle, as it were, between black leadership and Jewish leadership. During the course of this campaign, I expect to meet with some leaders and presidents of Jewish organizations very soon. I am not anti-Semitic. And I do hope that during these next few months that the charges can be put to rest.[12]

In a debate with one-minute answers and limited opportunities for follow-up, the issue might have been dropped after Jackson's hopeful but unspecific remarks. The open-ended format of the conversation and Walters' political neutrality allowed her to pursue the question.

WALTERS: Let's put it to rest here. Have you made these statements?
JACKSON: These statements are out of context. First of all, I am not one inclined to call people by names that would be insulting. I intend to insult nobody.
WALTERS: Did you ever make that statement? Did you call any New York Jews "hymies" or New York "hymietown" or anything like that?
JACKSON: I have no recollection of that, and, furthermore, I have indicated that those who've said it—I've not seen them make that statement face to face. And during the course of this dialogue, perhaps even tonight, it will become even clearer. I am not anti-Semitic. I've proven to desire dialogue. I think the constant confrontations have irreparable damage, both to blacks and to Jews.
WALTERS: I would just like to stick to the question. Do you recall making either of the other two statements. I have exactly what was said, if you want me to read it, but—
JACKSON: Do read that again.
WALTERS: All right. "I'm sick and tired of hearing constantly about the Holocaust. The Jews don't have a monopoly on suffering." And in speaking with Dan Rather, when he talked about the PLO engaged in terrorism, you said, "One could easily say . . ." He said, "How can you compare it to Israel?" And you say, "Well, one could identify with Israel with the continuous violations they express in dropping their bombs in south Lebanon and using U.S. equipment. It's also terrorism."

JACKSON: The point is, the context of that is that both groups—blacks and Jews—have known suffering. That's what we really have in common, and we have known suffering. We have, should have, a real sensitivity one toward the other. That statement really was taken out of context. I have been a supporter of Israel's right to exist. But I'm also a human rights activist. I support Palestinians' right to exist also. I support a mutual recognition policy. Furthermore, I am convinced that so long as Israel is in a posture where it has to occupy and expand on the West Bank, it has a way of undercutting Israel's ability to be a democracy and to, in fact, have the moral authority that she needs. If our nation in fact uses its moral authority, it can expand upon Camp David. It can raise peace in that troubled region.[13]

Flexibility and opportunity for follow-up are the most compelling advantages of the conversation, but they rely on more than format. Walters could pursue Jackson successfully because she knew her material and controlled the questioning.

An experiment at Harvard in the fall of 1987 and the winter of 1987/88 confirms that when controlled by a skillful interviewer, the conversational form can reveal both the person and the policies of a candidate. These nationally aired "conversations" were hosted by Marvin Kalb, director of the Joan Shorenstein Barone Center. For thirty minutes, an individual candidate was interviewed by Kalb. During the second half hour, the candidate took questions from Harvard students and faculty in the audience. Kalb, who served as a questioner in one of the Reagan–Mondale debates of 1984 and who moderated "Meet the Press" from 1980 to 1987, prefers the Harvard format. "In 1984 there were four of us lined up to ask questions," he recalls. "We asked a question and a follow-up. The questions were written down. It was mechanistic, not human. In the Harvard format the candidates had more of an opportunity to be themselves and to give answers that were honest and straightforward. In 1984 they were giving short pre-canned speeches. This fall we listened to the precanned speech and then had the opportunity to go beyond it."

The comparative advantage of the conversation was apparent in the interview with Massachusetts governor Michael Dukakis. "I had on the basis of my research an image of this man as an Eleanor Roosevelt Democrat somewhat to the left of center concerned about the use of American military power," notes Kalb. "I was able to ask a sustained set of questions that produced results quite different from my earlier understanding of the man. For example, 'If the Russians move into Nicaragua, will you use American military power to eliminate the threat?' 'Yes.'

'If Gorbachev said he'd never be the first to use nuclear weapons, do you think that in an administration you could share that promise with the Russians?' 'No. I will not do that so long as we have a conventional imbalance not in our favor.'

'Would you remove any troops from Western Europe as part of an effort to cut the budget?' 'No. I would not.' We went into four or five such areas. When we were finished with that five-minute sequence, one had a strong impression, at least I did, that this was not a man who measured up to his earlier image."

Without the presence of a tenacious moderator, the conversational form can produce confusion, if not chaos. Too many candidates, too little focus, and uncontrolled interjection marred a conversation-style Republican primary debate held at Dartmouth College on January 16, 1988. Moderator John Chancellor was unable to restore order in a free-for-all over Social Security. After listening to candidate Pete DuPont's explanation of his plan to overhaul the Social Security system, Chancellor turned the question toward Bob Dole.

CHANCELLOR: Gee, I'll sign up for that [DuPont's proposal] that's a good . . . I want to ask Senator Dole, I thought you all fixed Social Security?

DOLE: Well, I thought I fixed it too, but, George Bush says he fixed it here in his little circular. And I don't recall George being in the loop then either. You know I don't think he attended a single meeting. But we did save Social Security. He takes credit for a lot of things. I was almost ready to vote for ya after I read that.

BUSH: I think a lot of people will.

DOLE: But in 1983, we put together a Social Security package. In 1982, Social Security was technically insolvent. We were borrowing money from different funds, we could mail out checks to some people in this audience. We put together a commission; the long and the short of it is the commission didn't almost collapse. I met Pat Moynihan one day—a liberal Democrat, a conservative Republican—we can't give up, we gotta try it one more time. Eleven days later we had an agreement and now we have a good Social Security system. We got about seventy billion dollars in reserves, and Pete, don't worry about those young people. But

I do agree with you, if you can gets IRAs or some other program so they can supplement their income. Social Security was never meant to be a full retirement program.

DUPONT: Well Bob, those reserves would be wonderful if they were there, but every one of us who paid in our Social Security dollar on the first of the month, eighty percent of it went to pay benefits and the other twenty percent you spent. It didn't go into some trust fund.

DOLE (interjecting): Oh no, no.

DUPONT: It's not building up, it's been spent. We need to get to a system to save those young people's retirement and . . . (unintelligible as Dole cuts in)

DOLE: Well, well, I'll try to explain it to ya afterwards when ya get a little more time, but, the system is sound. That's the point I want to make. The system is sound. It's gonna stay that way because the reserves are gonna continue to go up. I don't think we spent twenty percent of it, it all goes right in the Social Security trust fund.

DuPont and Kemp simultaneously:

DUPONT: Ji-Jim Baker wrote me a letter. Jim Baker wrote . . .

KEMP: (unintelligible)

DUPONT: . . . me a letter last month . . . last month that points out there is not a dollar in the trust fund. It is promises, it is IOUs, and we better fund it because a lot of people out there [are] depending on it and one presidential candidate at least has got a plan . . .

DuPont, Kemp, and Robertson simultaneously:

ROBERTSON: Let's make it two people, 'cause I've had one for a number of years.

KEMP: Actually . . .

DUPONT: . . . to help those young people in their retirement.

CHANCELLOR (loudly): Last word from Congressman Kemp. Very briefly.

KEMP: Thank you. They're both wrong. They both are wrong. George Bush and Bob Dole voted to freeze Social Security and raise taxes on Social Security recipients; what saved Social Security was not the tax increase . . .

DOLE (interjecting): It was the 1983 bill you voted against; you voted against the '83 bill.

KEMP: . . . Bob, it was getting inflation down and getting the economy growing and . . . ah . . . Pete and Pat would dismantle it by forcing young people to invest twice, once in an IRA and once in Social Security.

ALL: (unintelligible)

CHANCELLOR: One word. How can we expect you people to run a government. I mean . . .

KEMP: Aaah, it's a healthy debate.

CHANCELLOR: Last word, really.

BUSH: The Social, the Social Security trust fund is sound and don't fool around with the future of the people that are putting money in and that have already put it in. And to scare the American people by saying it's . . . (unintelligible) . . . is wrong.

ALL: (unintelligible except for snippets)

ROBERTSON: . . . the Social Security trust fund . . . there's no money in it! There is none.

DUPONT: John, I want to come back . . . I want to come back to Jack Kemp, because that's the third time in the campaign . . .

BUSH (interjecting): Here, let me help you.

DuPont, Kemp, and Chancellor, simultaneously:

DUPONT: That he has misrepresented something I said.

KEMP: That is not a misrepresentation.

CHANCELLOR: After the program please!

DUPONT: There is not forcing of anybody to go into this plan. It is an optional plan, you can do it if you want to set aside some money tax free.

Dole and Kemp simultaneously:

DOLE: But it costs billions of dollars, billions of dollars.

KEMP: What's the cost? One hundred billion dollars? One hundred billion dollars.

DUPONT: The cost, about, about twenty billion dollars a year, but it's to help people save for their retirement and I don't understand why everybody here is against it . . .

Chancellor and DuPont simultaneously:

CHANCELLOR: Our next questioner . . .

DUPONT: . . . except for Pete DuPont.

ROBERTSON: And Pat Robertson.

DUPONT: And Pat Robertson.

CHANCELLOR: Fair enough.

Most would dispute Representative Kemp's assessment that this exchange constituted a "healthy debate." No pair of candidates consistently addressed the same question about Social Security.

None provided needed clarification about the status of the Social Security trust fund. Since the confusing claims and counterclaims had occurred in previous debates, a moderator, alert to the likelihood of a repeat of debacles past, might have prepared a clarifying statement to frame and direct the argument. Without a way for the confused viewer to reconcile or reject the contradictory claims of "fact," an absence complicated by the din created by competing discussants, this presidential debate degenerated into a schoolboys' squabble.

To the moderator and the candidates falls the task of penalizing the candidate who simplifies, engages in sloganeering, and distorts. As the predicament in which Chancellor found himself illustrates, the burden this places on the moderator is immense.

Permit Use of Visual Aids
Earlier we suggested that sponsors believe that only by inviting brief answers and focusing on multiple topics can they hold the attention of the electorate. Yet brief answers and a smorgasbord of subjects minimize the substance of the candidates' answers, invite sloganeering and ambiguity, and permit controversial assertions to go unexamined and, if false, uncorrected. To hold viewers' attention while concentrating on a single topic in longer statements, we would recommend that the candidates and debate sponsors use the audiovisual capacity of television to interest and educate the electorate.

Production aids could be used to familiarize the viewing audience with the issues being discussed, "If, for example," argues Brokaw, "there is a spirited discussion about the Persian Gulf, why shouldn't it be accompanied by a visually appealing map of the area, showing the locations of the Gulf countries and their stake in the struggle for control? Obviously these visual aids should not overwhelm the participants or the issues, but if they help the voter/viewer follow the discourse, they should be included."[14] The educational utility of visual aids is underscored by the finding that most high school students cannot locate Nicaragua or Vietnam on a map.

To avoid transforming debates into contests between media consultants, we would limit candidates to clips of actual statements made by their opponents and to the use of maps, charts, and graphs to clarify their claims. In his presidential speeches Reagan has made skillful use of the visual capacity of television to make statistics palatable and clear. As scholars of communication and TV news analysts have amply documented, such uses can increase attention, memorability, and learning. By barring such visual aids, the debates have denuded television of part of its power to educate and much of its capacity to engage hard-core prime-time addicts.

Support Party Sponsorship of These "Campaign" Events

In many ways political scientist James David Barber is correct when he contends, "The media in the United States are the new political parties."[15] Where parties once screened candidates, searching their lives and records as they assessed electability, the experiences of Gary Hart and Joseph Biden testify eloquently that this is now a role filled by the press.

Nonetheless, if any single force in American politics can institutionalize debates it is political parties. In 1988 the parties will attempt to do this by securing agreement to debate prior to the nomination. Institutionalizing party-sponsored general election debates would enhance somewhat the candidates' identification with party but would not necessarily give much of what traditionally was useful to the system and provided by the candidate's alliance with and accountability to the party structure.

Such debates would also foster a public identification between the candidates and the parties. But to expect a whole rehabilitation of parties as a result of party sponsorship is foolish. Nor will sponsorship ensure that the candidate identifies with party positions or that the parties offer coherent alternatives. Indeed, the Vietnam war and Watergate produced a flood of candidates running against party and "Washington" simultaneously. As in the past, candidates will ally with party when that alliance is beneficial and spurn it when the identification becomes burdensome.

If the parties succeed in institutionalizing debates, they will contribute to the quality of the public dialogue in at least one important way. Such agreement would eliminate the time-consuming debate about whether there will be debates and, if so, when and under what rules. Among all issues covered by United Press International during the campaign of 1980, for example, the debate about debates ranked fourth. On CBS "Evening News" there "was more hard campaign news about the debate than about the hostage 'issue' or the economy."[16]

Institutionalizing debates would minimize the likelihood that the stronger candidate would force the weaker to debate on his or her terms or give up the advantages gained by debates. No longer would the rules governing debates be forged in what debate negotiator and former FCC head Newton Minow describes as "the heat of the campaign at the last minute with the candidates' tactical advantage taking precedence over the public interest."[17]

The disadvantage of this proposal, and one conceded by the party heads in their press conference of February 17, 1987, is that it will exclude third-party candidates. Since third parties are generally both resource poor and meagerly covered in the press, such exclusion thwarts their chances of attaining major-party status. By channeling discontent into institutional channels, third parties aid the body politic. Additionally, they have been the originators of such important policy innovations as the direct election of senators, the graduated income tax, and women's suffrage. It is no coincidence that each of these policy proposals occurred before politics was dominated by the mass media.

Nonetheless, in two recent elections, third-party candidacies have played an important role. In 1980, Illinois congressman John Anderson won 6.6% of the vote; for a time in 1968 it appeared that Alabama Governor George Wallace would gain sufficient electoral college support to deny one of the major party nominees the presidency—propelling the decision into the House of Representatives. Ultimately, Wallace netted 13.5% of the general election vote.

Because debates not only grant access to a national audience but are, as we argued earlier, powerful means of asserting one's legitimacy and the legitimacy of one's cause, one major-party candidate or the other can be expected routinely to refuse to debate in the presence of a third-party candidate. In 1968, the presence of Wallace in the race became the excuse used by Nixon for not debating Humphrey. In 1980, Carter refused to debate Reagan if Anderson was included.

Even if parties sponsor the debates, nothing precludes a major party candidate from debating a third-party contender under the sponsorship of their choice. By debating John Anderson in 1980, Reagan confirmed this possibility. Since it is unlikely that including a third-party candidate would ever equally advantage both major-party nominees, and since the question Should the third-party candidate be included? has been an often-cited excuse of those major party candidates wishing to duck debates, sponsorship by parties provides a means of ensuring participation by the likely next president of the United States.

Another objection to party sponsorship of debates is that presidential nominees can coerce parties more readily than parties can coerce their standard-bearers. The nominee appoints the party chair and controls the party machinery. A candidate who does not want to debate can replace the party chair who insists on it. Walter Mondale sketched precisely this scenario during a seminar on presidential debates at Harvard University in 1986.[18] We acknowledge the power of the nominee and do not anticipate joyous compliance on the part of popular incumbents, but we do expect a regular, predictable series of debates to exert much more pressure on everyone to participate. Richard Nixon was returning to, not bucking, tradition when he declined to debate first Hubert Humphrey and then George McGovern. The situation will be very different for the would-be no-show who will emerge, at the earliest, in the 1992 elections. By that time, the previous six candidates and four presidents will have debated. Parties, voters, and the press will all expect debates as a matter of course. Nonparticipants will have to justify their choice and are likely to incur substantial political cost. In the expanded context of debating we have presented here, a refusal to debate would be interpreted as a refusal to campaign.

Good reasons exist as well for sponsorship by the League of Women Voters, the networks, the Congress, or some independent panel. Since the arguments for and against each are cogently presented in Joel Swerdlow's recent *Presidential Debates 1988 and Beyond* and since the issue of sponsorship will have been settled while this book is in press, we refer those interested in the comparative advantages of one sponsor over another to Swerdlow's fine work. Our conclusion that parties are best able to ensure participation by their candidates is consistent with that arrived at by a distinguished panel of scholars and professionals assembled under the auspices of the Twentieth Century Fund in 1986.

Invite Alternative Norms for Press Coverage

Empaneled or not, reporters play a central role in presidential debates. As rhetoric theorist Robert Scott argues, press coverage of the debate about whether Carter would or would not debate created expectations that disadvantaged the incumbent when such a debate finally occurred. By forecasting a Carter who would be tough, incisive, and a master of detail, press accounts heightened

Carter's vulnerability when he instead appeared stiff and ill at ease. By making the fairness of ducking debates an issue, by painting Carter as one who sought advantage in excluding Anderson, press coverage created a scenario in which "it was simple enough to perceive Reagan as long-suffering; denied an early confrontation with Carter through his insistence on being fair to John Anderson and finally granted a face-to-face encounter only when and under conditions that seemed upon the surface to favor Mr. Carter."[19] Within the debate itself "pushing hard to put Reagan on the defensive, Carter fulfilled the prophecy of the press. His efforts looked strategic because they had been so labeled well in advance for instant identification. . . . Carter's very presence in the debate after standing aloof the first time, as well as his hard struggling, underscored beliefs like Tom Wicker's wicked depiction of his 'hard won reputation for indecision, ineptitude and speed on the backtrack.' "[20] Carter's early refusal to debate fused with press accounts that suggested the advantage he sought to magnify his vulnerability to that decisive phrase "There you go again."

As its part of the equation, the press would cover the substance of debates as well as candidates' strategies. If broadcasters opened a debate on nuclear policy with the summary of positions in the *New York Times* editorial we cited earlier, the electorate would have been better served. Post-debate analyses should begin by summarizing the similarities and differences between the candidates, then indicate what was added to that knowledge by the clash of the debate. "What did we learn?" not "How, if at all, did they blunder?" would be the central question asked by broadcasters.

Since reliance on print to correct errors and clarify discussion does little to educate those who do not read newspapers, we need to find a way to move information now carried in print to the broadcast media and then to tie it to the analysis of the debate itself. "You can say anything you want during a debate," observed George Bush's press secretary in 1984, "and 80 million people see it." When reporters demonstrate that a candidate misinformed, "so what? . . . Maybe 200 people read it, or 2,000 or 20,000."[21]

To inform the 80 million requires that the national broadcast news channels do as the best newspapers have and correct misstatements of fact, clarify points of ambiguity, and point to nonanswers. There is no reason that the networks cannot do as Carter aide Jody Powell recommended in 1984 and "assemble a small squad of researchers" to "provide post-debate commentators and analysts with the information needed to call baloney on candidates who make clear misrepresentations."[22] In the past two elections, both major campaigns have assembled such teams to control the spin on news reports. In 1980, for example, Reagan established a special Debate Operations Center. "During and immediately following the debate approximately 50 researchers monitored closely Reagan's and Carter's remarks for errors or omissions which might draw the media's attention."[23]

Reporters should also abandon the win–lose mentality that pervades coverage of debates. At the minimum, the possibility that both candidates have won should be considered. A team of Carter's 1976 advisers concluded that those debates "helped both candidates by diminishing, if not eradicating, the general public's negative perceptions of each."[24]

More important is the fact that "winning" is in large part not a function of actual performance in the debate but is the by-product of audience predispositions. We tend to distort the positions of the candidates we favor and posit more agreement with them than we actually share. So, for example, in 1980 Carter's supporters magnified their agreement with Carter, and Reagan's supporters did the same with Reagan.[25]

An ideal debate model presupposes a disinterested audience able to act as an impartial judge swayed by the merits of one case rather than another. Instead, the audiences for debates turn on their sets primed to see their favored candidate vindicate their belief in his or her competence and virtue. Accordingly, 82% of those who supported Reagan for president in 1980 thought he had won the debate with Carter; 69% of Carter's supporters disagreed, believing that their candidate had done the better job.[26]

If the supporters of one candidate are more likely than those of the other to watch the debate, then national surveys reveal little other than which candidate had the larger number of viewing partisans. This was the case for Reagan in 1980 when 86% of his supporters and 81% of Carter's watched the debate.[27] The CBS/Associated Press poll gave Reagan the debate by 44 to 36%. Had a larger number of Carter's supporters been watching, the results would have been closer.

The tendency to view Reagan as the winner was magnified by ABC's use of a methodologically flawed phone survey to assess outcome. "Probably the most influential post-debate event was the telephone call-in conducted by ABC," recalled Reagan debate adviser Myles Martel.[28] "Although Carter's aides were quick to assail its methodology—and justifiably so—tens of millions of Americans saw Reagan outdistancing Carter in the poll by a 2 to 1 margin before they turned off their television sets. Additional millions of voters were exposed to lead stories about these results the following morning in the newspapers and on television news programs."

The sample of callers who paid for a call to ABC was self-selected. The fact that it cost money to call undoubtedly discouraged the poorer Democratic natural constituency. Since ideologues are more likely to engage in active communication behavior, the response could also indicate that Reagan's supporters felt more strongly about him than Carter's did about him—a rating of intensity, not an accurate representation of total support. We know from a Harris survey that Reagan's supporters were more intensely partisan than Carter's.[29]

These facts of political behavior led Leuthold and Valentine to postulate three principles governing perception of who won a debate:

1. The candidate with the most supporters in the debate audience is likely to be considered the winner, all other things being equal. This means that a candidate with a substantial lead in the polls is likely to be considered the winner, and to profit the most, if he performs as well as his opponent.

2. If the numbers of supporters of each candidate are equal, the candidate with the most intense supporters is likely to be considered the winner. The intense supporters will be more likely to watch and to declare their candidate the winner.

3. If the numbers of supporters are equal, the conservative Republican candidate is likely to be declared the winner, because his conservative Republican supporters will be more active, and this activity will include watching the debates and declaring their candidate the winner.[30]

The notion that we can immediately know who had made the best case should also be suspended. Initial appearances can deceive. As Edwin Yoder, Jr., of the *Washington Post* observed in 1984, Reagan at first appeared to many to be the winner "[R]esponses were deft, and brilliantly crafted for the limited attention level of television." When analyzed carefully after the debate, Reagan instead seemed "underinformed and imprecise about vital matters of detail."[31] Support for Yoder's observation comes from an unlikely source. After watching the Reagan–Carter debate, Reagan's pollster Richard Wirthlin concluded that Reagan had won. When he read the transcript he observed, "Thank God it was on television."[32]

Experiment in Primaries

Just as the conversational format was first tried in the primaries, so too should experiments test various ways in which changes in debates can better elicit information about potential presidential leadership. By barring candidates from bringing in notes, for example, debates have placed a high value on the ability to memorize data—a skill with a minimal correlation with governance. Primary debates might permit the candidates to bring a limited number of advisers or a set of notes with them to supply details. This model was used to good effect by Geraldine Ferraro in the press conference concerning her family finances in August 1984. When questions became too technical for her or required a level of accounting expertise she lacked, she turned to the family's accountants seated to one side. Her credibility was not hurt in the process. The level of accurate information increased, and the public was well served.

Democratic media consultant Tony Schwartz makes a related recommendation when he observes that: "The presidency is the only job in the world for which all of the applicants show up at the interview and attack each other." The style of the questions is equally unrelated to governance. "The only time when a president is called upon to respond immediately is for the decision about whether to respond to nuclear first strike. It would be more useful to find out what questions our presidential candidates would ask than what answers they have. We could have candidates gather with a 'brain trust' and ask questions of the experts." Precedent exists. On May 17, 1955, Ike engaged in a nationally telecast "keyhole" conversation with John Foster Dulles. This type of exercise more closely parallels the ways in which a sitting president obtains information and policy recommendations from advisory staff.

Once such an experiment has succeeded in the primaries, it could be refined for use in the general election.

Summary

The history of debate tells us that debate is most effective when we know what we want it to do; the form has to be adapted to the purposes at hand. The Latin *disputatio* was ideal for teaching logic and language to the children of the aristocracy, but poorly suited to training the legal classes in the American colonies. Press panels work well to elicit information from individuals, but fail to counterpose ideas in conflict. One problem in arriving at an adequate format for presidential debating is the diversity of our expectations. We want so many things from presidential debates that no single form can satisfy all.

Parceling the burden of debate across several formats increases not only the amount but also the kind of information generated. For voters interested in the way the candidates match up against one another, the confrontational approach offers direct competition. For those who want to see how the candidates withstand media scrutiny, the nationally televised press conference shows the presidential hopefuls in what will for one become a customary in-office joust with the White House press corps. The speeches that bracket the general election campaign provide additional advantages. Candidates have the opportunity to argue their cases without time pressures measured in seconds or the dislocations of rapid-fire topic changes. The public can evaluate the quality of the politician's thinking by examining the politician's own words. The conversations add a quieter dimension, at once more personal and more philosophical. Where the speeches provide sustained exposition, the conversation can contribute sustained inquiry.

All these devices would be useful on their own, but together they create a campaign that embodies the principles of sound communication. The first speeches forecast the substance of a candidacy, the debates subject that substance to the test of competition, and the press encounters penalize the candidate disposed to sloganeering or partisan distortion. The public is invited to treat the campaign as a coherent process, less a matter of surprise and staging than a means of providing persuasive support for a straightforward proposition. On election eve the public learns what the candidates have made of all this.

A diverse broadcast campaign rooted in the traditions of the nation's political past could improve democracy. Voters are enjoined to participate in a sustained way too often missing in the era of the spot. We do not suggest a return to log cabins and hard cider, but rather champion campaigns that exploit broadcasting for excitement and visual impact while offering predictability. By promising a series of events and pledging that the candidates seen in one debate will return for another, random advertisements gain context and running for office achieves a heft and seriousness of purpose not now evident to the great majority of Americans who receive their political educations on television.

Calvin Coolidge, no friend of innovation for its own sake, insisted on the importance of such diversity. "Progress depends very largely on the encouragement of variety," he wrote, "it is the ferment of ideas, the clash of disagreeing judgments, the privilege of the individual to develop his own thoughts and shape his own character, that makes progress possible."

The candidates will still be counseled by media consultants, dressed for success, steeped in briefing books, and armed with stock answers and set speeches, just as one of them will be in the White House. But in this expanded campaign, they would also be expected to answer tough questions and supply thoughtful analyses. Failing to do so would disadvantage a candidate against a more responsive opponent raising the risks in evasion and mere sloganeering.

In addition to making the election year more interesting and informative for a wider range of voters, the multiple debate system opens the field for a wider range of candidates. Less aggressive speakers who may not shine in the confrontational round might reveal themselves to be subtle theorists in the conversations. On the other hand, charmers who disarm audiences in debate may be proven more bluster than beef, more style than substance, in a setting bent on follow-up.

By working with a variety of necessarily imperfect formats, we hope to provide the political equivalent of the decathlon. No entrant is likely to excel in each event. A sense of overall superiority emerges from the total. In this evaluation of overall mettle, we would hope to reveal the presidential timbre of the intellectual heirs of the brilliant conversationalist who was hobbled as a public speaker. We venerate their ancestor as the author of the Declaration of Independence. At the same time we seek no penalty for those who are articulate, media savvy, and substantive, as was the ebullient, kinetic media master Teddy Roosevelt, who choreographed our remembrance of the charge up San Juan Hill. Each would have an opportunity to do what he or she did best. Aided by a vigilant press, voters would try to glean from the expanded range of evidence those qualities best suited to lead the nation. And, as they decide, the prospect that Teddy Roosevelt or Thomas Jefferson might indeed be elected in the electronic age is a thought that gives us comfort.

APPENDIX 1

Presidential Debates, 1948-1984

Year	Primary	General Election	Medium	Location	Candidates	Length	Sponsor/Broadcaster
1948 5/17	X		Radio	Portland, OR	Dewey, Stassen	20 min. opening 8½ min. rebuttal	KEX-ABC radio
1952 5/1	X		Radio	Cincinnati, OH	Harriman, Hoffman (Ike), Kefauver, Kerr, Stassen, Warren		ABC radio
1956 5/21	X		TV & radio	Miami	Kefauver, Stevenson	3 min. opening 5 min. closing	ABC
1960 5/3			TV	Charleston, WV	Kennedy/ Humphrey	5 min. opening 5 min. rebuttal	WCHS

Date	Convention		TV	City	Participants	Format	Sponsor
1960 7/12			TV	Los Angeles	Johnson/Kennedy	10 min. opening 5 min. rebuttal	CBS Texas & Mass. delegates
1960 9/26		X	TV & radio	Chicago	Kennedy/Nixon	8 min. opening 2½ min. response	Networks
1960 10/7		X	TV & radio	D.C.	Kennedy/Nixon		Networks
1960 10/13		X	TV & radio	Hollywood & N.Y.C.	Kennedy/Nixon		Networks
1960 10/21		X	TV & radio	N.Y.C.	Kennedy/Nixon	8 min. opening 3 min. closing	Networks
1968 6/1	X		TV & radio	San Francisco	R.F.K., McCarthy	Interview format	ABC
1972 5/28	X		TV	Burbank	Humphrey, McGovern	Interview format	CBS "Face the Nation"
1972 6/4	X		TV	Los Angeles	Chisholm, Humphrey, McGovern, Taylor, Yorty, a stand-in for Wallace	Interview format	ABC "Issues and Answers"
1976 2/23	X		TV	Boston	Bayh, Carter, Harris, H. Jackson, Shapp, Shriver, Udall		League of Women Voters

Year	Primary	General Election	Medium	Location	Candidates	Length	Sponsor/Broadcaster
1976 3/29	X		TV & radio	N.Y.C.	Carter, Church, Harris, H. Jackson, Udall		League PBS/NPR
1976 5/3	X		TV & radio	Chicago	Church/Udall		League
1976 9/23		X	TV & radio	Philadelphia	Carter/Ford	3/2 3 min. closing	League
1976 10/6		X	TV & radio	San Francisco	Carter/Ford	3/2 3 min. closing	League
1976 10/15		Vice Pres.	TV & radio	Houston	Mondale/Dole	2/2, 1/2 3 min. closing	League
1976 10/22		X	TV & radio	Williamsburg	Carter/Ford	2/2 3	League
1980 1/5	X		TV & radio	Des Moines, IA	Anderson, Baker, Bush, Connally, Crane, Dole	2/1 3 min. closing	Des Moines Register Networks/NPR
1980 2/20	X		TV & radio	St. Anselm's College, Manchester, NH	Anderson, Baker, Bush, Connally, Crane, Dole, Reagan	First hour 2/1; 2nd hr. 1½ min.; 1 min. closing	League PBS/NPR

Date				Location	Participants	Format	Sponsor / Network
1980 2/23		X	TV	Nashua, NH	Bush/Reagan	2/2 2 min. closing	Nashua Telegraph PBS
1980 2/28		X	TV	U. of S.C. Columbia, SC	Baker, Bush, Connally, Reagan	2/1; 1/1; 2 min. closing	PBS
1980 3/13		X	TV & radio	Chicago	Anderson, Bush, Crane, Reagan	Question Answer-Rebuttal 1 min. closing	League PBS/NPR
1980 4/23		X	TV & radio	Grapevine, TX	Bush/Reagan	1¾; Question Answer 1 min. closing	League PBS/NPR
1980 9/21	X		TV	Baltimore, MD	Anderson/Reagan	2½ min., 1¼ min, rebuttal 3 min. closing	League NBC/CBS
1980 10/28	X		TV	Cleveland	Carter/Reagan	2/1, 1/2; 3 min. closing	League ABC/NBC/CBS
1984 1/15		X	TV	Dartmouth College Hanover, NH	Askew, Cranston, Glenn, Hart, Hollings, Jackson, McGovern, Mondale	Questions, free-wheeling discussion	Dartmouth College, Democratic Caucus PBS

Year	Primary	General Election	Medium	Location	Candidates	Length	Sponsor/Broadcaster
1984 1/31	X		TV	Harvard Univ.	Cranston, Glenn, Hart, Hollings, Jackson, McGovern, Mondale	Question-answer closing	Harvard Institute of Politics, JFK School of Gov't., *Boston Globe* C-SPAN
1984 2/3	X		TV & radio	Emmanuel College	Glenn, Hart, Hollings, Jackson, McGovern	Question-answer closing	Emmanuel College and Women in Politics '84 WBZ-Boston available by satellite
1984 2/11	X		TV & radio	Des Moines, IA	Askew, Cranston, Glenn, Hart, Hollings, Jackson, McGovern, Mondale	2 min. opening, 3 round of cross questioning, 2 min. closing	*Des Moines Register* CNN, PBS, C-SPAN, state-wide radio in Iowa
1984 2/23	X		TV	St. Anselm's College	Askew, Cranston, Glenn, Hart, Hollings, Jackson, McGovern, Mondale	1 min. response 1½ response 1½ closing	League of Women Voters PBS
1984 3/11	X		TV	Atlanta	Glenn, Hart, Jackson, McGovern, Mondale	Question-answer cross-talk closing	League PBS
1984 3/18	X		TV	Chicago	Hart, Jackson, Mondale	Question-answer closing	Environmental Law Committee & Chicago Bar Assoc. WBBM C-SPAN

Date		TV		Location	Participants	Format	Network
1984 3/28	X	TV		Columbia U.	Hart, Jackson, Mondale	Question-answer 2 min. closing	CBS
1984 4/5	X	TV		Pittsburgh	Hart, Jackson, Mondale	1 min. response cross-talk, closing	League PBS, KDKA (CBS)
1984 5/2	X	TV		Dallas, Ft. Worth	Hart, Jackson, Mondale	Question-answer closing	League PBS, KERA
1984 6/3	X	TV		Los Angeles	Hart, Jackson, Mondale	Question-answer 1½ min. closing	NBC
1984 10/7		TV	X	Louisville, KY	Mondale/Reagan	2½ min. 1 min. rebuttal 4 min. closing	League Networks, PBS
1984 10/11		TV	X	Philadelphia	Bush/Ferraro	2½ min. 1 min. rebuttal 4 min. closing	League Networks
1984 10/21		TV	X	Kansas City, MO	Mondale/Reagan	2½ min. 2 min. rebuttal 4 min. closing	League Networks, PBS

The Law and Presidential Debates

1934. Section 315 of the Communications Act of 1934: A licensee who permits a legally qualified candidate for public office to use a broadcasting station must afford equal opportunities to all other candidates for that office.

1959. 1959 Amendment: Bona-fide newscasts, news interviews, news documentaries, and on-the-spot coverage were exempted from section 315 equal opportunity requirements.

1960. For the 1960 elections, Congress suspended the equal opportunity provisions of section 315. The Kennedy–Nixon debates took place during the suspension.

1975. In 1975, the Aspen ruling exempted debates that were bona-fide news events between or among legally qualified candidates if initiated by nonbroadcast entities and covered in their entirety live. The debates of 1976, 1980, and 1984 sponsored by the League of Women Voters were made possible by the Aspen ruling.

1984. In 1984 the Geller ruling exempted debates sponsored by broadcasters. The debates sponsored by the networks in the primaries of 1984 and 1988 occurred as a by-product of this ruling.

Notes

Introduction

1. *Washington Post,* September 24, 1980.
2. Sears and Chaffee, in Kraus, 1979, p. 231.
3. Babbitt on "MacNeil/Lehrer," February 17, 1988.
4. *Austin American Statesman,* February 29, 1988, B3.
5. Auer, in Kraus, 1979; Harold D. Lasswell, Introduction, pp. 19–24, in Kraus; Bitzer and Reuter.
6. Auer, 1962, p. 146.
7. Davis, 1889, pp. 195–96.
8. These were the national debate topics in 1980–81 and 1975–76, respectively. Freeley, p. 398.

Chapter 1

1. Bohman, in Brigance, pp. 18–22; Thomas, in Brigance, pp. 198–99.
2. *Ibid.,* p. 39.
3. Dwight.
4. Potter, in Wallace, p. 240.
5. *Diary of John Quincy Adams,* p. 123.
6. Sheridan, p. 3.
7. *Ibid.,* p. 4.
8. John Quincy Adams, *An Inaugural Oration,* p. 27.
9. John Adams, *Works,* v. 7, pp. 249–50, quoted in Bohman, in Brigance, p. 18.
10. Sampson, pp. 9–14.
11. Hall, pp. 7–18.
12. *Ibid.,* p. 10.
13. Bode, p. 101.
14. *Ibid.,* p. 50.
15. *Ibid.,* p. 54.
16. Thomas Jefferson to David Harding, April 20, 1824, in Lipscomb, pp. 30–31.
17. Bode, p. 27.
18. Aly and Tanquery, p. 96.
19. Sullivan, v. II, pp. 13–96.
20. McElligott, p. 14.
21. Freeley, p. 3.
22. Morris, pp. 86–87.
23. *Ibid.,* p. 86.
24. Jefferson, "Education of a Young Lawyer," in Padover, p. 1047.

25. Peterson, p. xiv.
26. William Matthews quoted in Miller, 1916, v. I, p. 154.
27. Padover, *The Complete Jefferson*, p. 1058.
28. Thomas Jefferson to James Madison, February 17, 1926, in Lipscomb, p. 156.
29. Sullivan, v. II, p. 95.
30. Wood, p. 607.
31. Hamilton and Jay, p. 79.
32. Miller, v. I, pp. 299–301.
33. Madison, *Notes of Debates*, p. 18.
34. *Ibid.*, p. 654.
35. Brant, pp. 21ff.
36. Scott, v. II, pp. 617–22.
37. "The Address and Reasons of Dissent of the Minority of the Convention of the State of Pennsylvania to their Constituents," *Pennsylvania Pack and Daily Advertiser*, December 18, 1787, in McMaster and Stone, p. 454.
38. Ford, pp. 91–111.
39. Jay, "Pamphlet to the People of New York."
40. Elliott, v. III.
41. Wiltse and Moser, v. I, p. 286.
42. Current, p. 63.
43. Wiltse and Moser, v. I, p. 384.
44. *Ibid.*, p. 393.
45. Boorstin, 1965, p. 312.
46. Hance, Henderson, and Schoenberger, in Brigance, v. I, pp. 136–44.
47. *Ibid.*, pp. 136–44.
48. Wilson, pp. 69–72.
49. James Madison to Thomas Jefferson, December 8, 1788, in Madison, *Letters and Other Writings*, v. I, p. 444.
50. James Madison to Edmund Randolph, March 1, 1789, in Madison, *Letters and Other Writings*, v. I, pp. 445–51.
51. *The Virginia Argus*, August 5, 1800, p. 3.
52. Sullivan, v. II, p. 118.
53. *Ibid.*, pp. 122–25.
54. Ostrogorski, pp. 181–88.
55. Basler, v. I, pp. 334–45.
56. *Ibid.*, p. 508.
57. Johannsen, p. 428.

Chapter 2

1. Thomas Jefferson, "A Bill for Establishing Religious Freedom," in Peterson, p. 253.
2. Wilson, pp. 143ff.
3. John Jay, "An Address to the People of the State of New York on the Subject of the Constitution," in Ford, 1888.
4. Miller, 1913, v. I, pp. 219–20.
5. *Ibid.*, p. 335.
6. *Ibid.*, pp. 332–33.
7. *Ibid.*, pp. 333–34.

8. Miller, *American Debate,* v. I, pp. 219–20.
9. Franklin, v. I.
10. Miller, *Great Debates,* v. IV, p. 345.
11. Leonard.
12. Maclay, pp. 7ff.
13. Quoted in Leonard, p. 84.
14. Report of the Hartford Convention, in Miller, v. V, p. 17.
15. Miller, 1913, v. V, p. 18.
16. *Ibid.,* pp. 25–26.
17. Garrison quoted in Bormann, p. 183.
18. *Ibid.,* pp. 192–93.
19. Barnes and Dumond, v. I, p. viii.
20. Stanton quoted in Bormann, p. 176. Rhetorical scholar Ernest Bormann argues that their vision of change was ultimately much more successful than Garrison's. Henry Stanton was one of the Lane Rebels. Compare his speech before a committee of the Massachusetts House of Representatives with the spleen of Garrison's Fourth of July address.

And now, Mr. Chairman, what do the petitioners ask you to request Congress to do? I answer;—merely to repeal these odious statutes immediately, and to enact others, if necessary, in their stead. By immediate abolition, they do not intend that the Slaves of the District should be turned loose:—nor, that they should be, as a *sine qua non* to abolition, immediately invested with all political rights, such as the elective franchise. But, simply, that Congress should immediately restore to every Slave, the ownership of his own body, mind, and soul. That they should no longer permit them to be deemed, held, and sold, as chattels personal, to all intents, constructions and purposes whatsoever; but should give the slaves a fee simple in their own blood, bones and brains. (Stanton quoted in Bormann, p. 176.)

This speech emphasizes the need to preserve order while working in the cause of abolition. The language itself is borrowed from the law. In the abolitionist strongholds of the North, arguments such as Stanton's were thought characteristic of the whole movement. Bormann observes that these abolitionists retained much more enduring influence after the Civil War than did the hotter heads banded under Garrison.

21. *Cincinnati Journal,* May 30, 1834, quoted in Barnes and Dumond, v. I, p. 143.
22. Sullivan, v. II, p. 95.
23. Hall, p. 6.
24. *Ibid.,* pp. 13–14.
25. *Ibid.,* p. 9.
26. *Sangamo Journal,* March 18, 1844.
27. *Sangamo Journal,* July 16, 1836.
28. Current, p. 61; Wiltse, v. I, p. xiii.
29. Current, pp. 61–62.
30. Wiltse, v. I, p. xiii.
31. Basler, v. I, p. 170.
32. For a complete discussion of the arguments used, see Zarefsky, pp. 162–84.
33. Johannsen, *The Lincoln-Douglas Debates,* p. 50.
34. *Ibid.,* p. 177.

35. *Ibid.,* p. 277.
36. *Ibid.,* p. 257.
37. *Ibid.,* p. 231. Emphasis in original.
38. *Ibid.,* pp. 270–71.
39. *Ibid.,* p. 12.
40. *Ibid.,* pp. v–vi.
41. *Ibid.,* p. 14.
42. *Ibid.,* p. 277.
43. Miller, 1913, v. IV, pp. 125–26.
44. Southern fears were raised by abolitionist discourse. "The South watched this high water of reporting with horror, particularly after learning that Denmark Vesey had used reports of congressional debates to organize a slave revolt in South Carolina." Vesey used a speech by Rufus King. Starobin, p. 48.
45. Miller, 1913, v. IV, p. 106.
46. *Ibid.,* p. 107.
47. *Ibid.,* p. 114.
48. *Ibid.,* pp. 114–15.
49. *Ibid.,* p. 116.

Chapter 3

1. Van Buren quoted in Schlesinger, 1945, p. 51.
2. Adams, *Memoirs,* v. IX, p. 64, quoted in Schlesinger, 1945, p. 52.
3. Adams, *An Inaugural Oration,* p. 27.
4. *Ibid.,* pp. 18–19, 26.
5. Jefferson to David Harding, April 20, 1824, in Lipscomb, vol. XVI, pp. 30–31.
6. Jefferson to James Madison, February 17, 1826, in Lipscomb, pp. 155–59.
7. Quoted in Current, p. 128.
8. Benton, in Miller, 1913, v. V, p. 72.
9. Zarefsky, p. 181; Whan, pp. 777–827.
10. Wiltse and Moser, v. I, pp. 285–87.
11. Brigance, p. 710.
12. *Writings,* Hawthorne, v. XXII, p. 160, quoted in Schlesinger, 51–52n.
13. In Current, p. 17.
14. Quoted in Miller, *Great Debates,* v. IV, p. 340.
15. Johannsen, *The Lincoln-Douglas Debates,* p. 351.
16. *Ibid.,* p. 352.
17. Alexander, p. 115.
18. Mattis, in Brigance, v. II, p. 82.
19. *Ibid.,* p. 84.
20. Leonard, pp. 81–82.
21. *Ibid.,* p. 82.
22. Current, p. 113.
23. Brownlow and Pryne, pp. 13–14.
24. *Ibid.,* p. 14.
25. *Ibid.,* p. 29.
26. *Ibid.,* p. 54.
27. Auer, 1968, p. 1.
28. Ahlstrom, p. 654.

29. Brownlow and Pryne, p. iii.
30. Phillips, n.p.
31. Japp, p. 338. The authors are indebted to Karlyn Kohrs Campbell for her counsel in nineteenth-century women's history.
32. Lerner, pp. 178–80.
33. *Ibid.*, pp. 194–95.
34. *Ibid.*, pp. 375–81; Japp, pp. 335–48.
35. Cazden, pp. 27–29.
36. *Ibid.*, p. 29.
37. Japp, pp. 337–38.
38. Cazden, pp. 81–82.
39. Cowperwaithe and Baird, "Intercollegiate Debating," in Wallace, p. 269.
40. Freeley, p. 395.
41. Zarefsky, pp. 162–84.
42. Argumentation scholars with an interest in academic debate have devoted a great deal of attention to producing clash. See Cox and Willard; Herbeck and Katsulas; Parson, in Ziegelmueller and Rhodes; Thomas and Hart; Toulmin; Willard.

Chapter 4

1. Chester, p. 28.
2. *Public Papers*, 1938, pp. 278ff.
3. Barnouw, p. 76.
4. Auer, in Kraus, 1962, p. 145.
5. *Ibid.*
6. Morrison, p. 197.
7. *New York Times*, October 6, 1980, p. A20.
8. *New York Times*, November 4, 1984, p. H27.
9. March 14, 1948, p. E3.
10. Quoted by Ray, p. 249.
11. Quoted by Ray, p. 253.
12. Chester, p. 53.
13. Smith, 1982, p. 493.
14. *Ibid.*
15. *New York Times*, May 22, 1956, p. 21.
16. Lippmann, p. 91.
17. *Ibid.*, p. 195.
18. Chester, p. 19.
19. Jamieson, 1984, p. 26.
20. *Ibid.*, p. 27.
21. *Ibid.*, p. 29.
22. Nie, Verba, and Petrocik, p. 2.
23. Atkin, Bowen, Nayman, Sheinkopf, 1973.
24. Atkin, Galloway, and Nayman, cited in Atkin.
25. Neuman, 1984, p. 137.
26. Data provided by Nielsen Co.
27. Mendelsohn and O'Keefe.
28. Patterson.

29. Quarles, pp. 407–36.
30. *Ibid.*
31. Roper.
32. Robinson and Sheehan, p. 280.
33. Bogart 77, Robinson 71.
34. Keeter and Zukin, p. 59.
35. Jamieson, 1984, pp. 158–61.
36. Chester, p. 75.
37. White, pp. 132–33.
38. Jamieson, 1984, pp. 260–61.
39. Tulis.
40. Juergens, pp. 17ff.
41. Sharp, p. 240.
42. *Ibid.*
43. Vermont Royster, "Reflections on the Fourth Estate," *Washington Post*, December 25, 1978.
44. Grossman and Kumar, pp. 12–13.
45. Chester, p. 287.
46. *Ibid.,* p. 272.
47. *Ibid.,* p. 92.
48. Hagerty diary in Hagerty papers, DDE Library. March 4, 1954.
49. Salinger, "Introduction," p. x.
50. "Call to glory," *The New Republic*, November 12, 1984, p. 25.
51. Cornwell, p. 381.
52. Grossman and Kumar, p. 247.
53. Manheim, p. 63.
54. Quoted by Keough, p. 24.
55. January 27, 1969.
56. Keough, p. 45.
57. Lammers, p. 263.
58. Salinger, 1966, p. 155.

Chapter 5

1. Katz and Feldman.
2. Data provided by Nielsen Co.
3. Becker and Lower, in Kraus, 1976, p. 18.
4. Sears and Chaffee, pp. 230–31.
5. Sears and Chaffee, in Kraus, 1979, p. 229.
6. Robinson, in Kraus, 1979.
7. *Ibid.*
8. *New York Times*, October 30, 1987, p. 8.
9. *New York Times*, November 19, 1987, p. 14.
10. Neuman, pp. 136–37.
11. Robinson, 1976, p. 143.
12. *Ibid.,* n. 16.
13. Bishop et al., 1978.
14. Jamieson, 1988, Ch. 1.

15. Atkin, Bowen, Oguz, and Sheinkopf; McClure and Patterson, 1974; O'Keefe and Sheinkopf; Mendelsohn and O'Keefe.
16. McClure and Patterson, 1974.
17. Atkin and Heald; Mendelsohn and O'Keefe.
18. Patterson and McClure.
19. Patterson.
20. *Ibid.*
21. Bechtel, Achelpohl, and Akers.
22. *Ibid.*
23. Neuman, 1976.
24. *Ibid.*
25. Graber, cited in John P. Robinson, Dennis K. Davis, and Mark R. Levy, "Television News and the Informed Public: Not the Main Source." A paper presented at the 94th annual meeting of the American Psychological Assoc. August 22–26, 1984, Washington D.C., pp. 6–7.
26. *Ibid.*, pp. 25–26.
27. Miller and MacKuen, 1979; Becker et al., 1979.
28. *Ibid.*
29. Wald and Lupfer; Miller and MacKuen.
30. Chaffee and Choe.
31. Becker, Sobowale, Cobbey, and Eyal.
32. Miller and MacKuen, 1979.
33. Mendelsohn and O'Keefe, p. 52.
34. McLeod, Durall, Ziemke, and Bybee.
35. Miller and MacKuen, 1979b.
36. *The Prince*, ch. 18.
37. *Political Behavior*, pp. 74–76.
38. "Introduction," Kraus, 1962, p. 21.
39. Brams, p. 29.
40. Fishel, p. 124.
41. Jamieson, 1984, p. 305.
42. Fishel.
43. Ellsworth.
44. *Ibid.*, p. 794. See also Page, p. 171.
45. Page, pp. 171–72.
46. *Ibid.*, p. 160.
47. *Ibid.*, p. 63.
48. p. 9.
49. *New York Times*, November 2, 1987, p. 15.
50. Kinder and Sears, p. 685.
51. *Ibid.*, p. 686.
52. Kinder and Kiewiet; Kinder, 1981.
53. Hess, p. 61.
54. Barber, 1985.
55. The term is Page's.
56. Page, 1978, p. 262.
57. *Ibid.*, p. 233. Cf. Chapter 8.
58. West, pp. 23–50.

59. Kagay and Caldeira, 1975, cited by Kinder and Sears, p. 690.
60. Markus.
61. Kinder et al., 1980.
62. *Ibid.*, pp. 315–38.
63. *Crisis*, p. 356.
64. Reagan, p. 297.
65. *New York Times*, October 13, 1984, p. 26.
66. Graber, 1987, pp. 74–78.
67. Ekman, P., and Friesen, W. V. "Felt, Palse, and Miserable Smiles," *J of Nonverbal Behavior*, 1982, 4:238–52.
68. Zuckerman, M., et al. "Face and tone of voice in the communication of deception," *J of Personality and Social Psych*, 1982, 43:347–57.
69. *New York Times*, October 30, 1987, p. 8.
70. *New York Times*, March 12, 1984, p. B9.
71. October 23, 1976.
72. Seltz and Yocham, in Kraus, 1976, p. 142.
73. *USA Today*, November 9, 1987, p. 4A.
74. Sorensen, p. 198.
75. Nixon, pp. 362–63.
76. Ford, p. 415.
77. *New York Times*, January 27, 1984, p. A16.
78. Jackson-Beeck, p. 335.
79. Chaffee, p. 337.
80. Kraus, 1962; Sears and Chaffee.

Chapter 6

1. Kraus, 1979, p. iii.
2. Minow and Sloan, p. 61.
3. Bitzer and Reuter, p. 204.
4. *Ibid.*, p. 207.
5. *New York Times*, October 23, 1984, np.
6. Drucker and Hunold.
7. Robinson and Sheehan, 1983.
8. Chaffee, p. 333.
9. Chaffee and Dennis, in Ranney, p. 84; Lang and Lang, in Kraus, 1979; McLeod, in *ibid.*
10. Graber, Doris A. "Kind pictures and harsh words: how television presents the candidates," in *Elections in America* ed. Kay Lehman Schulzman. Boston: Allen and Unwin, 1987, p. 137.
11. Lang and Lang, in Bishop et al.; Steeper, in *ibid.*
12. Graber, 1980; Hofstetter; Carey.
13. Crouse.
14. *Ibid.*
15. *New York Times*, October 14, 1984, np.
16. Bishop, Oldendick, and Tuchfarber, 1978; Graber and Kim, 1978; Neuman, 1986.
17. October 22, 1984, p. B7.
18. Sundquist, p. 196.

19. Burnham in Sundquist, p. 98.
20. Burnham, p. 133.
21. *New York Times Magazine*, October 30, 1960, pp. 13, 79–80.
22. Suedfeld and Tetlock, pp. 169–84.
23. *Ibid.*
24. Boorstin, 1964, p. 42.
25. Polsby, in Ranney, p. 179.
26. Rosenberg, Bohan, McCafferty, and Harris, pp. 108–27.
27. Carter, p. 565.
28. Cheney, in Ranney, pp. 117–18.
29. Jamieson, 1984, Chapter 1.
30. *Ibid.*
31. 42 inches.
32. *New York Times*, October 8, 1984, p. B7.
33. Nixon, p. 420.
34. *Reporter*, November 10, 1960, p. 18.
35. Kraus, 1976a.
36. Stockman, p. 47.
37. Cater, in Kraus 1960, p. 128.
38. Nixon, p. 399.
39. Kraus, 1976, p. 106.
40. Ellsworth.
41. *New York Times*, October 26, 1976.
42. Bitzer and Reuter provided the first comprehensive rhetorical analysis of debates.
43. Reston, in Minow and Sloan, p. 12.
44. *Ibid.*, p. 65.

Chapter 7

1. Dallas, February 18, 1988.
2. Brown-Black Coalition, transcription from videotape.
3. For a discussion of Ronald Reagan's role in the 1980 primary debates, see Blankenship, Fine, and Davis.
4. Minnow, Martin, and Mitchell, p. 162.
5. Mills, p. 43.
6. Theodore White Conference at Harvard, December 1986.
7. Auer, 1986, p. 6.
8. September 23, 1984, p. E22.
9. *Washington Post*, September 5, 1984.
10. See Cohen, "The Public Agenda Foundation: An Experiment in Issues Analysis," in Kraus, 1979.
11. Swerdlow, 1987, pp. 74–75.
12. Quoted in Swerdlow, 1987, pp. 142–43.
13. *Ibid.*, p. 143.
14. *Ibid.*, p. 75.
15. Quoted by Gary Orren in "Thinking about the Press and Government," in Linsky, p. 10.
16. Robinson and Sheehan, p. 209.

17. Speech Communication Association speech, November 2, 1984.
18. Neuman and Harian, in Swerdlow, 1979, p. 79.
19. Scott, p. 32.
20. *Ibid.*
21. *New York Times,* October 19, 1984. *Washington Post* editorial, October 20, 1984.
22. "The Envelope, Please, For Debate Award Winners," *Houston Post,* October 10, 1984, p. B2.
23. Martel, p. 45.
24. Lesher, Caddell, and Rafshoon, in Ranney, p. 139.
25. Brent and Granberg, pp. 393–403.
26. CBS Poll, October 29, 1980.
27. *Ibid.*
28. Martel, p. 45.
29. *Broadcasting,* November 3, 1980, p. 25.
30. Leuthold and Valentine, pp. 65–66. See also Vancil and Pendell.
31. October 24, 1984, nationally syndicated column.
32. Diamond and Friery, in Swerdlow, 1987, p. 45.

References

Abelson, R. P., Kinder, D. R., Peters, M. D., and Fiske, S. T. (1982). Affective and semantic components in political person perception. *Journal of Personality and Social Psychology, 42,* 619–30.

Adams, J. Q. (1806). *An inaugural oration, delivered at the author's installation as Boylston professor of rhetoric and oratory at Harvard University, Cambridge, Massachusetts.* Boston: Munroe & Francis.

Adams, J. Q. (1928) *The diary of John Quincy Adams, 1794–1845.* New York: Longman, Green, and Co.

Ahlstrom, S. E. (1972). *A religious history of the American people.* New Haven and London: Yale University Press.

Alexander, D. S. (1916). *History and procedure of the House of Representatives.* Boston: Houghton Mifflin.

Almond, G. A., and Verba, S. (1963). *The civic culture.* Princeton, NJ: Princeton University Press.

Aly, B., and Tanquery, G. B. (1960). In W. N. Brigance (ed.), The early national period, 1788–1860, *A history and criticism of American public address. Vol. I.* New York: Russell, 55–110.

Anderson, P. A., and Kibler, R. J. (1978). Candidate valence as a predictor of voter preference. *Human Communication Research, 5,* 4–14.

Arnston, P. H., and Smith, C. R. (1978). News distortion as a function of organizational communication. *Communication Monographs, 45,* 371–81.

Asher, H. B. (1980). *Presidential elections and American politics.* Homewood, IL: Dorsey Press.

Atkin, C. K. (1973). Instrumental utilities and information seeking. In P. Clarke (ed.), *New models for mass communication research.* Beverly Hills, CA: Sage, 205–242.

Atkin, C. K., Bowen, L., Oguz, B., and Sheinkopf, K. (1973). Quality versus quantity in televised political ads. *Public Opinion Quarterly, 37,* 209–24.

Atkin, C. K., Galloway, J., and Nayman, O. B. (1976). News media exposure, political knowledge and campaign interest. *Journalism Quarterly, 53,* 231–37.

Atkin, C. K., and Heald, G. (1976). Effects of political advertising. *Public Opinion Quarterly, 40,* 216–28.

Atwood, L. E. (1980). From press release to voting reasons: Tracing the agenda in a congressional campaign. In D. D. Nimmo (ed.), *Communication yearbook 4.* New Brunswick, NJ: Transaction Books, 467–482.

242   *References*

Atwood, L. E., and Sanders, K. R. (1975). Perception of information sources and likelihood of split-ticket voting. *Journalism Quarterly, 52,* 421–28.

Auer, J. J. (1962). The counterfeit debates. In S. Kraus (ed.), *The great debates: Carter vs. Ford, 1976.* Bloomington: Indiana University Press, 142–150.

Auer, J. J. (1981). Great myths about the great debates. *Speaker and Gavel, 18,* 14–21.

Auer, J. J. (1986). Presidential debates: Public understanding and political institutionalization. *Speaker and Gavel, 24,* 1–7.

Auer, J. J. (Ed.). (1968). *Antislavery and disunion, 1858–1861.* Gloucester: Peter Smith.

Bailey, G. (1978). How newsmakers make the news: Covering the political campaign. *Journal of Communication, 28,* 80–83.

Bailyn, B. (1967). *Ideological origins of the American Revolution.* Cambridge: Cambridge University Press.

Barber, J. D. (1985). In *The presidential character,* 3rd ed. Englewood Cliffs, NJ: Prentice-Hall.

Barber, J. D. (Ed.). (1978). *Race for the presidency: The media and the nominating process.* Englewood Cliffs, NJ: Prentice-Hall.

Barnes, G. H., and Dumond, D. L. (1970). *Letters of Theodore Dwight Weld, Angelina Grimké Weld and Sarah Grimké, 1822–1844.* New York: Da Capo Press.

Barnouw, E. (1982). *Tube of plenty.* New York: Oxford University Press.

Basler, R. P. (Ed.) (1953). *The collected works of Abraham Lincoln.* New Brunswick, NJ: Rutgers University Press.

Bechtel, R. B., Achelpohl, C., and Akers, R. (1972). Correlates between observed behavior and questionnaire responses on television viewing. In E. A. Rubinstein et al. (eds.), *Television and social behavior.* Washington, DC: U.S. Government Printing Office.

Bechtolt, W. E., Jr., Hilyard, J., and Bybee, C. R. (1977). Agenda control in the 1976 debates: A content analysis. *Journalism Quarterly, 54,* 674–81.

Becker, L., McCombs, M., and McLeod, J. (1975). The development of political cognitions. In S. Chaffee (ed.), *Political communication.* Beverly Hills, CA: Sage, 21–64.

Becker, L., Sobowale, I., Cobbey, R., and Eyal, C. (1978). Debates' effects on voters' understanding of candidates and issues. In G. Bishop, R. Meadow, and M. Jackson-Beeck (eds.), *The presidential debates.* New York: Praeger, 126–139.

Becker, L. B. (1979). Measurement of gratifications. *Communication Research, 6,* 54–73.

Becker, L. B., and Dunwoody, S. (1982). Media use, public affairs knowledge and voting in a local election. *Journalism Quarterly, 59,* 212–18.

Becker, L. B., Weaver, D. H., Graber, D. A., and McCombs, M. E. (1979). Influence on public agendas. In S. Kraus (ed.), *The great debates: Carter vs. Ford, 1976.* Bloomington: Indiana University Press, 418–28.

Becker, S., Pepper, R., Wenner, L., and Kim, J. (1979). Information flow and the shaping of meaning. In S. Kraus (ed.), *The great debates: Carter vs. Ford, 1976.* Bloomington: Indiana University Press.

Becker, S. L. (1983). *Discovering mass communication.* Glenview, IL: Scott, Foresman.

Berelson, B., Lazarsfeld, P. F., and McPhee, W. (1954). *Voting.* Chicago: University of Chicago Press.

Berquist, G. F., and Golden, J. (1981). Media rhetoric and the public perception of the 1980 presidential debates. *Quarterly Journal of Speech, 67,* 125–37.

Billingsley, K. F., and Ferber, P. H. (1981). Patterns of issues orientations: Their relationship to electoral behavior. *Western Political Quarterly, 34,* 528–42.

Bishop, G. F. (1980). Book review of S. Kraus (ed.), *The great debates: Carter vs. Ford, 1976. Public Opinion Quarterly, 44,* 598–599.

Bishop, G. F., Meadow, R. G., and Jackson-Beeck, M. (Eds.). (1978). *The presidential debates: Media, electoral, and policy perspectives.* New York: Praeger.

Bishop, G. F., Oldendick, R., and Tuchfarber, A. (1978a). The presidential debates as a device for increasing the "rationality" of electoral behavior. In G. F. Bishop, R. Meadow, and M. Jackson-Beeck (eds.), *The presidential debates.* New York: Praeger, 179–196.

Bishop, G. F., Oldendick, R. W., and Tuchfarber, A. J. (1978b). Debate watching and the acquisition of political knowledge. *Journal of Communication, 28,* 99–113.

Bitzer, L., and Reuter, T. (1980). *Carter vs. Ford: The counterfeit debates of 1976.* Madison: University of Wisconsin Press.

Blair, H. (1783). *Lectures on rhetoric and belles lettres.* London: W. Strahan, T. Cadell.

Blanck, P. D., Rosenthal, R., Snodgrass, S., DePaulo, B., and Zuckerman, M. (1981). Sex differences in eavesdropping on nonverbal cues: Developmental changes. *Journal of Personality and Social Psychology, 41,* 391–96.

Blankenship, J., Fine, M. G., and Davis, L. K. (1983). The 1980 Republican primary debates: The transformation of actor to scene. *Quarterly Journal of Speech, 69,* 25–36.

Blumler, J. G. (1979). The role of theory in uses and gratifications studies. *Communication Research, 6,* 9–36.

Blumler, J. G., and Katz, E. (1974). *The uses of mass communication: Current perspectives on gratifications research.* Beverly Hills, CA: Sage.

Blumler, J. G., and McQuail, D. (1969). *Television in politics: Its uses and influences.* Chicago: University of Chicago Press.

Bode, C. (1968). *The American lyceum: Town meeting of the mind.* Carbondale: Southern Illinois University Press.

Bogart, L. (1977). *How the public gets its news.* New York: Newspaper Advertising Bureau.

Boller, P. F., Jr. (1984). *Presidential campaigns.* New York: Oxford University Press.

Boorstin, D. (1965). *The Americans.* New York: Random House.

Boorstin, D. (1964). *The image.* New York: Harper.

Bormann, E. G. (1985). *The force of fantasy: Restoring the American dream.* Carbondale: Southern Illinois University Press.

Bowers, T. A. (1972). Issue and personality information in newspaper political advertising. *Journalism Quarterly, 49,* 446–52.

Boyd, R. W. (1969). Presidential elections: An explanation of voting defection. *American Political Science Review, 63,* 498–514.

Brams, S. J. (1978). *The presidential election game.* New Haven: Yale University Press.

Brams, S. J., and Davis, M. D. (1974). The 3/2's rule in presidential campaigning. *American Political Science Review, 68,* 113–34.

Branch, E. D. (1965). *The sentimental years.* New York: Hill and Wang.

Brant, E. (1950). *James Madison: Father of the Constitution, 1787–1800.* Indianapolis: Bobbs-Merrill.

Brent, E., and Granberg, D. (1982). Subjective agreement with the presidential candidates of 1976 and 1980. *Journal of Personality and Social Psychology, 42,* 393–403.

Brigance, W. N. (Ed.). (1960). *A history and criticism of American public address.* New York: Russell and Russell.

Broder, D. (June 15, 1980). Editorial, *Washington Post,* C7.

Brownlow, W. G., and Pryne, A. *Ought American slavery to be perpetuated? A debate between Reverend W. G. Brownlow and Reverend A. Pryne.* Miami: Mnemosyne.

Campbell, A., Gurin, G., and Miller, W. E. (1954). *The voter decides.* Evanston, IL: Row, Peterson and Company.

Campbell, J. E. (1983). Ambiguity in the issue positions of presidential candidates: A causal analysis. *American Journal of Political Science, 27,* 284–93.

Campbell, J. E. (1983). Candidate image evaluations: Influence and rationalization in presidential primaries. *American Politics Quarterly, 11,* 293–313.

Cannon, L. (1982). *Reagan.* New York: G. P. Putnam and Sons.

Carey, J. (1976). How media shape campaigns. *Journal of Communication, 26,* 50–57.

Carter, J. (1982). *Keeping faith.* New York: Bantam.

Carter, R. (1962). Some effects of the debates. In S. Kraus (ed.), *The great debates.* Bloomington: Indiana University Press, 253–270.

Cazden, E. (1983). *Antoinette Brown Blackwell: A biography.* Old Westbury: The Feminist Press.

Chaffee, S. (1978). Presidential debaters—Are they helpful to voters? *Communication Monographs, 45,* 330–46.

Chaffee, S. H., and Choe, S. Y. (1980). Time of decision and media use during the Ford-Carter campaign. *Public Opinion Quarterly, 44,* 52–69.

Chester, E. W. (1969). *Radio, television and politics.* New York: Sheed and Ward.

Chester, G., Garrison, G. R., and Willis, E. E. (1971). *Television and radio.* New York: Appleton-Century-Crofts.

Chodorow, N. (1978). *The reproduction of mothering.* Berkeley: University of California Press.

Clarke, P., and Fredin, E. (1978). Newspapers, television, and political reasoning. *Public Opinion Quarterly, 42,* 143–60.

Clarke, P., and Kline, F. G. (1974). Media effects reconsidered: Some new strategies for communication research. *Communication Research, 1,* 224–40.

Coolidge, C. (1929). *The autobiography of Calvin Coolidge.* New York: Cosmopolitan Book Corporation.

Cornwell, E. E. (1960). The presidential press conference: A study in institutionalization. *Midwest Journal of Political Science,* 370–89.

Cox, J. R., and Willard, C. A. (Eds.) (1982). *Advances in argumentation theory and research.* Carbondale: Southern Illinois University Press.

Crouse, T. (1972). *The boys on the bus.* New York: Ballantine.

Current, R. N. (1955). *Daniel Webster and the rise of national conservatism.* Boston: Little, Brown.

Danielson, W. A., and Adams, J. B. (1961). Completeness of press coverage of the 1960 campaign. *Journalism Quarterly, 38,* 441–52.

Davis, D. (1979). The vote decision process. In S. Kraus (ed.), *The great debates: Carter vs. Ford, 1976.* Bloomington: Indiana University Press, 331–347.

Davis, R. (1889). *Recollections of Mississippi and Mississippians.* Boston and New York: Houghton Mifflin.

Debate at the Lane Seminary, Cincinnati, Speech of James A. Thome, of Kentucky, Delivered at the Annual Meeting of the American Anti-Slavery Society, May 6, 1934. Also: Letter of the Reverend Dr. Samuel H. Cox, Against the American Colonization Society. (1834). Boston: Garrison and Kapp.

Debates of Conscience with a Distiller, a Wholesale Dealer and a Retailer. American Tract Society, no. 300. n.d.

Declercq, E., Hurley, T. H., and Luttbeg, N. R. (1975). Voting in American presidential elections: 1956–1972. *American Politics Quarterly, 3,* 222–46.

Deering, I. (1942). *Let's try thinking: A handbook of democratic action.* Yellow Springs, OH: Antioch Press.

Dennis, J., and Chaffee, S. (1978). Legitimation in the 1976 U.S. election campaign. *Communication Research, 5,* 371–94.

Deutschmann, P. (1962). Viewing, conversation and voting intentions. In S. Kraus (ed.), *The great debates.* Bloomington: Indiana University Press, 232–252.

DeVries, W., and Tarrance, L. (1972). *The ticket-splitter.* Grand Rapids, MI: William B. Eerdmans.

Diamond, I., and Hartsock, N. (1981). Beyond interests in politics: A comment on Virginia Sapiro's "When are interests interesting? The problem of political representation of women." *American Political Science Review, 75,* 716–21.

Donohue, G. A., Tichenor, P. J., and Olien, C. N. (1975). Mass media and the knowledge gap: A hypothesis reconsidered. *Communication Research, 2,* 3–23.

Donohue, M., and Tipton, L. (1973). A conceptual model of information seeking, avoiding and processing. In P. Clarke (ed.), *New models for communication research.* Beverly Hills, CA: Sage.

Douglas, J. (1972). The verbal image: Student perceptions of political figures. *Speech Monographs, 39,* 1–15.

Drucker, S., and Hunold, J. P. (1987). The debating game. *Critical Studies in Mass Communication, 4,* 202–207.

Dwight, T. (1803). *Decisions and questions discussed by the senior class in Yale college in 1813 and 1814.* New York: Jonathan Leavitt; Boston: Crocker and Brewster.

Eisenberg, N., and Lennon, R. (1983). Sex differences in empathy and related capacities. *Psychological Bulletin, 94,* 100–31.

Elliott, J. (Ed.). (1888). *Debates on the adoption of the Federal Constitution, Vols. I–III.* New York: Burt Franklin Research and Source Series 109.

Ellsworth, J. W. (1965). Rationality and campaigning: A content analysis of the 1960 presidential debates. *Western Political Quarterly, 18,* 794–802.

Erbring, L., Goldenberg, E. N., and Miller, A. H. (1980). Front-page news and real world cues: A new look at agenda-setting by the media. *American Journal of Political Science, 24,* 16–49.

Farrand, M. (Ed.) (1911). *The records of the Federal Convention of 1787, Vol. II.* New Haven: Yale University Press.

Fishel, J. (1985). *Presidents and promises.* Washington, DC: Congressional Quarterly.

Flora, C. B., and Lynn, N. B. (1974). Women and political socialization: Considerations of the impact of motherhood. In J. Paquette (ed.), *Women in politics.* New York: John Wiley & Sons, 37–43.

Foote, H. S. (1874). *Casket of reminiscences.* Washington, DC: Chronicle Publishing.

Ford, G. (1979). *A time to heal.* New York: Harper & Row.

Ford, P. L. (Ed.) (1888). *Pamphlets on the Constitution of the United States.* Brooklyn.

Franklin, B. (n.d.). *The complete works in philosophy, politics, and morals of the late Dr. Benjamin Franklin.* London.

Freeley, A. J. (1981). *Argumentation and debate,* 5th ed. Belmont: Wadsworth Publishing Company.

Garramone, G. M. (1984). Audience motivation effects: More evidence. *Communication Research, 11,* 79–96.

Germond, J. W., and Witcover, J. (1979). Presidential debates: An overview. In A. Ranney (ed.), *The past and future of presidential debates.* Washington, DC: American Enterprise Institute, 191–201.

Gill, M. (1986). Presidential debates: Political tool or voter information? *Speaker and Gavel, 24,* 36–40.

Gilligan, C. (1982). *In a different voice.* Cambridge: Harvard University Press.

Glass, D. P. (1985). Evaluating presidential candidates: Who focuses on their personal attributes? *Public Opinion Quarterly, 49,* 517–34.

Goot, M., and Reid, E. (1975). *Women and voting studies: Mindless matrons or sexist scientism?* London: Sage.

Gormley, W. J. (1975). Newspaper agendas and political elites. *Journalism Quarterly, 52,* 304–8.

Graber, D. (August 1984). Television news and the informed public: Not the main source. Cited in J. P. Robinson, D. K. Davis, and M. R. Levy. Paper presented at the 94th annual meeting of the American Psychological Association, Washington, D.C.

Graber, D., and Kim, Y. (1978). Why John Q. Voter did not learn very much from the 1976 presidential debates. In B. Rubin (ed.), *Communication yearbook 2.* New Brunswick, NJ: Transaction Books, 407–421.

Graber, D. A. (1980). *Mass media and American politics.* Washington, DC: Congressional Quarterly.

Graber, D. A. (1976). Press and TV as opinion resources in presidential campaigns. *Public Opinion Quarterly, 40,* 285–303.

Graber, D. A. (1987). Television news without pictures? *Critical Studies in Mass Communication, 4,* 74–78.

Grant, A. (1986). *The American political process.* London: Gower.

Greenburg, B. S., and Kumata, H. (1968). National sample predictors of mass media use. *Journalism Quarterly, 45,* 641–46, 705.

Grossman, M. B., and Kumar, M. J. (1981). *Portraying the president.* Baltimore: Johns Hopkins University Press.

Hagner, P., and Rieselbach, L. (1978). The impact of the 1976 presidential debates: Conversion or reinforcement? In G. Bishop, R. Meadow, and M. Jackson-Beeck (eds.), *The presidential debates.* New York: Praeger, 157–178.

Hall, C. C. (1890). The value of the debating society: An address to young men. Brooklyn.

Hall, J. A. (1978). Gender effects in decoding nonverbal cues. *Psychological Bulletin, 85,* 845–57.

Hamilton, A., Madison, J., and Jay, J. (Rpt. 1961). *The Federalist papers.* New York: New American Library.

Hamilton, C., and Ostendorf, L. (1963). *Lincoln lithographs: An album of every known pose.* Norman: University of Oklahoma Press.

Hardy-Short, D. (1986). An insider's view of the constraints affecting Geraldine Ferraro's preparation for the 1984 vice-presidential debate. *Speaker and Gavel, 24,* 8–22.

Hellweg, S. A., and Phillips, S. L. (1981). Form and substance: A comparative analysis of five formats used in the 1980 presidential debates. *Speaker and Gavel, 18,* 67–76.

Hellweg, S. A., and Phillips, S. L. (1981). A verbal and visual analysis of the 1980 Houston Republican presidential primary debate. *Speaker and Gavel, 47,* 23–38.

Herbeck, D., and Katsulas, J. (1985). The affirmative topicality burden: Any reasonable example of the resolution. *Journal of the American Forensic Association, 1*33–45.

Hess, S. (1974). *The presidential campaign.* Washington, DC: Brookings Institution.

Hofstetter, C. R. (1976). *Bias in the news.* Columbus: Ohio State University Press.

Hofstetter, C. R., Zukin, C., and Buss, T. F. (1978). Political imagery and information in an age of television. *Journalism Quarterly, 55,* 562–69.

Isenhart, M. W. (1980). An investigation of the relationship of sex and sex role to the ability to decode nonverbal cues. *Human Communication Research, 6,* 309–18.

Jackson, J. E. (1975). Issue, party choice, and presidential votes. *American Journal of Political Science, 19,* 161–85.

Jackson-Beeck, M., and Meadow, V. G. (1979). Content analysis of televised communication events: The presidential debates. *Communication Research, 6,* 321–44.

Jamieson, K. H. (1988). *Eloquence in an electronic age.* New York: Oxford University Press.

Jamieson, K. H. (1984). *Packaging the presidency.* New York: Oxford University Press.

Japp, P. M. (1985). Esther or Isaiah? The abolitionist-feminist rhetoric of Angelina Grimké. *Quarterly Journal of Speech,* 335–48.

Jaquette, J. (1974). Introduction. In J. Jaquette (ed.), *Women in politics.* New York: John Wiley & Sons, xiii–xxxvii.

Johannsen, R. W. (ed.) (1961). *The letters of Stephen A. Douglas.* Urbana: University of Illinois Press.

Johannsen, R. W. (ed.) (1965). *The Lincoln–Douglas debates of 1858.* New York: Oxford University Press.

Jordan, H. (1982). *Crisis.* New York: Berkeley Books.

Joreskog, K. G., and Sorbom, D. (1981). LISREL V: *Analysis of linear structural relationships by the method of maximum likelihood.* Uppsala, Sweden: National Educational Resources.

Juergens, G. (1981). *News from the White House.* Chicago: University of Chicago Press.

Kaid, L. L. (1977). The neglected candidate: Interpersonal communication in political campaigns. *Western Journal of Speech Communication, 4,* 245–52.

Karayn, J. (1979). The case for permanent presidential debates. In A. Ranney (ed.), *The past and future of presidential debates.* Washington, DC: American Enterprise Institute, 155–169.

Katz, E. (1979). The uses of Becker, Blumler, and Swanson. *Communication Research, 6,* 74–83.

Katz, E., and Feldman, J. J. (1962). The great debates in the light of research: A survey of surveys. In S. Kraus (ed.), *The great debates.* Bloomington: Indiana University Press, 173–223.

Kelley, S., Jr. (1960). *Political campaigning: Problems in creating an informed electorate.* Washington, DC: Brookings Institution.

Kelley, S., Jr., and Mirer, T. W. (1974). The simple act of voting. *American Political Science Review, 68,* 572–91.

Kendall, K. E., and Yum, J. O. (1984). Persuading the blue-collar voter: Issues, images, and homophily. In R. N. Bostrom (ed.), *Communication yearbook 8.* Beverly Hills, CA: Sage.

Kennedy, J. F. (1965). *Kennedy and the press.* H. W. Chase and A. H. Lerman (eds.). New York: Thomas Y. Crowell.

Kent, F. R. (1928). *Political behavior.* New York: William Morrow.

Keogh, J. (1972). *President Nixon and the press.* New York: Funk and Wagnalls.

Kimsey, W. D., and Atwood, L. E. (1979). A path analysis of political cognitions and attitudes, communication, and voting in a congressional campaign. *Communication Monographs, 46,* 219–30.

Kinder, D. (1978). Political person perception: The asymmetrical influence of sentiment and choice on perceptions of presidential candidates. *Journal of Personality and Social Psychology, 36,* 859–71.

Kinder, D. (1981). Presidents, prosperity and public opinion. *Public Opinion Quarterly, 45,* 1–25.

Kinder, D., and Kiewiet, D. R. (1979). Economic discontent and political behavior: The role of personal grievances and collective economic judgments in congressional voting. *American Journal of Political Science, 23,* 498–527.

Kinder, D., Peters, M. D., Abelson, R. R., and Fiske S. (1980). 1980 presidential prototypes. *Political Behavior, 2,* 315–38.

Kinder, D., and Sears, D. (1985). Public opinion and political action. *Handbook of Social Psychology, 2,* 659–741.

King, M. (1977). Assimilation and contrast of presidential candidates' issue positions, 1972. *Public Opinion Quarterly, 41,* 515–22.

Kirkpatrick, S. A., Lyons, W., and Fitzgerald, M. R. (1975). Candidates, parties, and issues in the American electorate: Two decades of change. *American Politics Quarterly, 3,* 247–83.

References   249

Kjeldahl, B. O., Carmichael, C. W., and Mertz, R. J. (1971). Factors in a presi-
dential candidate's image. *Speech Monographs, 38*, 129–31.
Kondracke, M. (November 12, 1984). Call to glory. *The New Republic, 21*, 23–25.
Kraus, S. (Ed.). (1962). *The great debates: Background, perspective, effects.* Bloom-
ington: Indiana University Press.
Kraus, S. (Ed.). (1979). *The great debates: Carter vs. Ford, 1976.* Bloomington:
Indiana University Press.
Kraus, S., and Davis, D. (1976). *The effects of mass communication on political
behavior.* University Park: Pennsylvania State University Press.
Kraus, S., Lang, C., Lang, L., and Davis, D. (1975). Critical events analysis. In
S. Chaffee (ed.), *Political communication.* Beverly Hills, CA: Sage.
Kraus, S., and Smith, R. K. (1962). Issues and images. In S. Kraus (ed.), *The great
debates.* Bloomington: Indiana University Press, 289–312.
Krauss, W. R. (1974). Political implications of gender roles: A review of the lit-
erature. *American Political Science Review, 68*, 1706–23.
Ladd, E. C., Jr. (1978). *Where have all the voters gone?* New York: Norton.
Lammers, W. (1981). Presidential press-conference schedules: Who hides, and
when? *Political Science Quarterly*, 261–77.
Lane, R. E. (1959). *Political life.* Glencoe, IL: The Free Press.
Lang, G., and Lang, K. (1978). The formation of public opinion: Direct and
mediated effects of the first debate. In G. Bishop, R. Meadow, and M. Jack-
son-Beeck (eds.), *The presidential debates.* New York: Praeger, 61–80.
Lang, G., and Lang, K. (1978). Immediate and delayed responses to a Carter-Ford
debate: Assessing public opinion. *Public Opinion Quarterly, 42*, 322–41.
Lang, K., and Lang, C. (1962). Reactions of reviews. In S. Kraus (ed.), *The great
debates.* Bloomington: Indiana University Press, 313–330.
Lansing, M. (1974). The American woman: Voter and activist. In J. Jaquette (ed.),
Women in politics. New York: John Wiley & Sons, 5–36.
Lazarsfeld, P. F., Berelson, B., and Gaudet, H. (1944). *The people's choice.* New
York: Duell, Sloan and Pearce.
Leonard, T. C. (1986). *The power of the press: The birth of American political
reporting.* New York: Oxford University Press.
Lerner, G. (1967). *The Grimké sisters from South Carolina: Rebels against slav-
ery.* Boston: Houghton Mifflin.
Leuthold, D. A., and Valentine, D. C. (1981). How Reagan 'won' the Cleveland
debate: Audience predispositions and presidential debate 'winners.' *Speaker
and Gavel, 18*, 60–66.
Linsky, M. (ed.) (1983). *Television and the presidential elections.* New York:
Lexington Books.
Lippmann, W. (1963). *The essential Lippmann.* C. Rossiter and J. Lare (eds.).
New York: Random House.
Lipscomb, A. (Ed.) (1904). *The writings of Thomas Jefferson.* Washington, DC:
The Jefferson Memorial Association.
The little debates. (December 6, 1962). *The Reporter*, pp. 36–38.
Lucas, W. A., and Adams, W. C. (1978). Talking, television and voter indecision.
Journal of Communication, 28, 120–31.
Maclay, E. S. (Ed.) (1890). *Journal of William Maclay.* New York: D. Appleton
and Company.

Madison, J. (1965). *Letters and other writings of James Madison.* Philadelphia: Lippincott.

Madison, J. *Notes of debates in the federal convention of 1787.* Athens: Ohio University Press.

Mahony, J., Coogle, C. L., and Banks, P. D. (1984). Values in presidential inaugural addresses: A test of Rokeach's two-factor theory of political ideology. *Psychological Reports, 55,* 683–86.

Manheim, J. B. (1979). The honeymoon's over: The news conference and the development of presidential style. *Journal of Politics, 41,* 55–74.

Markus, G. B. (1979). The political environment and the dynamics of public attitudes: A panel study. *American Journal of Political Science, 23,* 338–59.

Markus, G. B., and Converse, P. E. (1979). A dynamic simultaneous equation model of electoral choice. *American Political Science Review, 73,* 617–32.

Marshall, T. R. (1984). Issues, personalities, and presidential primary voters. *Social Science Quarterly, 65,* 750–60.

Martel, M. (1981). Debate preparation in the Reagan camp: An insider's view. *Speaker and Gavel, 18,* 34–46.

Mazanec, N., and McCall, G. (1975). Sex, cognitive categories, and observational accuracy. *Psychological Reports, 37,* 987–990.

McClure, R. D., and Patterson, T. E. (1976). Print vs. network news. *Journal of Communication, 26,* 23–28.

McClure, R. D., and Patterson, T. E. (1974). Television news and political advertising: The impact of exposure on voter beliefs. *Communication Research, 1,* 3–27.

McCombs, M., and Shaw, D. (1972). The agenda-setting function of mass media. *Public Opinion Quarterly, 36,* 176–87.

McCombs, M., and Shaw, D. (1977). The agenda-setting function of the press. In D. Shaw and M. McCombs (eds.), *The emergence of American political issues: The agenda-setting function of the press.* St. Paul, MN: West Publishing, 89–105.

McElligott, J. N. (1855). *The American debater.* New York: Ivison and Phinney.

McLeod, J. M., and Becker, L. B. (1974). Testing the validity of gratification measures through political effects and analysis. In J. Blumler and E. Katz (eds.), *The uses of mass communication: Current perspectives on gratifications research.* Beverly Hills, CA: Sage, 137–164.

McLeod, J. M., Becker, L. B., and Byrnes, J. E. (1974). Another look at the agenda-setting function of the press. *Communication Research, 1,* 131–65.

McLeod, J. M., Bybee, C. R., and Durall, J. A. (1979). Equivalence of informed participation: The 1976 presidential debates as a source of influence. *Communication Research, 6,* 463–87.

McLeod, J., Durall, J., Ziemke, D., and Bybee, C. (1979). Expanding the context of effects. In S. Kraus (ed.), *The great debates: Carter vs. Ford, 1976.* Bloomington: Indiana University Press, 348–367.

McMaster, J. B., and Stone, F. D. (1888). *Pennsylvania and the Federal Constitution, 1787–1788.* Philadelphia: The Historical Society of Pennsylvania.

Mendelsohn, H., and O'Keefe, G. (1976). *The people choose a president.* New York: Praeger.

Milic, L. T. (1979). Grilling the pols: Q & A at the debates. In S. Kraus (ed.),

The great debates: Carter vs. Ford 1976. Bloomington: Indiana University Press, 187–208.

Miller, A. H., and MacKuen, M. (1979b). Learning about the candidates. The 1976 presidential debates. *Public Opinion Quarterly, 43,* 326–46.

Miller, A. H., and MacKuen, M. (1979a). Informing the electorate: A national study. In S. Kraus (ed.), *The great debates: Carter vs. Ford 1976.* Bloomington: Indiana University Press.

Miller, M. M. (1916). *American debate: A history of political and economic controversy in the United States.* New York: G. P. Putnam's and Sons.

Miller, M. M. (Ed.) (1913). *Great debates in American history.* New York: Current Literature.

Miller, M. M., and Reese, S. D. (1982). Media dependency as interaction: Effects of exposure and reliance on political activity and efficacy. *Communication Research, 9,* 227–48.

Mills, S. (1986). Rebuilding the presidential debates. *Speaker and Gavel, 24,* 41–51.

Minow, N. N., Martin, J. B., and Mitchell, L. M. (1973). *Presidential television.* New York: Basic Books.

Minow, N. N., and Sloan, C. M. (1987). *For great debates.* New York: Priority Press.

Mitchell, L. M. (1979). *With the nation watching. Report of the Twentieth Century Fund task force.* Lexington, MA: D. C. Heath.

Morris, R. B. (1975). *John Jay: The making of a revolutionary.* New York: Harper & Row.

Morrison, T. (1974). *Chautauqua.* Chicago: University of Chicago Press.

Mullins, L. E. (1977). Agenda-setting and the young voter. In D. L. Shaw and M. E. McCombs (eds.), *The emergence of American political issues: The agenda-setting function of the press.* St. Paul, MN: West Publishing, 133–148.

Neuman, W. R. (1986). *The paradox of mass politics.* Cambridge: Harvard University Press.

Newman, B. I., and Sheth, J. N. (1984). The "gender gap" in voter attitudes and behavior: Some advertising implications. *Journal of Advertising, 13,* 4–16.

Nie, N., Verba, S., and Petrocik, J. (1976). *The changing American voter.* Cambridge: Harvard University Press.

Nimmo, D., and Savage, R. L. (1976). *Candidates and their images: Concepts, methods, and findings.* Pacific Palisades, CA: Goodyear.

Nixon, R. (1962). *Six crises.* Garden City, NY: Doubleday.

Norrander, B. (1986). Correlates of vote choice in the 1980 presidential primaries. *Journal of Politics, 48,* 156–66.

Norrander, B. (1986). Selective participation: Presidential primary voters as a subset of general election voters. *American Politics Quarterly, 14,* 35–53.

Norrander, B., and Smith, G. W. (1985). Type of contest, candidate strategy, and turnout in presidential primaries. *American Politics Quarterly, 13,* 28–50.

O'Keefe, G. J. (1975). Political campaigns and mass communication research. In S. S. Chaffee (ed.), *Political communication: Issues and strategies for research.* Beverly Hills, CA: Sage, 129–164.

O'Keefe, G. J. (1980). Political malaise and reliance on media. *Journalism Quarterly, 57*, 122–28.

O'Keefe, G. J. (in press). The changing context of interpersonal communication in political campaigns. In M. Burgoon (ed.), *Communication Yearbook 5*. New Brunswick, NJ: Transaction Books.

O'Keefe, G. J., and Mendelsohn, H. (1979). Media influences and their anticipation. In S. Kraus (ed.), *The great debates: Carter vs. Ford, 1976*. Bloomington: Indiana University Press, 405–417.

O'Keefe, G. J., Mendelsohn, H., and Liu, J. (1976). Voter decision making, 1972 and 1974. *Public Opinion Quarterly, 40*, 320–30.

O'Keefe, M. T., and Sheinkopf, K. (1974). The voter decides: Candidate images or campaign issues? *Journal of Broadcasting, 18*, 403–12.

O'Neill, T., with Novak, W. (1987). *Man of the House*. New York: Random House.

Orum, A. M., Cohen, R. S., Grasmuck, S., and Orum, A. W. (1974). Sex, socialization, and politics. *American Sociological Review, 39*, 197–209.

Osgood, C. E., Suci, G. J., and Tannenbaum, P. H. (1957). *The measurement of meaning*. Urbana: University of Illinois Press.

Ostrogorski, M. (1902). *Democracy and the organization of political parties, 2* vols. New York: The Macmillan Company.

Otis, J. (1762). *A vindication of the conduct of the house of the province of Massachusetts Bay*. Boston: Edes & Gill.

Padover, S. (Ed.). (1943). *The complete Jefferson*. New York: Duell, Sloan and Pearce.

Page, B. (1978). *Choices and echoes in presidential elections*. Chicago: University of Chicago Press.

Page, B. I., and Jones, C. C. (1979). Reciprocal effects of policy preferences, party loyalties, and the vote. *American Political Science Review, 73*, 1071–89.

Palmgreen, P., and Clarke, P. (1977). Agenda-setting with local and national issues. *Communication Research, 4*, 435–52.

Parker, E. B. (1963). The effects of television on magazine and newspaper reading: A problem in methodology. *Public Opinion Quarterly, 27*, 315–20.

Patterson, T. E. (1980). *The mass media election: How Americans choose their president*. New York: Praeger.

Patterson, T. E., and McClure, R. D. (1976). *The unseeing eye: The myth of television power in national elections*. New York: Putnam.

Patton, G. W. R. (1978). Effect of party affiliation of student voters on the image of presidential candidates. *Psychological Reports, 43*, 343–47.

Perry, J. M. (1968). *The new politics*. New York: Clarkson N. Potter.

Peterson, M. (Ed.) (1975). *The portable Thomas Jefferson*. New York: Penguin Books.

Phillips, W. (1905). The foundation of the labor movement (October 31, 1871). Delivered at the Music Hall in Boston, reprinted in *Speeches, Lectures, and Letters*. Boston.

Pierce, J. C., and Sullivan, J. L. (Eds.) (1980). *The electorate reconsidered*. Beverly Hills, CA: Sage.

Pomper, G. (1970). *Elections in America: Control and influence in democratic politics*. New York: Dodd, Mead.

Powell, L. (1977). Voting intention and the complexity of political images: A pilot study. *Psychological Reports, 43*, 343–47.

Quarles, R. C. (1979). Mass media use and voting behavior: The accuracy of political perceptions among first-time and experienced voters. *Communication Research, 6,* 407–36.

Ranney, A. (Ed.) (1979). *The past and future of presidential debates.* Washington, DC: American Enterprise Institute.

Rapoport, R. B. (1982). Sex differences in attitude expression: A generational explanation. *Public Opinion Quarterly, 46,* 86–96.

Rarick, G. (1975). *News research for better newspapers* (Vol. 7). Washington, DC: American Newspaper Publishers Association Foundation.

Ray, R. F. (1961). Thomas E. Dewey: The great Oregon debate of 1948. In *American public address: Studies in honor of Albert Craig Baird.* Columbia: Missouri University Press.

Reich, R. B. (1988). *The power of public ideas.* Cambridge, MA: Ballinger Publishing Co.

Reiss, A. J. (1971). *Occupations and social status.* New York: Free Press.

Repass, D. E. (1971). Issue salience and party choice. *American Political Science Review, 65,* 389–400.

Riley, P., and Hollihan, T. A. (1981). The 1980 debates: A content analysis of the issues and arguments. *Speaker and Gavel, 18,* 47–59.

Ringelstein, A. C. (1985). Presidential vetoes: Motivations and classification. *Congress & the Presidency, 12,* 43–55.

Ritter, K. W. (1981). Introduction: An inaugural issue on presidential debates. *Speaker and Gavel, 18,* 12–13.

Rivers, D., and Rose, N. L. (1985). Passing the president's program: Public opinion and presidential influence in Congress. *American Journal of Political Science, 29,* 183–96.

Roberts, C. L. (1981). From primary to the presidency: A panel study of images and issues in the 1976 election. *Western Journal of Speech Communication, 45,* 60–70.

Roberts, C. I. (1979). Media use and difficulty of decision in the 1976 presidential campaign. *Journalism Quarterly, 56,* 794–802.

Roberts, D. F. (1971). The nature of communication effects. In W. Schramm and D. F. Roberts (eds.), *The process and effects of mass communication.* Chicago: University of Illinois Press.

Robinson, J. P. (1976). Interpersonal influence in election campaigns: Two step-flow hypothesis. *Public Opinion Quarterly, 40,* 304–19.

Robinson, J. P. (1979). The polls. In S. Kraus (ed.), *The great debates: Carter vs. Ford, 1976.* Bloomington: Indiana University Press.

Robinson, J. P. (1974). The press as king-maker: What surveys from last five campaigns show. *Journalism Quarterly, 51,* 587–94, 606.

Robinson, J. P., and Jeffres, L. W. (1979). The changing role of newspapers in the age of television. *Journalism Monographs, 63.*

Robinson, M. J., and Sheehan, M. A. (1983). *Over the wire and on TV.* New York: Russell Sage, 1–31.

Rohde, D. W., and Simon, D. M. (1985). Presidential vetoes and congressional response: A study of institutional conflict. *American Journal of Political Science, 29,* 397–427.

Roper Reports (1983). New York: Roper Organization.

Roosevelt, F. D. (1938). *Public papers of the president.* Washington, D.C., 1939.

Rosenberg, S. W., Bohan, L., McCafferty, P., and Harris, K. (1986). The image and the vote: The effect of candidate presentation on voter preference. *American Journal of Political Science, 30,* 108–27.

Rosenthal, R., and DePaulo, B. (1979). Sex differences in eavesdropping on nonverbal cues. *Journal of Personality and Social Psychology, 37,* 273–85.

Rubin, L. (1983). *Intimate strangers: Men and women together.* New York: Harper Colophon Books.

Russeonello, J. M., and Wolf, F. (1979). Newspaper coverage of the 1976 and 1968 presidential campaigns. *Journalism Quarterly, 56,* 360–64, 432.

Salinger, P. (1965). Introduction. In H. W. Chase and A. H. Leeman (eds.), *Kennedy and the press.* New York: Thomas Y. Crowell.

Salinger, P. (1966). *With Kennedy.* Garden City, NY: Doubleday.

Samovar, Larry A. (1965). Ambiguity and unequivocation in the Kennedy-Nixon television debates: A rhetorical analysis. *Western Speech, 24,* 211–18.

Sampson, I. P. C. (1817). *A valedictory delivered at the forum.* New York: Van Winkle, Wiley and Co.

Sapiro, V. (1983). *The political integration of women: Roles, socialization, and politics.* Urbana: University of Illinois Press.

Sapiro, V. (1981). When are interests interesting? The problem of political representation of women. *American Political Science Review, 73,* 701–16.

Savage, J. (Ed.) (1853). *History of New England from 1630–1649.* 2 vols. Boston: Little, Brown & Company.

Schlesinger, A. M., Jr. (1945). *The age of Jackson.* Boston: Little, Brown.

Schlesinger, A. M., Jr. (1973). *The imperial presidency.* Boston: Houghton Mifflin.

Scott, E. H. (Ed.) (1894). *The Federalist and other constitutional papers by Hamilton, Jay, Madison and other statesmen of their time.* 2 vols. Chicago: Albert, Scott.

Scott, R. L. (1981). You cannot not debate: The debate over the 1980 presidential debates. *Speaker and Gavel, 18,* 28–33.

Sears, D. O., and Chaffee, S. (1979). Uses and effects of the 1976 debates: An overview of empirical studies. In S. Kraus (ed.), *The great debates: Carter vs. Ford, 1976.* Bloomington: Indiana University Press, 223–261.

Settel, I. (1967). *A pictorial history of radio.* New York: Grosset and Dunlap.

Shabad, G., and Andersen, K. (1979). Candidate evaluations by men and women. *Public Opinion Quarterly, 43,* 18–35.

Sharp, W. (July 1927). President and press. *Atlantic Monthly, 240.*

Shaw, D. L., and McCombs, M. E. (Eds.) (1977). *The emergence of American political issues: The agenda-setting function of the press.* St. Paul, MN: West Publishing.

Shepherd, J. (1981). Social factors in face recognition. In G. Davies, H. Ellis, and J. Shepherd (eds.), *Perceiving and remembering faces.* London: Academic Press.

Sheridan, T. (1759). *Course of lectures on elocution and the English language.* London: A. Miller in the Strand.

Short, B. (1986). A goals criteria approach: Preparing the public to evaluate presidential debates. *Speaker and Gavel, 24,* 23–35.

Simonston, D. K. (1987). *Why presidents succeed.* New Haven: Yale University Press.

Slagter, R., and Miller, R. (April 1978). The impact of the 1976 presidential debates on candidates' images: An experimental study. Paper presented to the Midwest Political Science Association, Chicago, Illinois.

Smith, M. S., Stone, P. J., and Glenn, E. N. (1966). A content analysis of twenty presidential nomination acceptance speeches. In P. J. Stone, D. C. Dunphy, M. S. Smith, and D. M. Ogilvie (eds.), *The general inquirer: A computer approach to content analysis.* Cambridge, MA: MIT Press.

Smith, R. (1977). The Carter-Ford debates: Some perceptions from academe. *central States Speech Journal, 28,* 250–57.

Smith, R. N. (1982). *Thomas E. Dewey and his times.* New York: Simon and Schuster.

Sorensen, T. (1965). *Kennedy.* New York: Harper & Row.

Starobin, R. S. (Ed.). (1970). *Denmark Vesey: The slave conspiracy of 1822.* Englewood Cliffs, NJ: Prentice-Hall.

Steeper, F. T. (1978). Public response to Gerald Ford's statements on Eastern Europe in the second debate. In G. F. Bishop, R. G. Meadow, and M. Jackson-Beeck (eds.), *The presidential debates: Media, electoral, and policy perspectives.* New York: Praeger, 81–104.

Stiles, W. B., Au, M. L., Martell, M. A., and Perlmutter, J. A. (1983). American campaign oratory: Verbal response mode use by candidates in the 1980 American presidential primaries. *Social Behavior and Personality, 11,* 39–43.

Stokes, D. E. (1966). Some dynamic elements of contests for the presidency. *American Political Science Review, 64,* 1167–85.

Stricker, G. (1963). The use of the semantic differential to predict voting behavior. *Journal of Social Psychology, 59,* 159–67.

Suedfeld, P., and Tetlock, P. (1977). Integrative complexity of communication in international crises. *Journal of Conflict Resolution, 21,* 169–84.

Sullivan, M. (1926). *Our times: The United States, 1900–1925.* New York: Charles Scribner.

Sundquist, J. (1987). Strengthening the national parties. In A. J. Reichley (ed.), *Elections American style.* Washington, DC: Brookings Institute.

Swerdlow, J. L. (1984). *Beyond debate.* New York: Twentieth Century Fund.

Swerdlow, J. (Ed.) (1987). *Presidential debates 1988 and beyond.* Washington, DC: Congressional Quarterly.

Tan, A. S. (1980). Mass media use, issue knowledge and political involvement. *Public Opinion Quarterly, 44,* 241–48.

Tetlock, P. E. (1981). Pre- to postelection shifts in presidential rhetoric: Impression management or cognitive adjustment. *Journal of Personality and Social Psychology, 41,* 207–12.

The Reporter. (December 6, 1962). Pp. 36–38.

Thomas, D. A., and Hart, J. (Eds.) (1987). *Advanced debate: Readings in practice and teaching.* Lincolnwood, IL: National Textbook Company.

Tichenor, P. J., Donohue, G. A., and Olien, C. N. (1970). Mass media flow and differential growth in knowledge. *Public Opinion Quarterly, 34,* 159–70.

Tiemens, R. K. (1978). Television's portrayal of the 1976 presidential debates: An analysis of visual content. *Communication Monographs, 45,* 362–70.

Tipton, I., Haney, R. D., and Baseheart, J. R. (1975). Media agenda-setting in city and state election campaigns. *Journalism Quarterly, 52,* 15–22.

Toulmin, S. (1958). *Uses of argument.* Cambridge: Cambridge University Press.

Tuckel, P. S., and Tejara, F. (1983). Changing patterns in American voting behavior, 1914–1980. *Public Opinion Quarterly, 47,* 230–46.

Tugwell, R. G. (1969). *The democratic Roosevelt.* Baltimore: Penguin Books.

Tulis, J. (1987). *The Rhetorical Presidency.* Princeton: Princeton Univ. Press.

Tulis, J. (1987). *The rhetorical presidency.* Princeton: Princeton Univ. Press.

Vancil, D. L., and Pendell, S. E. (1984). Winning presidential debates: An analysis of criteria influencing audience response. *Western Journal of Speech Communication, 48,* 62–74.

Volgy, T. J., and Schwarz, J. E. (1980). On television viewing and citizens' political attitudes, activity and knowledge: Another look at the impact of media on politics. *Western Political Quarterly, 33,* 153–66.

Wagner, J. (1983). Media do make a difference: The differential impact of mass media in the 1976 presidential race. *American Journal of Political Science, 27,* 407–30.

Wald, K. D., and Lupfer, M. B. (1978). The presidential debate as a civics lesson. *Public Opinion Quarterly, 42,* 342–53.

Wallace, K. (Ed.). (1954). *History of speech education in America: Background studies.* New York: Appelton-Century-Crofts.

Weaver, D. H., McCombs, M. E., and Spellman, C. (1975). Watergate and the media: A case study of agenda-setting. *American Politics Quarterly, 3,* 458–72.

Weisberg, H. F., and Rusk, J. G. (1970). Dimensions of candidate evaluation. *American Political Science Review, 64,* 167–85.

Weiss, R. O. (Winter 1981). The presidential debates in their political context: The issue-image interface in the 1980 campaign. *Speaker and Gavel, 18* 22–27.

Welch, S. (1977). Women as political animals? A test of some explanations for male-female political participation differences. *American Journal of Political Science, 21,* 711–30.

West, D. (1980). Cheers and jeers: Candidate presentations and audience reactions in the 1980 presidential campaign. *American Politics Quarterly, 12,* 23–50.

White, T. (1961). *The making of the president 1960.* New York: Atheneum.

Whitney, D. C., and Goldman, S. B. (1985). Media use and time of vote decision: A study of the 1980 presidential election. *Communication Research, 12,* 511–29.

Willard, C. A. (1983). *Argumentation and the social grounds of knowledge.* Tuscaloosa: University of Alabama Press.

Wilson, W. (Rpt. 1973). *Congressional government.* Reprint. Gloucester, MA: Peter Smith.

Wiltse, C. M., and Moser, H. D. (Eds.) (1980). *The papers of Daniel Webster.* Hanover and London: Dartmouth College by University Press of New England.

Winter, J. P., and Eyal, C. H. (1981). Agenda-setting for the civil rights issue. *Public Opinion Quarterly, 45,* 376–83.

Wirt, W. (1817). *Sketches of the life and character of Patrick Henry.* Philadelphia: James Webster.

Wood, G. S. (1969). *The creation of the American Republic, 1776–1787.* New York: Norton.

Zarefsky, D. (1986). The Lincoln–Douglas debates revisited: The evolution of political argument. *Quarterly Journal of Speech, 72,* 162–84.

Ziegelmueller, G., and Rhodes, J. (1981). *Dimensions of argument: Proceedings of the Second Annual Conference on Argumentation.* Annandale: Speech Communication Association.

Zukin, C., and Snyder, R. (1984). Passive learning: When the media environment is the message. *Public Opinion Quarterly, 48,* 629–38.

Index